University of London
Institute of Commonwealth Studies

COMMONWEALTH PAPERS

General Editor
Professor W. H. Morris-Jones

13
Nigerian Politics and Military Rule:
Prelude to the Civil War

COMMONWEALTH PAPERS

1. *The Vocabulary of Commonwealth Relations.* S. A. de Smith, 1954
2. *Imperial Federation: A Study of New Zealand Policy and Opinion, 1880–1914.* Keith Sinclair, 1955
3. *Richard Jebb and the Problem of Empire.* J. D. B. Miller, 1956
4. *The Investigation of National Income in British Tropical Dependencies.* A. R. Prest, 1957
5. *The Inter Se Doctrine of Commonwealth Relations.* J. E. S. Fawcett, 1958
6. *The Commonwealth and Regional Defence.* W. C. B. Tunstall, 1959
7. *The Nyasaland Elections of 1961.* Lucy Mair, 1962
8. *Political Parties in Uganda, 1949–62.* D. A. Low, 1962
9. *Population Characteristics of the Commonwealth Countries of Tropical Africa.* T. E. Smith and J. G. C. Blacker, 1963
10. *Problems of Smaller Territories.* Edited by Burton Benedict, 1967
11. *Canadian-West Indian Union: A Forty-Year Minuet.* Robin W. Winks, 1968
12. *Louis Botha or John X. Merriman: The Choice of South Africa's First Prime Minister.* N. G. Garson, 1969
13. *Nigerian Politics and Military Rule: Prelude to the Civil War.* Edited by S. K. Panter-Brick, 1970

Guide to Resources for Commonwealth Studies in London, Oxford and Cambridge, with bibliographical and other information. A. R. Hewitt, 1957

Union List of Commonwealth Newspapers in London, Oxford and Cambridge. A. R. Hewitt, 1960

Nigerian Politics and Military Rule: Prelude to the Civil War

edited by

S. K. PANTER-BRICK

*London School of Economics
and Political Science*

UNIVERSITY OF LONDON
Published for the
Institute of Commonwealth Studies
THE ATHLONE PRESS

Published by
THE ATHLONE PRESS
UNIVERSITY OF LONDON
at 2 Gower Street, London W C I
Distributed by Tiptree Book Services Ltd
Tiptree, Essex

U.S.A.
Oxford University Press Inc.
New York

First edition, 1970
Reprinted, 1971
First paperback edition, 1971

0 485 17613 0 *cloth*
0 485 17600 9 *paper*

First printed in Great Britain by
WESTERN PRINTING SERVICES LTD
BRISTOL

Reproduced by photo-lithography and made in Great Britain at
THE PITMAN PRESS LTD
BATH

FOREWORD

THIS BOOK is mainly concerned with developments in Nigeria leading to the outbreak of civil war and aims to provide an understanding of how and why secession was declared. It looks at the various sources of conflict, at the nature of disagreements arising over attempts to formulate constitutional and administrative arrangements for the preservation of unity and peace in Nigeria, and at the structure and character of the army and its interrelations with the political environment. Although the civil war has tended to overshadow the preceding period of military rule and to pose its own problems, the resort to arms has not in itself either settled all the outstanding issues or brought about an entirely new situation. Even before the war began Colonel Adebayo, the Military Governor of the Western Region, had this to say:

I need not tell you what horror, what devastation and what extreme human suffering will attend the use of force. When it is all over and the smoke and dust have lifted, and the dead are buried, we shall find as other people have found, that it has all been futile, entirely futile, in solving the problems we set out to solve.*

A wider understanding of how blunt an instrument is civil war may make possible the settlement which hitherto has proved so elusive. One gains an appreciation of the difficulties when one studies the situation as it developed under military rule during 1966 and the first half of 1967.

The book is in two parts, a collection of essays and a reproduction or summary analysis of documentary material. Some of the essays were originally presented at a seminar organized by Professor Dennis Austin and myself at the Institute of Commonwealth Studies, University of London, in May and June 1968, and have since been revised. Others have been specially written. All the contributors have close personal experience of Nigeria in recent years. Dr Dudley is a Nigerian scholar now teaching at Manchester University. Dr Lloyd, Dr Luckham and I have taught in Nigerian universities. Mr Dent and Mr Dawson have had administrative experience in Nigeria. Mr Whiteman is on the editorial staff of *West Africa*.

* Broadcast 3 May 1967, as reported in the *Daily Times*, 5 May 1967.

The documentary material in the appendices is both a selection and an abridgement. Some of the most important records are either too voluminous or too repetitious and technical to be reproduced in full and their presentation in summary form will, I hope, satisfy the reader who wishes to be acquainted with the documentary evidence yet not submerged by it.

My special thanks are due to Professor W. H. Morris-Jones, Director of the Institute of Commonwealth Studies, for his very valuable encouragement, to Professor Austin for his ever helpful and friendly advice, and to Miss Valerie Beard and Miss Sonja Jansen for their indispensable secretarial assistance; also to the Geography Department of the London School of Economics for assistance in the preparation of the Maps.

June 1969   Keith Panter-Brick

CONTENTS

Chronology   viii

Abbreviations   xii

1. The Ethnic Background to the Nigerian Crisis   I
   P. C. LLOYD

2. From Military Coup to Civil War, January 1966 to May 1967   14
   S. K. PANTER-BRICK

3. The Nigerian Military: Disintegration or Integration?   58
   A. R. LUCKHAM

4. The Military and the Politicians   78
   M. J. DENT

5. Western Nigeria and the Nigerian Crisis   94
   B. J. DUDLEY

6. Enugu: The Psychology of Secession, 29 July 1966 to
   30 May 1967   III
   K. WHITEMAN

7. The Creation of New States in the North   128
   S. K. PANTER-BRICK and P. F. DAWSON

Notes   139

Appendices

A. Analysis of proposals submitted to the Ad Hoc Constitutional
   Committee, September and October 1966, and of the
   Committee's Progress Report   154

B. Selected Decrees issued by the Military Government,
   January 1966 to May 1967   177

C. Selected Speeches   184

D. Draft Minutes of the meeting of the Supreme Military Council
   held at Aburi, Ghana, 4–5 January 1967   240

E. Extract from the Minutes of a meeting attended by officials
   of the Federal and Regional Military Governments, held
   at Benin 17–18 February, 1967   252

F. Petitions to Lt-Col Gowon for the creation of more states
   in the West, June 1967   267

MAPS

1. Nigeria as a federation of four Regions, 1966   x

2. Nigeria as a federation of twelve States, 1967   x

3. Location of oilfields, terminals, and pipelines (1969)   xi

CHRONOLOGY

1966

14–15 January   Small group of army officers attempt to take power. The Federal Prime Minister, the Prime Ministers of the Northern and Western Regions, and several senior army officers killed. Proclamation by Major Nzeogwu.

16 January   General Ironsi assumes power as Head of the Federal Military Government. Military Governors appointed to administer the Regions.

21 February   General Ironsi outlines constitutional and administrative reforms to be introduced.

24 May   Formal abolition of the Regions and Federation (Decree No. 34). Ban on political activities for period of three years (Decree No. 33).

29/30 May   Riots and massacre of Ibo civilians in the North.

29 July   Mutiny by Northern troops. General Ironsi, Colonel Fajuyi, and some two hundred Ibo officers and men killed.

1 August   Lt-Col Gowon takes over as Supreme Commander of the Armed Forces and Head of the National Military Government. Not recognized by Lt-Col Ojukwu, the Military Governor in the East.

9 August   Meeting of representatives of the Military Governors in Lagos recommends that the Supreme Commander should take immediate steps to post military personnel to barracks within their respective Regions of origin, and to repeal any centralizing Decrees.

1 September   Repeal of Decree No. 34. Nigeria reverts to its previous status as a Federation.

12–29 September   Ad Hoc Constitutional Committee, attended by delegates from all the Regions and from Lagos, meets in Lagos. Submission and examination of delegates' proposals. Issue of Progress Report.

29 September   Wholesale massacre of Ibo civilians in the North which continues for several days.

24–31 October	Ad Hoc Constitutional Committee meets. Eastern delegates absent. Revised proposals submitted.
16 November	Lt-Col Gowon adjourns indefinitely the Ad Hoc Constitutional Committee.
30 November	Broadcast by Lt-Col Gowon outlining constitutional proposals.

1967

4–5 January	Meeting of the Supreme Military Council at Aburi, Ghana, attended by Lt-Col Ojukwu. Declaration renouncing the use of force. Decisions on the reorganization of the army and of the Military Government.
10–11 March	Meeting of Supreme Military Council (without Lt-Col Ojukwu) at Benin to discuss the draft of Decree No. 8.
12–15 March	Meeting of Law Officers of all the Regional and Federal Governments at Benin.
17 March	Publication of Decree No. 8.
Late March	Negotiations on financial questions in Benin and Accra. Meetings between Lt-Col Ojukwu and several members of the Supreme Military Council.
1 April	East sequestrates federal revenues, followed by other similar measures and retaliatory action by the Federal Military Government.
20–22 April	Meeting of the Supreme Military Council (without Lt-Col Ojukwu) in Lagos to discuss measures to be taken against the East.
1–4 May	Meetings of 'leaders of thought' and of traditional rulers in the North, West, and Mid-West. Speeches by Chief Awolowo and Colonel Adebayo in favour of a negotiated settlement.
4–5 May	Meeting of a National Reconciliation Committee. A 'peace-mission' sent to Enugu.
25 May	Announcement that non-Yoruba troops were being withdrawn from the Western Region.
26–27 May	Meeting of the Eastern Region's Consultative Assembly. Lt-Col Ojukwu authorized to secede.
27 May	Lt-Col Gowon declares a state of emergency, assumes full powers, and divides Nigeria into twelve States.
30 May	Eastern Region secedes.

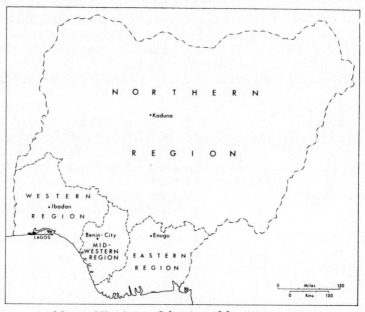

Map 1. Nigeria as a federation of four Regions, 1966

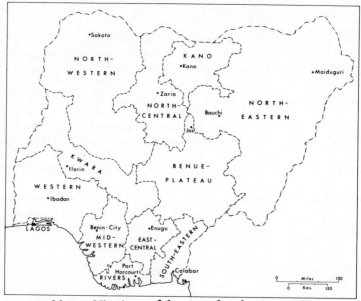

Map 2. Nigeria as a federation of twelve States, 1967

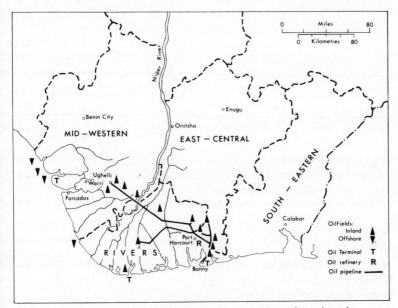

Map 3. Location of oilfields, terminals, and pipelines (1969)

ABBREVIATIONS

AG   Action Group
NCNC National Council of Nigerian Citizens (before 1961: National Council
        of Nigeria and the Cameroons)
NEPU   Nigerian Elements Progressive Union (before 1962: Northern Ele-
        ments Progressive Union)
NNA   Nigerian National Alliance
NNDP Nigerian National Democratic Party
NPC   Northern Peoples' Congress
UMBC United Middle Belt Congress
UNIP   United National Independence Party
UPGA   United Progressive Grand Alliance
UPP   United Peoples' Party
COR   Calabas-Ogoja-Rivers

THE ETHNIC BACKGROUND TO THE
NIGERIAN CRISIS

P. C. Lloyd

THE NIGERIAN CIVIL WAR was between the Regions and over the right of one of them to secede from the Federation. But the impetus for the war and its prolongation derived from the hostility which had developed between the major ethnic groups of the country. Social anthropologists are sometimes prone to see all opposition in ethnic terms—a category with which they are better acquainted than, for instance, social stratification. Be that as it may, Nigeria's problems do, I believe, derive in large measure from the tensions which have arisen between the larger ethnic groups.

Africa's new states have many characteristics in common and one of these is that all are composed of a number of clearly distinguishable ethnic groups. Is the Nigerian war, therefore, a foretaste of things to come in other states? Inasmuch as ethnic hostility and rivalry is already apparent in the political life of any country, is a further deterioration into armed struggle inevitable? I shall show that the Nigerian situation is peculiar in that ethnic differences are of greater magnitude here than elsewhere and that historical factors, not inevitable elsewhere, have been exploited by these differences.

THE SCALE OF ETHNIC DIFFERENCES

Nigeria is dominated by the Hausa (approximately 15 million), Ibo (approximately 10 million), and Yoruba (approximately 10 million) peoples. Together they constitute well over half of the country's population; each alone is more numerous than most of the new states of tropical Africa. Each is dominant in one of the Regions which composed the newly independent Federation. These Regions, furthermore, were based upon earlier administrative divisions of the country: the River Niger formed an obvious boundary between the Eastern and Western Provinces, even though half a million Ibo were left on the western banks; the division into North and South derives from the process of consular administration along the coast and its hinterland, and from the grant of a charter to the Royal Niger Company to exploit and administer the hinterland. (A million Yoruba were placed in the Northern Provinces, their territory having been overrun or conquered by the Fulani.)

Each of the three dominant ethnic groups—Hausa, Ibo, and Yoruba —has a relatively uniform culture; the discontinuities at the boundaries with neighbouring ethnic groups are most marked. In the present century, furthermore, ease of movement, schooling and a cultural renaissance among the educated elite have tended to produce greater uniformity; for instance, dialects, once pronounced, are disappearing.

It is, however the difference between the cultures of the major ethnic groups which is most pronounced. Such differences are not capable of precise measurement, save perhaps in terms of language. Thus both the Yoruba and Ibo languages belong to the Kwa group of the Niger-Congo family, a group which embraces most of the languages of the Guinea Coast from the Cross River to Liberia. But the difference between Yoruba and Ibo, and indeed even between Yoruba and neighbouring Edo, is of the same order, very approximately, as that between English and Russian. Such linguistic differences indicate that the peoples have developed their cultures largely independently of one another over thousands of years. The languages of the interior belong to yet other families. Thus Tiv and many of the languages of the Jos plateau are semi- (or proto-?) Bantu (another group within the Niger-Congo family), Tiv being as close to Ibo as it is to Swazi. Hausa is a Chadic language, belonging to the Afro-Asiatic family which includes the Semitic, Berber and Cushitic groups. Cultural differences of this order are paralleled, for example, in Kenya. But over most of Bantu-speaking Africa the linguistic, and hence cultural, range within the state is of a far smaller degree.

In Nigeria the cultural differences are frequently reinforced by legends of origin which give each ethnic group uniqueness. Thus Oduduwa, the Yoruba progenitor, is variously said to have come down from the heavens or to have come from 'the east'. Reputable African historians frequently argue that their own ethnic group migrated to its present home over thousands of miles and hundreds of years, preserving its individual identity. It is a lone voice which stresses, as Okoi Arikpo[1] did in his broadcast Lugard Lectures, that cultural traits are often of widespread occurrence, indicating a considerable immigration of people over the centuries, so that no ethnic group can be considered a 'pure' stock.

The scale of ethnic differences alone would pose problems for a new nation but a further factor in Nigeria is the ranking of the societies in terms of complexity of organization and hence, in the eyes of their people, in prestige. The Hausa live in walled cities, centres of trade and administration; political power resides with the Fulani aristocracy, the original Habe kingdoms having been conquered in the *jihad* at the beginning of the nineteenth century. In scale and complexity (measured by the differentiation of offices) the Hausa-Fulani emirates equal the kingdoms of medieval Europe. The Ibo, in contrast, are organized in a large number of small village groups, the people of each claiming descent from a founding ancestor, whose sons in turn founded the constituent villages. Centralized authority is absent, and few titled offices exist. The Ibo are strongly egalitarian and accord less respect to age than most Nigerian peoples. The Yoruba fall between these two extremes, having kingdoms of some complexity yet possessing a social organization in which the descent group is the basic unit. The Muslim Hausa-Fulani scorn all non-Muslims — and Muslims are negligible among the Ibo, though there are as many Yoruba Muslims as Yoruba Christians. The Hausa-Fulani are apt to describe the Ibo as cannibals, human sacrifice being recorded as late as the early years of this century. The Yoruba see town dwelling as a mark of 'civilization' and deride those who live in villages. Dress, too, is a ready symbol of civilization, and in Nigeria varies from the elaborate robes of Hausa and Yoruba to the loin-cloth of many Ibo groups and the decorated nudity of Plateau peoples.

Kenya was cited earlier as an example of comparable ethnic diversity but these differences are not hierarchically ordered as in Nigeria; neither the Bantu-speaking peoples, such as the Kikuyu, the Luo, nor the Somali had created a centralized state.

The social and political structure of the various Nigerian peoples produces values which are variously appropriate to modernization; in particular, their achievement orientation differs markedly. Furthermore, the hierarchical ordering described above is revealed. In psychological tests measuring 'achievement motivation, concern with self-improvement, non-authoritarian ideology, a favourable attitude towards technological innovation, and rapid advancement in Western education and the Western type of occupational hierarchy'[2] the Ibo scored highly, being followed by the Yoruba, with the Hausa lowest on these scales. In other words, it is the despised (in Hausa eyes) Ibo who are best able to exploit the opportunities presented by modernization to assure for themselves a dominant role. The traditional ranking is reversed in the modern economy.

COLONIAL RULE AND THE PRESERVATION OF ETHNIC DIFFERENCES

These ethnic differences have been described in the present tense because they are still marked. British rule has frequently been blamed for maintaining these differences rather than, by measures not explained, obliterating them.

Policies of administration by Indirect Rule did, indeed, preserve the indigenous social and political units and the values associated with them. Lugard had little alternative but to govern through the Fulani political elite and his success here was followed by the introduction of his principles to Yoruba country. A more direct administration of the Ibo through Warrant Chiefs was a failure, culminating in the Aba riots of 1929. Under colonial rule traditional office-holders maintained their positions though their roles were often substantially altered.

In modern government too, the traditional units have been reorganized, often forming local government wards or parliamentary constituencies. Thus, when the policies of the rival parties appear, to the electorate, to be indistinguishable, ancient rivalries can provide the basis of opposition.

Nigeria has its wealthy areas; apart from the modern towns, the cocoa-producing areas of the Yoruba, the oil palm area of the Ibo, and the cotton and groundnut areas in the North are all relatively affluent. New occupations have created relationships outside those of the corporate descent groups, thus weakening the solidarity of the latter. But at the same time the use of the land for export crops and the growing population have resulted in land shortage which has intensified descent group loyalties—a man whose allegiance falls short of expectations may find himself with a minimal allocation of land.

Agricultural products form the greater part of Nigeria's exports, and the crops cited above have not occasioned any great displacement of population; they are all grown by peasant farmers. Population movements have been less in Nigeria, relative to its size, than in most African states. Much migration is for short periods only: men from the northern savannah margins emigrate for the dry season only; southerners often go to the towns as 'target workers', accepting unskilled jobs until they have accumulated a specified sum of money, perhaps for bride wealth. Clerks and teachers, committed to modern occupations and, in most cases, town life, have in the past been transferred frequently from one place to another. They have formed no attachments to the towns of such temporary domicile. One result is the strength of ethnic associations in these towns, particularly among those peoples such as the Ibo, whose social structure is based upon localized descent groups.

In doing so little to break down traditional patterns of residence and allegiance, economic development has not contributed to any reduction in inter-ethnic differences. In fact, it may be said to have exacerbated them. For economic development is notoriously uneven, and these new inequalities are superimposed on all existing rivalries. Lugard would, I think, have set up schools and technical colleges for the Hausa; but his local lieutenants were so impressed with the need to protect the indigenous political system and the religion which upheld it that Christian missions were excluded from the towns of the emirates. The Hausa remained educationally backward—in the late 1950s only 2 per cent of the children of Sokoto Province were in primary schools. The mines and the commercial firms were obliged to rely on immigrant southerners; and even the Zaria Native Authority, for example, had 59 southern clerks and technicians on its staff in 1945.[3] These were mainly Ibo, the Yoruba having a preference for independent trade. The southerners lived in settlements close to the government residential and commercial areas, well outside the walls of the indigenous town in whose social and political life they participated not at all. The situation was self-perpetuating. Not only did the southerners almost alone possess the qualifications for jobs in the modern sector, but with their family and clan obligations they successfully preserved vacant posts for their own people. Hausa resentment developed as increasing numbers left primary schools to search for jobs in the modern sector.

ETHNIC COMPETITION AND HOSTILITY

So far I have stressed the range of ethnic differences within Nigeria and suggested a few reasons for the maintenance of these differences in the present century. But the scale of ethnic differences does not determine the degree of hostility between the groups. The world has seen bitter struggles between peoples of substantial cultural similarity—the English and Irish for example in the second decade of this century. The hostility derives, of course, not from the ethnic differences but from competition between peoples for wealth and power. One might as well have begun with the analysis of these factors, for I believe it is the intensity of this competition which is probably the prime determinant of the degree of ethnic hostility. Nevertheless, wide cultural divergence between competing ethnic groups does render communication difficult and reduce the chances of settlement by peaceful means.[4]

Colonial rule is autocratic and to some degree impartial. Some areas are more favoured in the provision of schools (though local demand is an important factor in allocation) or in economic development (determined usually by natural resources). Administrative officers in Northern Nigeria clearly favoured the Hausa-Fulani; the 'punishment stations' were not in the emirates. But with independence there has been a struggle between competing groups for leadership in the new state. At stake is not only the right to govern. It is widely believed by the electorate that those in power will give preference to their own kin, communities, and areas in allocating scarce resources. This is a traditional value subscribed to by both Ibo and Hausa, and most other ethnic groups. Not only will some areas be favoured with new social services, new economic opportunities, but their inhabitants will benefit from the patronage exercised by those in positions of power. Examples of such favouritism are easily found to support this viewpoint. There *are* main roads which are tarred as far as the Minister's own village and no further.

In Nigeria, political parties assumed an ethnic complexion well before independence. The split between the Nigerian Youth Movement and the NCNC of Nnamdi Azikiwe in the early 1940s to some extent followed ethnic divisions between Yoruba and Ibo. The Action Group developed from the political wing of the cultural association of the Yoruba educated elite, the Egbe Omo Oduduwa; the NCNC was closely allied with the Ibo State Union. The NPC was founded by the Fulani aristocracy. In the smaller ethnic groups, a local political party was often indistinguishable from the cultural association.[5]

The fears of the minority areas were argued before Willink's Minorities Commission but allegations of discrimination were often poorly grounded. Furthermore the minority areas tended to lack internal cohesion or economic viability. Eventually only the Mid-West Region was created; the Middle Belt Region and the Calabar-Ogoja Rivers Region remained a hope for an ever-decreasing number. For the price of services and patronage was seen to be joining the dominant party in the Region and thus sharing in its power—a process which at least weakened the ethnic exclusiveness of the dominant party.

A second factor producing ethnic hostility is the inter-personal competition for offices in the modern sector of the economy. Primary and secondary education in southern Nigeria was relatively (by African standards) well developed in the early 1950s. But a deliberate policy of Nigerianization in the public services was late in developing. Only in 1953 did the last new British administrative officers arrive in Western Nigeria and in 1954 the first big recruitment of Nigerians began. Within a very few years most British officers on the permanent establishment had left. At the same time, the size of the public services expanded with the administration of new and increasing social services —the politicians' reward to their electorate. This expansion was made possible by the growth of the educational system at all levels simultaneously. Thus University College Ibadan, opened in 1948, increased in size before the new secondary schools were able to supply it with enough graduating fifth- and sixth-formers.

One result of this expansion was the very rapid promotion enjoyed by most of those Nigerians who were early entrants to the public services. The first Nigerian permanent secretaries in the Western Region's civil service had, on average, but ten years' service on appointment. In the University of Ibadan seven years, on average, saw a

Nigerian rise from assistant lecturer with a newly won Ph.D to professor and head of department.

This rapid expansion was halted in the early 1960s almost as quickly as it had started, with the depletion of the sterling balances, the reduction in foreign aid, and the like. New entrants to the bureaucratic hierarchies were faced with very slow promotion as those at the top, still only in their forties and fifties, were ensconced for another decade or two. The supply of educated men began to exceed the demand. The returning university graduate in the mid-1950s was welcomed into a government post with all its privileges and perquisites; in the mid-1960s the Western Region inaugurated civil service examinations of the English type and was no longer bound to find employment for those whose training it had financed.

Rapid promotion and shortage of posts both, in their own way, foster a high degree of inter-personal competition; both result in a high rate of failed expectations. These failures, furthermore, are experienced not only by the individuals concerned but by a wide circle of kin hoping for the benefits of patronage and indeed expecting them as a due reward for financing the education of their 'son'. The processes resulting in failure are frequently misunderstood. The criteria for promotion in a bureaucratic system are alien to them; it is not appreciated that a boy who shines in secondary school may perform less well in a university. A characteristic response to failure is extrapunitive; the failure is ascribed to the machinations of enemies. Among southern Nigerians witchcraft by near kin is often alleged. But a common explanation—common because it is acceptable to all hearers— is that one has been the victim of nepotism or ethnic favouritism. If the chairman of the Selection Committee was an Ibo, what chance had a Yoruba candidate? Such rationalizations enhance ethnic hostility; nevertheless, they also detract from criticism of the structure of employment itself—a structure which has produced the over-supply of educated men and can be altered only by a radical change of government policies or of its personnel.

A third factor which engenders hostility is the image of the modern society to be created in Nigeria. In southern Nigeria the educated elite have come largely from humble homes. The traditional elite of obas, chiefs, and lesser title-holders today have insignificant roles at the national level; their remaining prestige is confined to their own communities. The educated elite are thus free to construct a modern society unencumbered by that of their past. In Northern Nigeria, however, the Fulani aristocracy, through the NPC, retain their elite status. Their problem has been to modernize their society only so far as leaves their superior position unimpaired. This they have substantially achieved through their control of the political party, the Native Authorities, and the Alkali's courts. The introduction of institutions from the south—elected local government councils, centrally controlled and politically independent courts—threatens their status.

A correlated factor affecting the Western-educated elite concerns the criteria for social mobility within the society. In southern Nigeria education is so often both the determining qualification for getting a job and the limiting factor in subsequent promotion that it is seen as the only legitimate criterion for elite status. In the emirates, one's position within the Fulani aristocracy is pre-eminent. Northerners have violated (in southern eyes) the usual career expectations when, for instance, a Federal minister returns to take up an office in the Native Authority of his home area. When southerners and Northerners are competing for elite-type offices, the lack of agreement over the legitimate criteria for appointment and promotion leads to strain.

Of the factors cited here, the first—the struggle for power—is inevitable in a new African state, though it is not inevitable that the struggle should be between ethnic groups—in Nigeria it is merely probable that it should be so. The inter-personal competition for offices is a feature of southern Nigeria which is less apparent in the North or in those African states which have not yet begun to produce too many educated people. The third factor is somewhat peculiar to Nigeria. (In a different context Liberia has its traditional elite, still in power and circumspect in its modernizing policies.)

To the extent that ethnic hostility is rife, it may be, and frequently is, increased by politicians who use ethnic issues to enhance their electoral support. Ethnic arguments will be used when policy differences between the rival parties is minimal or where the policies of a party are unlikely to win popular support. Thus, at the grass roots level, AG politicians often asserted that an NCNC victory in Western Nigeria would mean that the Yoruba would be ruled by the Ibo. Overtly ethnic propaganda reached its height in Akintola's attempts to win popular support before the Regional election of 1965.

ETHNICITY AND POLITICAL TENSIONS IN NIGERIA, 1952-68

Let us now glance quickly at Nigeria's recent history, interpreting some of its events in the light of the ethnic hostility described above. First, the fear on the part of Northern Nigeria, and particularly the Fulani aristocracy, of domination by the southerners, and particularly by the Ibo. This is not simply the fear that the southerners will govern, if in power, to their own advantage. At stake, for the Fulani, is the entire structure of their society and their privileged position in it. Should they lose, it is most probably the Ibo who will emerge dominant over them. In the early 1950s the North tried to retard progress towards independence. But when it became evident that the demands of the southern politicians could no longer be contained the northerners joined them, intending not to be co-equal partners in the federation but to be dominant over them. The size of the Northern Region, as expressed by the 1952/3 population census, gave it an initial advantage in the Federal legislature; this was enhanced as the NPC came to win most of the seats in the Region. It was threatened by the 1962 census, preliminary figures for which showed that the population of the southern Regions exceeded that of the North. A recount gave the North the same proportion of the total population as in 1952! Northern control was seen to be threatened too by the dominance of southerners in the Federal civil service; thus in the early 1960s, as southerners went on leave, northerners with lower educational qualifications were placed in acting positions—and tended to remain substantively.

In attempting to win recognition as a national party, the AG campaigned, in the 1959 Federal elections, in the Northern Region using ethnic minority propaganda in the non-Hausa areas, but in the emirates the appeal was on class lines, urging the *talakawa* commoners to oppose the Fulani aristocracy. The defence of the NPC here lay in cultural terms—southern domination would be a threat to Islam, and would introduce alcoholism and debauchery. The AG campaign was, in terms of seats won, not very successful, but it seems to have created considerable apprehension in the North.

The Northern Region also had its own internal problems. The Hausa-Fulani emirates comprised only half of its population, the remainder being made up of Bornu and non-Hausa emirates and acephalous peoples, such as the Tiv, in the 'Middle Belt'. Some of the latter areas, largely non-Muslim, far outpaced the Hausa in acceptance of education, and Yoruba from Kabba, for instance, and other neighbouring peoples began to dominate the Regional civil service. But although the values of these men were similar to those of the southern educated elite they had a vested interest in preserving regional autonomy, for, with their relatively meagre qualifications, they could rise much higher than if they were competing with southerners. NPC electoral successes in the Middle Belt meant that men from these areas came to assume ministerial office; but the dominance of these people came only after the military coups, for it is from the Middle Belt that the Nigerian army was largely recruited. The recent creation of six states in the North can, perhaps, be seen as the result of Fulani attempts to maintain their superior status in their emirates; having lost power at the Federal and Regional level, they see in the new states, with their substantial autonomy, their best safeguards.

Hostility between Yoruba and Ibo is of a somewhat different character. There is a general fear by each of dominance by the other, increased both by the difference in their cultural levels and by the fact that the Yoruba received an early start in the race for education; their educated elite founded the first nationalist movements. The Ibo have, rather self-consciously, been trying to catch up—with such success that their secondary school output came to equal and perhaps exceeded that of the Yoruba. But the values of the educated elite and the goals of the political parties have been very similar—at least in comparison with those of the Hausa-Fulani. Why, then, have they been so unsuccessful in combining against the Fulani, allowing the latter to play one off against the other—even to the extent of accepting the NCNC as partners in the Federal government from 1959 onwards? The answer lies, I believe, in the intensity of inter-personal competition for office, in Federal services, between the Yoruba and Ibo.

In the 1960s the control of public corporations, with the patronage to be dispensed by their chairmen, was a recurrent issue in the press. The University of Ibadan proved not to be a locus of academic detachment. A nice balance between an Ibo Vice-Chancellor and a Yoruba Registrar resulted in court actions between the two; control of the University Council became an ethnic/political issue and almost every professorial appointment (or delayed appointment) was seen as a move in the struggle for dominance between the rival ethnic groups. Had those in high places behaved with some rectitude, any qualms surrounding their appointment might have been forgotten. But the commissions of enquiry, court actions, and the like disclosed that not only politicians used their offices for private gain but that senior civil servants and professors were, in many instances, equally corrupt. Bitterness, especially within the elite, was intensified. (The masses were more apt to feel 'a plague on both your houses'.)

Ethnic hostility had reached such a pitch by the time of the military coup of January 1966 that subsequent events were interpreted only too often in these terms. The coup was, in my view, the action of a section of the educated elite, possessed of physical power and free from the taint of corruption, against elected politicians whose failure to control the masses threatened the stability of the country—and, in particular, the privileged position of the educated elite. It was not an 'Ibo coup', but most of the young army officers were Ibo and it was reasonable that the conspirators should not share their secrets with members of other ethnic groups. General Ironsi, in all probability, did not see himself as a leader of the Ibo; but he probably erred in leaning more on the advice of Ibo colleagues and in tolerating those Ibo who rushed to State House to proffer advice. The promotion of Ibo officers to fill ranks depleted in the coup was probably fair in the sense that they were next in seniority. It was probably not significant that a senior and very able Ibo federal civil servant was in charge of the preparation of plans for a more centralized national administration—one in which the Ibo would be expected to achieve a large share of high offices. Many intellectuals, both Yoruba and Ibo, favoured a stronger Federal government and administration. But all these events were construed as an attempt by the Ibo to take over the whole country.

The Ibo, judging their own actions in terms of values appropriate to the modern state, seem to have been unaware of the degree of hostility which they inspired in others. Tactlessness in high places was paralleled by insensitivity among the masses. Such were the religious divisions within Islam in the Northern Region that many Hausa were not displeased by the assassination of the Sardauna of Sokoto, but they resented the manner in which the Ibo in the North rejoiced at the event. The growing lack of tolerance towards the Ibo in the Northern towns ultimately led to the first wave of massacres in May, the spark perhaps being provided by the publication of the plans for a unified administrative structure. In this and other outrages it seems that atrocities were directed specifically against the Ibo and that members of other ethnic groups were spared—although in the mêlée many who could not be distinguished from the Ibo were killed. Significantly, too, the massacres were not fanned by religious sentiment; Muslims did not attack churches. In the second army coup of July 1966 Northern officers, aggrieved by the death of their compatriots in January (when only one Ibo officer lost his life and then, apparently, more by fortuitous circumstances than by design) and fearful of current Ibo dominance, led an attack on not only Ibo officers but other ranks as well. The September/October massacres, this time sparked off by reports on Radio Cotonou of the killing of Hausa in Onitsha market, followed the same pattern.

The scale of the massacres brought death or mutilation to humble members of thousands of Ibo villages. Ethnic hostility was no longer seen as a characteristic of relationships within the educated elite. In their sudden shock, the Ibo leaders talked in terms of genocide and demanded reparations—claims which were certainly justified but were pursued with such intolerance as to impede settlement. Threats of secession led to its ultimate declaration.

As ethnicity came to dominate all relationships the Yoruba elite again failed, after much indecision, to join the Ibo in a common ideological cause. They opted for the Federation in which, with the Fulani aristocracy politically weakened and with Ibo excluded, they might be dominant.

I have drawn contrasts between Hausa, Yoruba, and Ibo in stark and dramatic terms. But the picture is infinitely more complicated than this, for within each group there are divisions. Thus the popular stereotype of the Ijebu is of greater achievement orientation than other Yoruba. Ijebu and Egba, who gained an early lead in the race for education, tend to predominate in the higher offices. As each new state is created, it is found to contain minority areas whose people demand their own autonomy. This is a process which can, logically, continue *ad infinitum*. Members of the educated elite, feeling that their prestige depends ultimately not on their income or the general importance of their jobs but on the patronage controlled, are apt to abet the proliferation of political and administrative units.

Finally, having outlined the reasons for the intensity of ethnic hostility in Nigeria, I feel obliged to offer, even if in summary form, some means of reducing the tensions created. I must, however, provide a caveat that measures which reduce ethnic hostility may be inimicable to the economic or political development of the country generally. The gains in any measure must be measured against costs in other spheres.

Neither the scale of ethnic differences nor the size of the major ethnic groups can be altered. The cultural renaissance, an integral part of the nationalist movement, has tended to produce greater uniformity within each ethnic group and so differentiate it more sharply from neighbouring groups. Thus among the Yoruba, for instance, a standard dialect is emerging and dress styles, both for rich and poor, have a similarity that did not exist a century or two ago. There is in fact a consciousness of being Yoruba which is recent—the term Yoruba applied formerly only to the Oyo Kingdom. Thus stronger cohesion has been produced within ethnic groups; this process has its advantages and, in any case, can hardly be reversed. Nevertheless if national unity and consciousness is to be stimulated and maintained a national symbolism must be fostered. American children, of diverse ethnic origins, each morning recite the oath of allegiance and salute the national flag. This is certainly not the only method of attaining unity, but it does exemplify the conscious methods which might be used. Again, while cultural pride is legitimate, ethnic exclusiveness, such as the belief in the migration of one's own ethnic group as an exclusive unit over thousands of miles and hundreds of years must be shown to be a myth which denies implicitly such intermixing of peoples and cultures as must have occurred. Ethnic groups should not form single political units; the larger ones should be subdivided. Inter-personal competition can be reduced only through equating, to a greater degree, the output of schools and colleges with the number of jobs available; it will then, as in the years before 1955, be a struggle to get an educational qualification; the job then almost automatically followed. Today, as the numbers of candidates qualified for each post increases, the attainment of an educational certificate merely allows one to enter the employment lists where the struggle really begins. GCE certificates and university degrees are won by merit—not (as yet, at any rate) by ethnic favouritism; jobs are, in contrast, seen to be allocated according to ethnic principles. But these, I again add, are but partial solutions to Nigeria's problems.

2

FROM MILITARY COUP TO CIVIL WAR
JANUARY 1966 TO MAY 1967

S. K. Panter-Brick

THE NIGERIAN political system had passed through so many political and constitutional crises both before and since independence that it had come to be regarded as relatively well constituted, despite the country's great size, cultural diversity, and uneven economic development. But doubts remained and uncertainty increased as the struggle for control of the central government intensified and as contesting political forces sought to extend and consolidate their positions by means which were anything but constitutional.[1] The muted confrontation between the President and the Federal Prime Minister, arising out of the 1964 Federal elections, was a portent of the gathering storm. The rigged elections in the Western Region in October 1965, and the resulting breakdown of law and order in that Region, were clearly the prelude to further, more desperate, measures, involving in all probability the use of the army. Rumours to this effect were rife when, in the night of 14–15 January 1966, a small group of army officers staged a coup, murdering in the process several leading politicians and senior military officers. On the evening of the 16th General Ironsi took control of the Federal Government and by the 18th had established his authority throughout the country.[2] It was a blow which ended the regime but not the political difficulties besetting Nigeria. All the previous tensions persisted, despite the profession of good intentions on the part of the military leaders. In the end all negotiations failed and Nigeria disintegrated. The coup of 15 January 1966 is, therefore, not merely the advent of military rule in Nigeria, it is also the beginning of a crisis far more acute, far less amenable to peaceful resolution than any previous crisis in Nigerian political history. The purpose of this chapter is to provide an analysis of the central issues and to trace the development of the crisis from its inception in the coup of 15 January 1966 to its culmination in civil war at the end of May 1967.

Looking back over the course of events one can discern a dialectical pattern. The coup heralded a period of centralization, or attempted centralization, under General Ironsi. This initial trend was sharply reversed on 29 July when the army, inflicting upon itself a second and still more serious internal haemorrhage, effectively ceased to respond to any central command and consequently ceased to be a unifying force. The country then moved into a period of decentralization and dislocation. The final stage of this dialectical conflict was the attempt by Lt-Col Gowon to impose a synthesis on these contradictory centralizing and disintegrative forces by reconstituting Nigeria as a federation of twelve states.

As in all dialectical movements, the first stages were marked by internal contradictions. Long before 29 July the initial impulse towards a unitary system of government was being opposed but it was not until 29 July that these opposing forces had gathered sufficient strength to bring about a change. Similarly, the reverse movement towards regional autonomy soon attracted opposition. It is only in the third and final stage of a dialectical movement that the contesting forces are superseded by a synthesis which resolves the contradiction. It is at this point that events might fail to conform to the suggested pattern, for it is one still to be consolidated. The account which follows therefore deals solely with the events of the first two stages, that is, up to the end of May 1967.

THE IRONSI GOVERNMENT

January–May 1966

The initial movement towards a more centralized form of government was slow to express itself in concrete terms. In a sense the military regime was in itself a switch to a unitary form of government. The strictly hierarchical structure of military command is inconsistent with a federal division of powers constitutionally guaranteed. Once 'formally invested' as Head of the Federal Military Government and Supreme Commander of the Armed Forces, General Ironsi decreed that the Federal Military Government was the supreme authority.[3] This was the formal constitutional position, backed of course by the military chain of command. In practice, however, the federal structure was left to function much as before. Regional authorities were not abolished but replaced by Military Governors who inherited their legislative and executive powers in a modified form. At the centre a Supreme Military Council was established in which the four Military Governors sat *ex officio*.[4] Thus the central authority retained a quasi-federal character and the regional administrators continued to act in much the same autonomous fashion as under the 1963 Constitution.[5] This contrast between the formal position and actual practice helps to explain the official designation of the central government as the *Federal* Military Government. Although something of a misnomer because of General Ironsi's overriding legislative and executive powers, it reflected administrative continuity. This element of continuity was reinforced in three other ways. The Military Governors were all drawn from their respective Regions, the former Regional Governors were appointed as Political Advisers to the Military Governors, and each Region retained its own separate civil service and judiciary.

No immediate and definite steps were taken to centralize the administration, not because of any doubts about its desirability and necessity—there was a clear intention to move in that direction—but because the Military Government was fully stretched attending to more pressing matters. Its main concern was to restore and maintain law and order, especially in the Western Region where the rigged elections of October 1965 had led to widespread bitterness, thuggery, lawlessness, damage to property, and loss of life.[6]

The Military Government was also preoccupied with laying down new codes for the conduct of public affairs, with checking on corrupt practices and bringing offenders to court, with enforcing the proper collection of taxes and the repayment of loans out of public funds, and with trying to alleviate popular discontent in matters such as inadequate housing, high rents, and the rising cost of staple foods. It was not the moment to add to the burden by undertaking a fundamental reorganization of legal and administrative structures. Nor was it the moment for precipitate action of a kind that might confirm suspicions, especially strong among many Northerners, that the 15 January coup, in which certain political leaders and senior army officers were murdered but others spared, was simply part of a wider conspiracy to bring the whole country under Ibo domination. Furthermore, discipline in the army itself was shaken.[7] The strength of the armed forces was, in any case, only about 10,000. There were 18,000 Nigeria Police but the local police forces in the Northern and Western Regions, now brought under the operational control of the Nigeria Police, had local loyalties and could not be relied upon to any great extent. Given the paucity and uncertainty of the forces at its command the Government had every reason to proceed cautiously.

The first intimations of the Military Government's intention to centralize—its necessity and desirability being very much taken for granted—came in a speech by General Ironsi on 28 January.[8] Denouncing the evils of the previous regime and outlining the necessary reforms, he mentioned as the root-causes of Nigeria's troubles corruption, nepotism, inefficiency, and 'regionalism'. 'All Nigerians', he declared, 'want an end to regionalism. Tribal loyalties and activities which promote tribal consciousness and sectional interests must give way to the urgent task of national reconstruction. The Federal Military Government will preserve Nigeria as one strong nation.' He then went on to promise 'administrative reforms' and referred specifically to several matters in which regional as well as personal interests were known to have had decisive influence. These were official appointments, public investments, and the universities. He promised that 'in the public service, efficiency and merit will be the criteria for advancement', that industrial development would be 'coordinated to avoid wasteful duplication of industrial projects', and that the universities would be 're-orientated to serve the genuine interest of our people'.[9]

Immediately following this speech, Lt-Col Ejoor, the Military Governor in the Mid-West, was reported as saying that the 'National Government' set up by the army was the prelude to the reintroduction of a unitary form of government.[10] Shortly afterwards the Military Government announced that a senior government official, Mr Nwokedi, had been asked to consider and to report to the Supreme Military Council on the 'establishment of an administrative machinery for a united Nigeria' and the 'unification of the Public Services and Judicial Services'. Another official was to help in a review of 'statutory corporations, State-owned companies and related organizations throughout the Federation'.[11]

This fairly clear indication of the Military Government's intentions was soon openly questioned, if not directly challenged, in the press. A leader in the *Daily Times* raised the question 'What Next?' after the military had completed 'the task of preparing the site for a new nation'.[12] It commented: 'There seems to be the misconception among some people that because of the myriad weaknesses of the last constitution, and because of the universal impatience with its shortcomings, we can now take it for granted that Nigerians have picked a unitary form of government for the Second Republic. Maybe. But only maybe. . . . are we already satisfied that Nigerians necessarily want a particular form of unitary government? . . . some probably want a Government that is strong at the centre, but which has weak units as well. Such people would say that in spite of the many faults of the last constitution, at least we were saved an outright dictatorship by one man, because of the division of power . . . We may find that . . . an administration in which counterbalancing powers are granted provincial administrators would be our security against a dictator in the unseen future. An outright unitary government could leave too much room for goodwill, the way the old Constitution left too much room for goodwill among the regions. On the other hand, there will be those who will say that federalism in any form is an evil . . . Which of these two will be the popular choice is anybody's guess.'

Having thus suggested that there were reasonable differences of opinion, the *Daily Times* added a warning against claiming to know what the people wanted without consulting them. 'The major failure in the drafting of the previous constitution was that the British and the politicians took the people for granted. The leadership presumed to know what the people wanted and signed up for it.' To avoid a repetition, the *Daily Times* urged the Military Government to entrust the drafting of a new constitution to a committee of experts, whose draft would be debated, and if necessary amended, in a constituent assembly and finally submitted to the electorate for its approval. More tentatively, it suggested that the fixing of a time limit for the completion of the whole process, although possibly 'premature', was certainly 'not beyond imagination'. Meanwhile people were urged to 'speak out', on the assurance that the Government was 'eager for suggestions' and 'sensible to reasoned argument'. General Ironsi could scarcely ignore this astutely worded call for popular participation in the constitution-making process. The military certainly enjoyed widespread support but relief at the abdication of the corrupt politicians in no way implied a renunciation of the right to be heard and of the right to be honestly represented. Indeed, the military authorities were already being overwhelmed by the flood of suggestions pouring in from citizens and associations of all kinds, so much so that a leader in the *New Nigerian* referred to the new game of 'Let's make a constitution'. The *Daily Times* was thus on strong ground in urging its readers to 'speak out', and in giving them a forthright, albeit cautiously worded, example: public interest was too strong to ignore.[13] All the more important therefore was the lead given to public opinion. Although the *Daily Times* expressed the opinion that 'a majority of vocal Nigerians want a stronger government in Lagos' and hoped that when the time came the people would choose a strong, united government, the overall effect was to raise the question 'how strong a central government' and to encourage those who opposed the institution of a unitary form of government to speak up and say so. Since this was a direct challenge to the Military Government's own assumption, it certainly could not be ignored.

Four days after the appearance of the *Daily Times'* article, General Ironsi called a press conference. While conceding the demand for a constituent assembly and a referendum, he restated even more strongly the need for centralization. '. . . the experiences and mistakes of the previous governments in the Federation have clearly indicated that far-reaching constitutional reforms are badly needed . . . it has become apparent to all Nigerians that rigid adherence to "regionalism" was the bane of the last regime and one of the main factors which contributed to its downfall. No doubt, the country would welcome a clean break with the deficiencies of the system of government to which the country has been subjected in the past. A solution suitable to our national needs must be found. The existing boundaries of government control will need to be readjusted to make for less cumbersome administration. In the new order of things there should be no place for regionalism and tribal consciousness. The country needs a sort of nerve centre which will give the necessary direction and control in all major areas of national activities, so that we will be in a position to plot a uniform pattern of development for the whole country. Matters which were formerly within the legislative competence of the regions will need to be reviewed so that issues of national importance could be centrally controlled and directed towards overall and uniform development in the economic and social fields. Effective liaison and co-ordination should be established between the Federal authority and its provincial counterparts.'[14]

This vigorous restatement of the Military Government's determination to centralize was accompanied, as might be expected, by an appeal to the press 'to exercise a sense of loyalty, responsibility and restraint' and by an assurance that the Military Government was without 'political affiliation or ambition', and had 'no desire to prolong its interim administration of government longer than is necessary for the orderly transition of the country to the type of government desired by the people'. But the military, 'the trustees of the nation', were to be given 'the time to accomplish the great task before it'. Meanwhile the press, 'moulders of public opinion', were allotted 'a responsible and constructive role' and the citizens 'a useful part to play'.

For many the crucial part of this press conference was no doubt the promise of a constituent assembly and referendum. Although no date had been fixed, it did seem to exclude any arbitrary action on the part of the Military Government. Unfortunately, doubts soon arose because of the way the Government set about the first stage, that of preparing the proposals to be submitted to the constituent assembly. The Government did not limit itself to setting up a committee to advise on the constitutional issues. It commissioned a whole set of reports, all concerned with administrative centralization, and appointed various working parties and committees to advise on national policy. The work of these different bodies and the importance of each needs to be explained in greater detail, for it is crucial to an understanding of subsequent events.

In a class by itself, because of its obvious importance and wide-ranging terms of reference, was the nine-man committee appointed to carry out a review of constitutional questions. These included not only the form of government best suited to Nigeria and the related question of 'possible territorial divisions' but also the equally controversial question of party politics. It was 'to identify those faults in the former constitution of Nigeria which militated against national unity and against the emergence of a strong central government; to ascertain how far the powers of the former legislative governments fostered regionalism and weakened the Central Government; and to consider the merits and demerits of (a) a unitary form of government, (b) a federal form of government as a system of Government best suited to the demands of a developing country like Nigeria . . .'. On the question of party politics the committee was asked to establish how far it had contributed to tribal consciousness, nepotism, and abuse of office; to consider whether the one-party system or the multi-party system would be more suitable for Nigeria; to report on electoral procedures; and to recommend 'safeguards' for chieftaincies and other traditional institutions.[15]

Secondly, some senior officials were asked to report on certain specific administrative problems. The Government had already called for reports on administrative machinery for a united Nigeria, on the unification of the public services and of the judicial services, and on the state-owned commercial undertakings. These were to be continued, with the responsibilities partly reallocated and, in addition, reports were to be made on the educational services, the information services, police, and prisons.[16] Each of the seven topics was assigned to an individual official but collectively they constituted 'the study group on national unity', and they had similar terms of reference. The task was to identify the problems arising from existing administrative arrangements, to assess how far 'regionalism' had accentuated these problems, to indicate whether administrative unification would create any particular difficulties and, if so, to recommend the means of overcoming such difficulties. In some cases they were assisted by 'working parties'. For instance a working party on education was set up 'to formulate a national and unified policy in Primary and Secondary Education, . . . to consider the type and content of education . . . to examine the implications of introducing universal free primary education'.[17]

Thirdly, the Government established two important advisory committees to advise on questions of economic and agricultural policy. The National Planning Advisory Group was to review economic developments since independence, to recommend any urgent government action or modifications of existing policy thought necessary, and to advise on long-term trends.[18] The National Agricultural Advisory Committee was appointed to advise on the provision of an adequate and well-balanced food supply, the development of agricultural exports and of secondary industries using local agricultural resources, and the kinds of organization needed to accelerate agricultural production on a national scale.[19]

The overall impression created by this proliferation of study groups, working parties, and advisory committees was confusion as to their relative importance. Some thought the review of constitutional issues obviously took pride of place and that, pending a decision on whether the country was to be governed under a unitary or a federal constitution, it was premature and illogical to prepare for a centralization of the administration and an expansion of the central government's responsibilities over matters of policy. The Government appeared to them to be jumping the gun. Others thought that in acting thus the Government was simply engaged in contingency planning, a typical military operation, justifiable in the circumstances. Some centralization was probable and it was wise to prepare the technicalities of it well in advance. A third view was that the country was in a transitional period of military rule, the 1963 Constitution having been largely suspended and a new constitution still to be agreed, and that the military should be allowed to govern the country in its own way. In any case the formulations of national economic, agricultural, and educational policies were the proper responsibility of the Federal Government under the 1963 Constitution. The Military Government was merely making use of powers which the 'regionalism' of the previous regime had rendered inoperative.[20]

Naturally the view taken depended very much upon the intensity of one's preference for a unitary or a federal form of government, and upon the extent of one's confidence in the good intentions of the military. Those convinced of the need for federalism and suspicious of the Military Government's obvious desire to centralize naturally stressed the primacy of agreement on new constitutional arrangements and the inadmissibility of any change in existing administrative arrangements which prejudged the issue. On the other hand, ardent supporters of a unitary form of government saw in the Military Government a powerful ally and had no objection to an anticipation of what they hoped would be the eventual outcome. The middle ground was held by those who, having a more open mind and perhaps also a little naïvety, saw little objection in contingency planning or even a temporary centralization, provided it was perfectly clear that this in no way prejudged the discussions on constitutional issues. In other words, the announcement that a committee was to carry out a thorough review of fundamental constitutional questions—an announcement apparently contradicted by the appointment of a whole series of other committees concerned solely with the centralization of authority—failed to provide a safety valve for the fears of those who had still to be convinced of the military's good intentions. Indeed it may be said to have strengthened those fears by increasing uncertainty. Thus a move which should have brought together people of differing views in an atmosphere of mutual confidence tended, if anything, to push them even further apart.

April was the start of a new financial year and, since the degree of centralization existing in any system of government depends very largely on the way financial powers are exercised, there was some doubt whether the established budgetary procedures would be followed or amended so as to strengthen the Federal Military Government's control.[21] There was talk of a single 'national budget' to supersede the separate federal and regional budgets. But the Federal Military Government had too little time at its disposal to do much more than rubber-stamp the Estimates already under consideration when the military came to power in mid-January and determined largely by established policies. The Federal Military Government could hardly hope to introduce changes before the various advisory committees and working parties had reported and these began work only towards the end of March; some did not begin until near the end of April. Such was certainly the position as regards expenditure on current account. There was a little more flexibility about proposals for capital expenditure, although these also were determined to a considerable extent by existing policies, as well as by commitments to various Regional development projects for which outside financial and technical assistance had already been negotiated. Unquestionably the 'regionalism' of the past was too firmly embedded in the 1966/7 estimates for them to be discarded at this late stage.[22]

Nevertheless, General Ironsi managed to make it sound as if important changes in procedure had been put into effect. He broadcast on 31 March and, after dealing at some length with the state of the economy, he referred to a 'historic' meeting held the previous day with the four Military Governors. He claimed that 'for the first time . . . fiscal, economic and industrial projects are being considered and directed by one central authority'.[23] This remark, more the expression of an aspiration than a description of reality, nonetheless indicated the procedure to be followed on future occasions. He stated that 'any important issues relating to such subjects as education, agriculture, industry and health' would in future be examined centrally, adding: 'I am convinced that the bulk of our people want a united Nigeria and that they want in future one government for Nigeria and not a multitude of governments.' 'In future' meant 'henceforth'. He had that same morning signed a Decree appointing the four Military Governors to the Federal Executive Council, a decision taken, he said, 'to underline the fact that there is now only one government of Nigeria'. This new style Executive Council 'would now ensure that government will be run from one central point'.

Nothing could have been plainer. The Federal Military Government was clearly not confining itself to contingency planning. By the end of March it had come full circle. Having at first adapted its own structure of military command to the established federal pattern of civilian administration, it had now brought the civilian administration more into line with accustomed military practice.

General Ironsi's budget speech of 31 March gave no assurance that this centralization of the civilian administration was to be regarded as an interim arrangement. There was no mention of the committee which was to report on the relative merits of unitary and federal forms of government, no confirmation that a final decision rested with the electorate after full discussion in a constituent assembly, no assurance that a decision by the electorate in favour of some form of federal government would be respected. These omissions inevitably reinforced the impression that the military was irrevocably committed to a unitary form of government, in the belief that this was the popular wish as well as in the best interests of the country. Those who preferred some form of federal government or were undecided or accepted centralization only in certain conditions resented this apparent attempt to bring about a *fait accompli*, and the growth of serious opposition to Ironsi's Government can be dated from this time. The financial calendar, by bringing the military face to face with the reality of regional autonomy, had precipitated a clearer formulation of opposing points of view.

May–July 1966

The scene was thus set for the dramtic turn of events at the end of May. On 24 May General Ironsi announced further measures, most notably Decrees Nos. 33 and 34.[24] The first of these dissolved a large number of organizations, mainly political parties and tribal associations, and banned the formation of any new associations of a political nature until January 1969, although General Ironsi did say that the ban might be lifted earlier 'if the Military Government accomplishes its aims before then'. The other Decree renamed the Federal Military Government the *National* Military Government, redesignated the Regions as *Groups of Provinces*, and incorporated all civil servants, federal and regional, into a single public service.

The ban on political activity was nothing new. The display of party flags and party symbols and the shouting of party slogans had long been proscribed,[25] and the holding of party political meetings had been declared 'inopportune' at the beginning of March.[26] A great deal of informal political activity had, however, continued and only rarely had the military authorities used their arbitrary powers of detention to curb what they considered to be undesirable political activity. Presumably the present formal ban meant that the Military Government was about to make more active use of its powers. Perhaps even more ominous was the duration of the ban—i.e. nearly three years—and the implication that the new constitutional arrangements would be finalized during the period of the ban. General Ironsi's assurance that the constitutional review committee was hard at work and that the unification accomplished by Decree No. 34 in no way prejudiced its findings was, in the circumstances, no assurance at all. It would be difficult to organize any expression of opinion while such a ban remained in force.

It was, however, the 'unification decree', and that part of it which related to the civil service, which caused most immediate concern. Northern civil servants had already shown their anxieties on this score two months earlier when Lt-Col Hassan Katsina, in Lagos for a meeting of the Supreme Military Council, was reported to have 'condemned' the policy of 'Northernization' in the making of appointments. On his return to Kaduna he was besieged with demands for an explanation.[27] It was feared that in a unified service Northerners would be at a disadvantage. It was no consolation that the Decree provided for the delegation of appointments and promotions, except the most senior, to Provincial Civil Service Commissions. It was the senior officials who controlled the administration. Moreover there was no assurance as to the qualifications which were to be taken into consideration when making appointments and promotions. If only formal educational qualifications were to be taken into consideration, to the exclusion of experience, local knowledge, and character, then it was feared that the majority of the senior positions would be filled by southerners, unversed in and unsympathetic to the ways of those they were administering. These fears may have been exaggerated but they were real. They were accentuated by the knowledge that Mr Nwokedi had made his report on the unification of the civil service to General Ironsi without having had it approved by the other members of the committee.[28] This manner of proceeding was taken as a demonstration of the scant attention likely to be given to the claims of Northerners when it came to making appointments.

A few days after the announcement of these new measures protest demonstrations were organized by civil servants in Kaduna and by students in Zaria and Kano. The tension rose, rumour spread, and the mob was organized. There followed, in most Northern towns, a wave of vengeance, in which many hundreds of Ibo civilians were selectively massacred and their property destroyed, the police and the army being powerless to prevent it.[29] It was a deliberate defiance of the Military Government's authority, a warning that there were limits to Northern acquiescence, a delayed reaction to the January coup in which Ibo

officers had organized the equally selective killing of the most prominent Northern political leaders and the most senior Northern officers,
an expression of resentment at the manner in which some of the Ibo
in their midst had unwisely begun to assume an air of dominance.

With its authority challenged and shown to be weak, at least in large
parts of the North, the National Military Government had little option
but to proffer its assurances and to explain its actions. The Supreme
Council met on 7 and 8 June and issued the following statement:

the public must not be led to confuse the Military Government with government by a civilian regime under a constitution approved by the people. Nobody
will expect the present Military Government to cease to function until the new
constitution has been approved or to be compelled to operate the old system of
government with its obvious weaknesses. It cannot be too seriously emphasised
that the Military Government while in office can only run the government as a
military government under a unified command. It cannot afford to run five
separate governments and separate services as if it were a civilian regime . . .
Final decisions on the territorial structure of the country and the public service
will be matters for the constituent assembly and the referendum.[30]

The Supreme Military Council also decided that General Ironsi
should invite traditional rulers from all parts of the country to a
meeting to be held in Lagos as soon as possible and that the Military
Governors would immediately summon similar meetings in their own
Regions. This was presumably an attempt to improve the channels of
communication. There had in fact already been a meeting of Northern
Emirs and Chiefs at Kaduna on 4 June and the Military Governor had
been given a list of grievances and recommendations to take to Lagos.
The Emirs and Chiefs met again on 16 June to receive General Ironsi's
reply. On the face of it the outcome was eminently satisfactory to all
concerned. Lt-Col Hassan Katsina was able to assure the Emirs and
Chiefs that they were part of the machinery of government, sharing
in the duty to preserve law and order and to run the administration,
that they were the Government's main source of knowledge about
public feeling, and that their representatives would be regularly invited
to Lagos for consultation. The Sultan of Sokoto then went on the air
to say that the explanations and assurances given by General Ironsi were
'sufficient to allay our fears and anxieties'.[31]

In the light of subsequent events, however, one wonders whether
this exchange of views really was satisfactory. It is believed that the
Emirs and Chiefs requested that those responsible for the 15 January
coup should be brought to trial, as a test of the National Military
Government's good faith, but that a disappointing reply was received.
Be that as it may, the months of June and July were calm only on the
surface pending General Ironsi's next move. Towards the end of July,

only a few days before the national conference of traditional rulers was due to be held in Ibadan, General Ironsi announced plans to rotate the Military Governors and to appoint military 'prefects' responsible for carrying out government policy at provincial level. There was also to be some transfers of army units, e.g. the 4th Batallion stationed since 1957 at Ibadan and the 1st Battalion stationed at Enugu were to interchange.[32] All this promised a more direct form of military administration and, since Ibo predominated among the higher ranks of the officer corps, a tightening of Ibo control over the North. As in May there was immediate and violent reaction, this time within the army itself. Northern troops mutinied and systematically slaughtered close to 200 Ibo officers and men, including General Ironsi who had come to Ibadan to address the conference of traditional rulers. It was in all probability a premeditated coup, but like that of 15 January the precise political objectives of those who organized it remain obscure; one can, in the present state of knowledge, merely record the resort to violence and its consequences.[33]

General Ironsi is criticized by some Nigerians for not having acted decisively enough and early enough.[34] It is argued that he should have instituted a unitary form of government immediately on taking power, when the military enjoyed great popularity and all the politicians ran for cover. The fallacy of this point of view should be obvious from what has already been said. It overlooks the need for prudence, given the suspicion that the military were less 'the trustees of the nation' than the instrument of the Ibo seeking to establish their hegemony over the other peoples of Nigeria. It also begs the question, for the growing opposition to General Ironsi's government was perhaps not so much to centralization itself as to the manner in which it was being imposed. The attempt at a *fait accompli* was the cause of his downfall. The only hope for a unitary form of government was its acceptance after ample opportunity to discuss safeguards against possible domination. Thus General Ironsi is to be criticized not for his indecision and slowness of action but for his attempt to centralize the administration unilaterally in the face of growing opposition.

He was perhaps unaware of the strength of this opposition. It is, of course, difficult, especially in moments of crisis, to keep a balance between responsible leadership and popular participation, but it is impossible if there is a total lack of confidence. Had the Military Government quickly brought to trial those involved in the 15 January coup the necessary degree of confidence might have been established. But to many Nigerians these men were national heroes, not murderers, and General Ironsi had himself promised Major Nzeogwu safe conduct. Yet the fact that General Ironsi was caught in this kind of dilemma merely underlines the folly of centralizing the administration in advance of some agreement on the prior constitutional issues. This was compounded when he sought to overcome opposition by announcing his intention to stay in power for three years and at the same time prohibit all political activities. There was no lack of warning of the probable consequences. Lt-Col Hassan Katsina, returning from the meeting of the Supreme Military Council immediately preceding the promulgation of Decrees Nos. 33 and 34, remarked that the egg was about to break. It cracked and then finally broke, under the impact of two opposing forces: a Military Government set on imposing its own form of centralized command, at least as an interim measure, and an opposition movement, less clearly led and less openly asserted, but sustained by growing fears of a *fait accompli*.

THE GOWON GOVERNMENT
August 1966

The July coup brought about a radically different situation. Following the January coup, the military had led the movement for national unity conceived in terms of a more unitary form of government. Despite opposition, it had remained undeterred even by the violent Northern reactions to the May decrees. But in July the army itself became a casualty with far-reaching consequences. It ceased to be a cohesive force obeying a single command, and so ceased to be an integrating force for the country as a whole. Its dislocation under the impact of the July coup unleashed widespread political demands for regional atutonomy, not only in the Eastern but also in the Northern and Western Regions. The situation in August 1966 was thus the reverse of that which prevailed in mid-January. Instead of the Regions drawing together they were moving apart, endangering Nigeria's very existence, except as a loose confederation.

The disintegration of the army was twofold. First, many were obliged to decamp for their own safety. Nearly all the surviving Ibo soldiers and many others of Eastern origin sought refuge in their home areas, as did some Mid-Westerners.[35] There was also a reverse flow of Northern troops out of the Eastern Region.[36] Secondly, the army command was disrupted. Lt-Col Gowon, who succeeded General Ironsi as Supreme Commander, was not in fact recognized as such by the Military Governor of the Eastern Region. Lt-Col Ojukwu's objections were based partly on military and partly on political grounds.[37] Lt-Col Gowon was not the next in line of command by order of seniority; thus a vital principle of military organization was at issue which, if ignored, would 'write something into the Nigerian Army which is bigger than all of us, and that thing is indiscipline'.[38]

In addition, Lt-Col Ojukwu accused Lt-Col Gowon of having taken over by 'force of conquest' as the head of a political faction within the army, or at least as someone acceptable to it; moreover, of having done so despite Lt-Col Ojukwu's own strong objections expressed at the time on the telephone.[39] This was quite unacceptable to Lt-Col Ojukwu. It was 'not possible for the East to accept blindly leadership from Lagos. For this we have fought . . . and for this the East will continue to struggle and fight, if necessary.'[40]

Lt-Col Gowon, however, was supported by the other members of the Supreme Military Council. Far from regarding him as the leader of a rebel faction, they acknowledged him as the most senior officer capable, at the time of the July mutiny, of re-establishing command over the army and of restoring the Supreme Military Council's authority. Had he not accepted the leadership that circumstances thrust upon him, the situation would have been much worse. Commodore Wey, Head of the Navy, Kam Salem, the Inspector-General of Police, and Colonel Adebayo, Military Governor of the Western Region, all testified to the inability of more senior officers to make themselves obeyed and they expressed the opinion that if Lt-Col Gowon had not intervened to take command they themselves would certainly have paid with their lives.[41]

With the army in some disarray and unitary government shown to be impossible, the decisive influence over political and constitutional developments tended to shift from Lagos to the Regions. It also shifted, for a time, away from the military towards the politicians for, by the second week of August, almost all those held in detention had been released. The major beneficiaries were the leaders of the Action Group, notably Chief Awolowo, imprisoned since 1963. Hailed as 'Leader of the Yoruba', he enjoyed an authority which rivalled that of the Military Governor. This change in the balance of forces affected the whole conduct of government. The Supreme Commander was reduced rather to the status of a convener; decisions affecting the country as a whole were made dependent upon negotiations between regional delegates, and regional opinion itself tended to be much more openly discussed and formulated in consultative assemblies, composed partly of traditional leaders and partly of 'leaders of thought', that is, people recognized to have a political following. It became quite common for the Military Governors of the Regions and for the Administrator of Lagos to convene meetings of consultative assemblies whenever some crucial decision had to be taken. These assemblies were, of course, no more than advisory bodies and their claim to be fully representative could sometimes be questioned,[42] but their influence, varying somewhat from Region to Region and from time to time, was often considerable.[43]

This dispersed, and not always easily identifiable pattern of *de facto* authority, between the centre and the Regions, between the military and the politicians, further complicated by cross-currents within each Region and within the military, formed the rather fluid background to the ensuing deliberations on Nigeria's future. These began in early August 1966 and dragged on for many months but ended in a basic disagreement and eventual civil war. Two fundamentally opposed points of view quickly emerged and although there was some attempt to bridge these differences the belief on both sides that their own point of view could be made to prevail was a permanent obstacle to a negotiated settlement.

On the one view, the only viable arrangement, at least for the immediate future, was some form of confederation.[44] Events had shown that the basis for any closer form of political association was lacking. According to this view, it was 'folly . . . to pretend . . . there are no differences between the *peoples* of Nigeria'.[45] 'Brought together by recent accidents of history', they were now beset by 'fears of one another', some fearing 'the sheer weight of numbers of other parts', others fearing 'the sheer weight of skills and the aggressive drive of other groups'. Their 'political differences . . . are no longer just matters of words, but are now matters of life and death'. The only sure way to prevent a recurrence of 'national suicide', and to preserve some degree of unity, was the decentralization of authority, to an extent far greater than ever before, in other words 'to examine the areas which have caused conflicts in the past and remove them as far as possible to the Regions'. Moreover, the central authority would need to be reconstituted in such a way as to preclude a struggle for its control, this having been 'the perennial source of friction, mistrust and tension' in the past. It could be avoided by equality of representation on the central executive, unanimous decisions on all major issues, and the rotation of offices. Nigeria would thus become a 'union of autonomous states', an 'association of regions', or a 'Commonwealth' in which each state (or region) would have a recognized right to secede.

This line of reasoning includes an important assumption, namely that the existing Regions were to be the constituent parts of any such union. It was an assumption easily made because three of the Regions contained the three largest 'internal nations'[46] of Nigeria: the Ibo, the Yoruba, and the Fulani-Hausa. Each of these would become master of its own affairs. Two of them, the Ibo and the Hausa-Fulani, would however be in a better position to dominate the various minorities who had long been demanding regional status for themselves. Thus the advocates of confederation gave much greater weight to the mutual fears of the three largest 'internal nations' than to the corresponding fears of the minorities.

The alternative point of view attempted to take into account the fears of all groups, large and small, by proposing the creation of several new states out of the existing Regions, and the continuation of Nigeria as a federation. It was not denied that there were problems in determining the precise number and the precise boundaries of any new states, requiring somewhat arbitrary settlement even if plebiscites were to be held, but within the context of a federation these problems were not considered insurmountable. Such a federation would allay the fears of minorities, because it would have sufficient authority of its own to allow the creation of relatively small states. All minorities of sufficient size to aspire to a certain measure of autonomy could be satisfied. It would also allay the mutual fears of the three 'internal nations'. The larger number of states, all more or less equally represented at the centre, would be some guarantee that central authority would not be abused.

Manifestly, these two opposing points of view expressed different interests. A confederation of the existing regions was acceptable to many Ibo, Yoruba, and Fulani-Hausa, for they were of a size which enabled them to live separately from each other, at least in political terms. The minority peoples, on the other hand, saw their best hope in a more fragmented but still fairly closely integrated federation.

In the ensuing trial of strength between these two viewpoints, the preferences of the military, especially of the army, were obviously crucial. The army, however, was itself divided very roughly into three factions. One, predominantly Ibo and concentrated for the most part in the Eastern Region, looked to Colonel Ojukwu as their military commander and spokesman; it unquestionably advocated confederation and opposed any subdivision of the Eastern Region.[47] The second faction consisted of soldiers drawn from minority areas, mainly the 'Middle Belt' of the Northern Region. The officers in this group worked closely with political leaders such as Mr Tarka, who had long advocated the creation of a Middle Belt State, and were determined to achieve this by exploiting their disproportionate strength within the army. With the departure of the Ibo their position was stronger than before and they could look to the Supreme Commander for support, since Lt-Col Gowon was himself from a minority tribe. The third faction had as its hard core some of the Fulani- or Hausa-speaking Muslim troops, working in league with ex-NPC politicians and in favour of Northern secession, but it appears not to have had any single overriding objective and this probably accounts for its comparative ineffectiveness.

The Ad Hoc Constitutional Committee, September 1966

August and the first part of September were spent preparing for a constitutional conference to be attended by delegates from each of the Regions and Lagos. Most of the delegates (three from each Region, two from Lagos) were politicians, in many cases former Ministers; their advisers were mainly traditional chiefs and lawyers. No military personnel attended, nor was the Federal Military Government represented,[48] but Lt-Col Gowon addressed the Committee at its opening session on 12 September. Although he left the issue of federation or confederation open, he gave some hint as to his own point of view. He urged delegates not to 'minimize the advantages that will derive from our remaining together as one strong political and economic entity'. He reminded them of similar occasions in the past when 'after many years of constitution-making exercises, it was eventually agreed to adopt a Federal system of government, which the former politicians failed to make workable'. He also listed among the matters that might have to be considered 'the territorial divisions of the country'.

Although no overall agreement was reached, the conference did force the debate more into the open and revealed a little more clearly the balance of forces. It showed that the Eastern Region was firmly committed to confederation based on the existing Regions, that the Mid-West, itself a recent creation, strongly favoured the creation of more states and the maintenance of the Federation, but was prepared to make some concessions to the confederal point of view for the sake of general agreement, and that official policy in the North, West, and Lagos was much more open to fluctuation, and more difficult to pin down.[49]

At the start of the conference the balance of opinion appeared to favour a confederation of the existing Regions; the question of the creation of new Regions (or states) was firmly relegated to a later stage and left for each Region to settle as its own internal affair. The Northern and Eastern delegates tabled very similar proposals to this effect. The Western and Lagos delegations, acting jointly, were prepared to follow suit, even though they stated a preference for a federal constitution and the immediate creation of more states. The Mid-West was left as odd man out, too small by itself to carry much weight. This near-consensus was, however, more apparent than real. It is not at all clear how far the North's proposals had the support of Mr Tarka, who had been included in the Northern delegation. Certainly they failed to offer the people of the Middle Belt any immediate prospect of autonomy and in all probability never had his full approval. There was the same kind of doubt about the proposals from the Eastern Region; as soon as they were made known, spokesmen for the minority areas declared them unacceptable. These minorities of the Northern and

Eastern Regions were none the less faced with the immediate prospect of an agreement made over their heads by the three largest 'internal nations', an agreement which promised not to be to their advantage. The most they could hope for was some form of local self-government on a provincial basis.[50] Quick and decisive action was needed if their case was not to go by default. Pressure was therefore brought to bear where it was most likely to succeed, namely on the Northern delegation, by Middle Belt leaders, backed by their counterparts in the army. This brought about a revision of the North's stand. Its new proposals still retained certain features more characteristic of a confederation than a federation, such as the rotation of executive offices, equal state representation, both in government and in parliament, state armies, and state police. But the right to secede disappeared and the federal government was to have its own powers instead of powers delegated by the states with the possibility of their being withdrawn. It was also to have its own independent sources of finance. On the question of new states there was a very careful reformulation. It remained a question to be decided by ascertaining in a referendum the 'wishes of the people concerned'; no Region, except the Mid-West, was to be 'left out of the operation', and there were 'grave doubts' about the wisdom of creating states based on 'ethnic and linguistic affinities', one of the criteria set out in the joint proposals submitted by the Western Region and Lagos. The implication was clear: the creation of states in the North was conditional on the creation of states in the East and West. But the cause of the minorities had been advanced for it was now a question for discussion immediately and not at some later stage.

This restatement of the North's position brought about a quite different realignment. The highest common factor was now to be found in the proposals of the North, West, and Mid-West, leaving the East as the odd man out. It was not, however, a realignment that brought overall agreement any nearer. The East was not prepared to abandon its basic standpoint, especially as there were obviously some divisions of opinion in the North and the West. The delegates therefore spent their time drawing up a balance sheet, listing points of agreement and issues which were still in dispute.[51] After submitting this to Lt-Col Gowon on 29 September, the Committee adjourned.

It was at this point that the terrible massacre of Ibo civilians broke out in all its fury throughout most of the Northern Region. The people responsible, their degree of responsibility, their motivation, and their objectives are still matters for speculation and may never be established with any reasonable measure of certainty. It is difficult to see how these massacres advanced the cause of those Northerners who advocated a confederation of the existing regions. It was not the Ibo who stood in the way of such a settlement. Nor is it easy to see how they helped the Northern minorities in their stand for the creation of new states. Probably there is no explaining them in terms of cold-blooded calculation. Tension had remained high throughout August and September and there were many isolated incidents long before the end of September. No doubt the deadlock reached in the Committee, the widespread assumption that the East was about to secede, and reports that Northerners were being attacked in the Eastern Region, acted as a flash-point, releasing an accumulation of hatred and frustration. Whatever the cause, the effects were clear to see: first, a large-scale redistribution of civilian population, brought about not only by Easterners returning for safety to their own Region but also by the displacement of non-Easterners, ordered by the Eastern Regional Government to leave; and, secondly, an ever-deepening mistrust dividing the different peoples of Nigeria. The idea of a federation, based on new states and a strong central government, seemed more remote than ever before.

The Ad Hoc Constitutional Committee met again on 24 October, but no delegates from the East attended, despite various appeals and attempts to find a meeting place acceptable to all concerned. After an exchange of revised proposals which brought agreement no nearer, the Committee adjourned once again on 2 November. A fortnight later a statement from the Federal Military Government made known Lt-Col Gowon's decision 'that no useful purpose would be achieved by the continued sitting' of the Committee in the absence of the delegates from the East and that therefore it 'should remain adjourned indefinitely'. It was mentioned that Lt-Col Gowon had himself drawn up proposals for lessening tensions and for constitutional reform'. These were to be discussed with the Regional Military Governors. In short, he had decided to make his own proposals in an attempt to break the deadlock. These were announced in a broadcast on 30 November as 'measures which the Federal Military Government will implement to save the country from disintegrating'. His speech is an important document in the history of the crisis, not because everything went according to plan—quite the contrary—but because it was the first public statement clearly indicating Lt-Col Gowon's own standpoint and because he never really abandoned it even though he had to retreat, momentarily, on more than one occasion.[52] By this speech Lt-Col Gowon committed himself to 'the preservation of one Nigerian army and one country'. He rejected 'a temporary confederation' as 'unworkable', on the grounds that there would be 'no effective central authority', that each region 'as a virtually sovereign state' could 'contract out or refuse to join any common service', and that it would be 'hard to come together again'. He then referred to 'the generally expressed desire for a stable Federation' in which 'no one Region or tribal group should be in a position to dominate the other' and 'no Region should be large enough to be able to threaten secession or hold the rest of the Federation to ransom in times of national crisis'. There followed his 'definite commitment on the states question' and a statement of principles for the creation of new states, on the basis of which Nigeria would divide into 'not less than eight and not more than fourteen states'. A Constituent Assembly was to be summoned. Meanwhile, civilians would be brought on to the Federal Executive Council to assist in implementing these measures and 'in projecting the national image'. They would be 'persons known to believe strongly in the continued existence of Nigeria as an effective Federation, of undoubted integrity and of independent character'.[53]

This unqualified commitment to a federation of eight to fourteen states was backed by an unequivocal statement on the stationing of troops—a question which had some bearing on Lt-Col Gowon's chances of being able to put his plans into effect. A meeting of representatives of Regional Governors on 9 August had recommended that 'immediate steps should be taken by the Supreme Commander to post military personnel to barracks within their respective Regions of origin'.[54] Compliance with this recommendation would have meant withdrawing all Northern troops from the Western Region, something Lt-Col Gowon was obviously reluctant to do in view of the West's strategic position and the uncertainty of its support for his policy. With so few Yoruba in the army, Lt-Col Gowon was able to dismiss the demand as 'not practicable' until more Westerners had been recruited. Similarly the demand for the withdrawal of Northern troops from Lagos (which the 9 August meeting had not specifically recommended but which Lt-Col Ojukwu and some Yoruba leaders were now openly demanding) was countered with the assertions that the security of Lagos, the seat of the Federal Government, was the responsibility of the Head of the Federal Military Government. Lt-Col Gowon thus made it clear that he intended to keep his grip on Lagos and the Western Region, adding that he could easily 'mobilise enough forces to deal with any dissident or disloyal group', and would, if necessary, 'preserve the integrity of Nigeria by force'.

The authoritative tone of this speech was not, in fact, matched by the power to give it immediate effect. Indeed, within a few weeks it had been overtaken by a meeting of the full Supreme Military Council at Aburi, Ghana, the first to be attended by Lt-Col Ojukwu since Lt-Col Gowon had assumed the position of Supreme Commander. There was immediate agreement to rule out the use of force, and the question of creating states was never mentioned. Lt-Col Gowon's 30 November programme had been put in cold storage.

The Aburi Meeting

The two-day meeting on 4–5 January marked a fresh start. The military were once again meeting on their own, with politicians entirely excluded; one of the resolutions taken at Aburi was to exclude them for at least the next six months.[55] Yet this attempt on the part of the Supreme Military Council to resume control and to start afresh soon degenerated into an additional source of disagreement, for what was actually decided at Aburi itself became a matter of some dispute.

The major issues discussed—all interlocking—were the recognition of Lt-Col Gowon as Supreme Commander and Head of the Federal Military Government, the reorganization of the army, the powers of the Federal and Regional Governments, and the functioning of the Supreme Military Council. Lt-Col Ojukwu stated his case clearly and persuasively, his basic argument being a simple one. Since the troops of the Eastern Region did not acknowledge any command other than his own and the civilian population rejected any central authority over which their own regional government did not have a power of veto, some form of confederation was the only practical solution. The following extracts from the verbatim report illustrate the argument.

Ojukwu . . . who will stand up here and tell me that he commands and controls the Eastern Army or the Army in the East . . . any attempt to put somebody and say he commands the entire army is eyewash; it does not work, not in the present circumstances. Therefore we must accept that the army should be regionalised: whether we like the term or not, we all understand what we mean by that. I do not think at the moment what we need is a Supreme Commander because Supreme Commander does involve commanding. I think what we need is a Commander-in-Chief who is just titular so that people will take orders from people at least they have confidence in. Whoever you put in Lagos will not command the loyalty of the East. That is the fact of today . . . there should be a coordinating group to which each region would send somebody but just for the façade of Nigeria there should be a titular Commander-in-Chief not a Supreme Commander which involves and which means somebody who commands over and above the various entities . . .

Johnson . . . May I ask one question, gentlemen . . . Is there a central government in Nigeria today?

Ejoor That is the question.

Ojukwu That question is such a simple one that anybody who has been listening to what I have been saying all the time would know that I do not see a central government in Nigeria today . . . any government set-up now in Nigeria that does not take into cognisance Regional loyalties is complete eyewash . . . I do submit that the only realistic form of Government today until tempers are cooled is such that will move people slightly apart and a Government that controls the various entities through people of their areas. It is better that we move slightly apart and survive. It is much worse that we move closer and perish in the collision. Therefore I say no single person today in Nigeria can command the entire loyalty of the people of Nigeria. People can command loyalties of various groups and therefore to save suspicion and enable us to settle down it is essential that whatever form of Government we have in the Centre must be limited or controlled by a consensus on which we all agree . . . what I envisage is that whoever is at the top is a constitutional chap—constitutional within the context of the Military Government—that is, he is the titular head but he would only act when we have met and taken a decision. . . . whoever we decide to sit on the Chair will have limited functions and only act with our agreement . . . can only act in consultation, and his action would, of course, be limited by our own agreement.[56]

The other members of the Supreme Military Council did not really dispute Lt-Col Ojukwu's basic analysis but they were reluctant to follow him all the way. From Lt-Col Ojukwu's point of view it was not sufficient to secure the private agreement of his colleagues; it was essential to offer the people of the Eastern Region some overt proof that they were no longer subject to any centralized military command or any centralized political authority, other than of a formal 'titular' or 'constitutional' kind. This could only be achieved by some change of names, particularly in the title 'Supreme Commander', and by some formal enactment of new institutional arrangements and procedures. Lt-Col Ojukwu's colleagues, on the other hand, were more concerned with emphasizing their own determination to act in unison and to hold together what still remained of Nigerian unity. They accepted the need to decentralize government as much as possible to the Regions and to reorganize the army. But they argued that the fabric of both a central military command and a central government authority needed to be preserved. Because of the loss of contact and deep mistrust at lower levels, both in the armed forces and in the population generally, public confidence could only be restored by working from the top downwards. This they held to be possible, since no member of the Supreme Military Council had blood on his hands.[57] They prided themselves on not being self-seeking politicians out to take advantage of the situation. Nor was Lt-Col Gowon's lack of seniority thought to be a reason for not recognizing him as Supreme Commander, since he owed his position not to any intrigue or favour by some rebellious faction but solely to his own courage and skill in re-establishing command over mutinous troops after others, more senior to himself, had tried and failed. The members of the Supreme Military Council were therefore well placed to work together as a team and by setting an example gradually to restore confidence in the country at large.

Consonant with this line of thought, it was argued that some 'mixing and mingling' at lower levels was to be positively encouraged; for example some exceptions could be made to the general principle that military personnel should be stationed in their own home regions. This 'locality rule' could be waived in instances where harmony still prevailed. Similarly, a start should be made in allowing Mid-Westerners and Westerners expelled from the Eastern Region to return, for if this was not allowed then the demand to expel Easterners still employed in the West and Mid-West would prove irresistible. Retaliatory action of this kind could only worsen the situation and was avoidable only if the idea of some 'mixing and mingling' was accepted.

This second point of view was voiced by several members of the Council and was expressed by different speakers in a variety of ways, as, for example, by Colonel Adebayo:

I would agree with the majority here that our association should be tightened up at the top. This will enable us to see whether we can bring that association down to the bottom when the time comes, that is when the troops have got more confidence in themselves. As Jack [Gowon] and I have always said we do not want to break the Army completely into pieces . . . if we can tighten up the Army at the top then those of us who are at the top now will help to bring the confidence of the troops back.[58]

The Aburi meeting aroused new hopes but it is clear from the above analysis that a basic difference in approach still stood in the way of a definite settlement. Lt-Col Ojukwu continued to view matters in terms of a breakdown of central authority, whereas Lt-Col Gowon regarded its maintenance as both possible and desirable. Ostensibly both had the same aim, the preservation of Nigerian unity, but their methods of achieving it were radically different. For this reason it may be doubted whether there was ever much chance of reaching agreement on the most vital matters. None the less, there appeared to be substantial agreement on a number of specific points, as follows:[59]

(1) on the reorganization of the Army:
    '(a) The Army is to be governed by the Supreme Military Council the chairman of which will be known as Commander-in-Chief and Head of the Federal Military Government
    (b) There will be a Military Headquarters on which the Regions will be equally represented and which will be headed by a Chief of Staff
    (c) In each Region there shall be an Area Command under the charge of an Area Commander and corresponding with the existing Regions
    (d) All matters of policy including appointments and promotions of

persons in top executive posts in the Armed Forces and Police shall be dealt with by the Supreme Military Council

(e) During the period of the Military Government, Military Governors will have control over their Area Commands in matters of internal security

(f) Creation of a Lagos Garrison including Ikeja Barracks'

(2) on appointments to certain posts:

'The following appointmenets must be approved by the Supreme Military Council

(a) Diplomatic and Consular posts

(b) Senior posts in the Armed Forces and the Police

(c) Super-scale Federal Civil Service and Federal Corporation posts'

(3) on the functioning of the Supreme Military Council:

'Any decision affecting the whole country must be determined by the Supreme Military Council. Where a meeting is not possible such a matter must be referred to Military Governors for comment and concurrence.'

Two consequential questions were, however, referred to committees for further detailed consideration:

(1) A Military Committee, on which each Region was to be represented, was to collect information on the actual distribution of manpower and equipment and to indicate what were the deficiencies and future requirements of each Area Command. It was to complete its work within two weeks of receiving instructions and to report to the Supreme Military Commander;

(Pending this report, there was to be no further recruitment, but thereafter sufficient Westerners were to be recruited and trained, as a matter of urgency, as to enable all personnel of Northern origin to be withdrawn from the West.)

(2) The Solicitors-General of the Federal and Regional Governments were to meet in Benin on 14 January and list whatever changes needed to be made to the Military Decrees issued since 15 January 1966. They were given a week in which to report.

These decisions, and the question of their implementation, almost immediately became the subject of bitter controversy, resulting in an even more serious breakdown of confidence. Lt-Col Ojukwu took it for granted that his views had prevailed and that the decisions, recorded in the draft minutes, left no room for any further serious disagreement. Only technical details remained to be settled by the Military Committee and by the Law Officers. At a press conference, held on 6 January immediately on his return from Aburi, he stated in answer to questions: 'The East believes in confederation, and I believe that this is the only answer. I have not moved from that, neither am I likely to move from that point of view ... We have ... gone a long way towards that, as a result of this meeting.'[60] Lt-Col Gowon, on the other hand, regarded the Aburi meeting and its decisions as a basis for further discussion. Many matters, discussed and settled in principle, had to be considered in greater detail, with the help of expert advice, and would no doubt require some further clarification if not also qualification in order to take account of the different views expressed at Aburi.[61] Given these conflicting interpretations of the meeting, 'the spirit of Aburi' quickly evaporated in a welter of accusations and counter-accusations of bad faith.

It is scarcely possible to come to any conclusion as to which interpretation is to be considered the more justifiable. Lt-Col Ojukwu had some grounds for his presumption, in that the actual wording of the decisions recorded in the draft minutes was largely copied from prepared resolutions which he himself had brought to the meeting. But if one turns to the discussions for guidance in interpreting these decisions one faces certain difficulties. The verbatim report of the meeting is incomplete, its recording having been suspended twice so that the discussions could continue in private. One such break came after Mr Omo Bare, the Deputy Inspector-General of Police, had remarked: 'We cannot sit here ... and divide up Nigeria, because the way things are now moving is towards regionalisation of everything, and I do not think it is safe or that we are right to divide up Nigeria at this table.'[62] When the recorded discussion was resumed Mr Omo Bare was able to announce that agreement had been reached on the reorganization of the Army. This was a matter of obvious and vital importance; as Lt-Col Ojukwu had remarked earlier, 'the Army problem . . . is mixed up very closely with the political problem, with the question of Government'.[63] In the absence of any evidence as to precisely what was said at this crucial point in the proceedings one can only base a judgement on the part of the discussion that was recorded. Here also there are difficulties. Much of the discussion was an exchange of views, expressed in general terms, not always clearly and consistently. There was, moreover, some conflict of opinion, as well as agreement. Thus the only conclusions to be drawn on the evidence available are that Lt-Col Ojukwu came to the meeting with certain concrete proposals which, at least in his own mind, were clear and precise; that several of his colleagues made statements which were basically irreconcilable with Lt-Col Ojukwu's proposals; but decisions were minuted apparently conceding much of what Lt-Col Ojukwu had demanded. It is perhaps unfortunate there were no official advisers present at Aburi; they might have been able to draw attention to some of the difficulties of interpretation which arose when the Law Officers met later to give legal shape to the decisions reached.[64]

It is a moot question whether those present at Aburi came away with the impression that a settlement had been reached in principle—an impression conveyed to the general public by the communiqués issued during and at the end of the meeting.[65] What is certain is that, within a fortnight, the possibility of a settlement was shown to be as remote as ever. When the Law Officers met on 14–15 January they reported that they had been handicapped by not having before them an 'authentic copy' of the Aburi decisions and by the fact that some came only 'on purely verbal instructions or with very sketchy instructions in writing'.[66] But their disagreement on all the vital issues was quite plainly rooted in the differing conceptions of government held by those they represented. The major points of disagreement all concerned the respective powers of the centre and the Regions, and the fundamental principle of Regional consent for action taken by the centre. For example, the principle that Federal legislation required Regional consent could be applied in various ways. If there were to be matters for which the Federal Military Government had exclusive responsibility and if Regional consent was refused, was legislation then made altogether impossible, or could the Regions legislate in default of Federal legislation? If the Federal Military Government and the Regional Military Governments had some concurrent powers, was Regional legislation to override Federal legislation, or vice versa?

It was agreed that the first question needed further consideration by the Supreme Military Council, since it had not been made clear whether the Federal Military Government was to retain any such exclusive responsibility. On the second question relating to concurrent powers, there was a straight disagreement. The Law Officers of the Eastern Region interpreted the principle of Regional consent to mean that 'the Regions can legislate in relation to Federal law', whereas all the other Law Officers took the view that 'where there is an inconsistency between a Federal Decree . . . and a Regional Edict on the same matter, the Federal Decree will prevail'.

There was similar disagreement concerning the functioning of the Supreme Military Council. Was a Regional Governor to have an absolute veto over its proceedings, in the sense that it would be unable to take any decision except by and with the express consent of each Military Governor? Some of the Law Officers questioned this. An absolute veto over all the proceedings of the Supreme Military Council would have stripped it of any independent powers, and it was doubtful whether many of its members had accepted the principle of Regional consent to that extent. Unable to agree what should be the precise rules for the taking of formal decisions, the Law Officers referred the whole question back to the Supreme Military Council.[67]

Closely related to these two questions was a third, whether or not to incorporate a provision of the 1963 Constitution whereby a Region was precluded from exercising its executive authority in such a way as 'to impede or prejudice the exercise of the executive authority of the Federation or to endanger the continuance of the Federal Government of Nigeria'. The inclusion of such a provision was either contradictory or highly necessary, depending on one's particular point of view. It purported to give the Federal Military Government authority to declare that a Regional Governor was abusing his powers. To the advocates of confederation, like Lt-Col Ojukwu, it was an inadmissible contradiction, inconsistent with the principle of Regional consent. To those advocating federalism, like Lt-Col Gowon, a provision of this kind was absolutely essential, especially if Regional Governors were normally to have a right of veto over the proceedings of the Supreme Military Council and if the Regions were to have unlimited legislative powers, as seemed to be suggested.

The doubts and difficulties reported by the Law Officers were echoed and amplified in an official memorandum submitted by the Acting Secretary of the Federal Military Government to members of the Federal Executive Council.[68] It not only rejected several of the Aburi decisions on the grounds that they were incompatible with the maintenance of effective control in essential matters; it also advised quite bluntly that 'the immediate political programme announced to the nation on 30 November 1966 by the Supreme Commander should be implemented and the country must be so informed'.[69] The publication of this document—it was leaked to Lt-Col Ojukwu—naturally added fuel to the flames. In the eyes of those who claimed, like Lt-Col Ojukwu, that the Aburi decisions instituted new arrangements of a confederal type, it was confirmation that the Federal Military Government had no intention of implementing these decisions. It was also presented as proof that Lt-Col Gowon had come under the sinister influence of officials, who had not been present at Aburi and whose vested interest in the maintenance of their own positions in the federal service blinded them to a proper appreciation of the Nigerian problem. This is questionable. The views expressed in the memorandum were made on the assumption that Lt-Col Gowon had not abandoned his policy of preserving 'one Nigerian Army and one country', that is, an army under effective central command and a Nigeria reconstituted as a well-integrated Federation. This was probably a correct assumption.

At most Lt-Col Gowon was hesitant, and since it was questionable whether the Aburi decisions could be said to constitute a hard and fast agreement which required the federal officials to look at the whole question again with a fresh mind, their critical comments, drawing attention to some of the implications, were not out of place. The advice that Lt-Col Gowon should stick to the pre-Aburi policy must, however, be considered as the expression of a political judgement unusual in civil servants.

On 26 January Lt-Col Gowon held a press conference.[70] Carefully taking into account all the points raised, and following very closely the advice given in the memorandum, he offered his own account of the Aburi decisions and revived the plans which had been in abeyance for nearly two months. These, he said, had never been abandoned and were now more urgent than ever. He continued to reject confederation as unworkable and sounded the warning which he had already expressed at Aburi: 'I am sure that if this country were to fall apart, it will disintegrate into more than the existing regions. Without an effective central authority to hold the country together, the minorities in each region will definitely assert their right to self-determination.' He restated his intention to create additional states 'for those who want them in accordance with the criteria laid down', adding that it was an issue which 'will have to be given early consideration'. The appointment of a committee to draft a new constitution and the convening of a constituent assembly would, it was now admitted, have to await 'normal conditions', but he confirmed the intention to bring civilian members on to the Federal Executive Council.

As far as Lt-Col Gowon was concerned, the Aburi decisions had to be seen in this context. 'We did not go to Aburi to write a new constitution for Nigeria' was how he expressed it. He passed over in silence the principle of Regional consent, confirming only an agreement 'to return to the status quo ante 17 January', this being 'in keeping with my earlier public pronouncements that Decrees or parts of Decrees which tended towards overcentralisation should be repealed'. He added: 'we will continue to operate the existing Federal Constitution and the Federal system of government until a new Constitution is drawn up'. The agreements on the reorganization of the army, being more specific, required particularly careful exegesis and on one specific point the turning of a blind eye if Lt-Col Gowon was to safeguard his position as Supreme Commander. He contended:

We reviewed the situation in the Nigerian Army and we all agreed that there should be one Nigerian Army under a unified command as at present. We recognized that in the context of the events of 1966 the most practical way of achieving this aim is to organize the Army into area commands. The preponderance of the army personnel in each command will be drawn from the indigenes of that area. Each area command will be under an Area Commander who will take operational instructions from the Military Headquarters which will be directly under me as the Supreme Commander of the Armed Forces. Under the proposal, the Military Governors can use the area command for internal security purposes but this will normally be done with the express permission of the Head of the Federal Military Government. We definitely decided against Regional armies.

It will be noticed that Lt-Col Gowon still referred to himself as Supreme Commander. The reason is to be found in the memorandum referred to earlier. This had objected to any such change of title lest it might be said to create a vacancy, to be filled by the unanimous decision of the Supreme Military Council, in which case 'there would be considerable instability caused by political and military manœuvres to fill the post'. This was not idle speculation. The question had been raised at Aburi, momentarily, during a brief exchange between Colonel Adebayo and Lt-Col Ojukwu:

Adebayo   The Commander-in-Chief and myself agreed . . .
Ojukwu   No: we have not appointed anyone Commander-in-Chief.
Adebayo   Can we not appoint a Commander-in-Chief now?
Ojukwu   We will see about that later . . .[71]

Lt-Col Ojukwu had raised it again, this time in a slightly different form, when in a press interview he called for a meeting of Military Governors to designate a successor to General Ironsi as Supreme Commander.[72] Lt-Col Gowon was questioned during his press conference about this statement and he replied: 'There is no question of a successor to the late Supreme Commander, and Lt-Col Ojukwu knows that himself. I do not have to depend on the East Military Governor or anyone else to say that I am Supreme Commander.'[73]

Similarly, in stating that under the reorganization of the army he would command Military Headquarters and control the use of troops by Military Governors, Lt-Col Gowon was taking careful account of points raised by his official advisers. They had warned that under the terms of the Aburi decisions the Commander-in-Chief 'would have no power of control or dismissal over the Military Governors', little or none over Military Headquarters, and none over Military Governors in the use they might make of the Army for the maintenance of internal security. This last point was considered to have 'serious political implications in respect of the creation of states', in that the Commander-in-Chief would be unable to guarantee 'the status of minorities'—a warning that Military Governors could, under the Aburi decisions, use the Army to silence minorities who demanded states of their own.

Once Lt-Col Ojukwu and Lt-Col Gowon had made known their quite contrary interpretations of the Aburi meeting, and repeated in uncompromising fashion their conflicting views on the twin issues of limiting the powers of the centre and of satisfying minority demands, there was a return to the deadlock which the meeting at Aburi was supposed to have overcome. A two-day meeting of officials held at Benin in mid-February produced some hopeful concessions, especially from Lagos, but not sufficient to constitute a break-through. (See Appendix E.) Yet the need to break the deadlock was becoming more and more urgent with the approach of the new financial year. The preparation of the Estimates for the coming year was, as in 1966, an operation that brooked no delay, and, just as General Ironsi's first positive steps towards introducing a more unitary form of government came towards the end of March when the 1966/7 budgets came up for approval, so also Lt-Col Ojukwu's first tentative steps towards greater regional autonomy and eventual secession came in March 1967 in the field of finance. It was on 25 February in a dawn broadcast that he announced: 'We are coming to the end of the fiscal year and estimates must be finished and plans made for the coming year. This is not possible under the present unsettled state. For this reason I have recently informed my fellow military leaders that if the Aburi agreements are not fully implemented by March 31, I shall have no alternative but to feel free to take whatever measures may be necessary to give effect in this region to those agreements.'[74]

It was thought at the time that this implied immediate secession, and consequently during March every effort was made to arrive at some settlement so that this could be avoided. Less is known about the details of the negotiations during this period but sufficient has been disclosed to make clear the general pattern. First, the West and Mid-West held the balance, politically if not militarily. Neither Region had any vital interest in giving outright support to Lt-Col Ojukwu's demand for a loose confederation of existing Regions or to Lt-Col Gowon's demand for a closely integrated federation of eight to twelve states. They were not directly and immediately affected by the proposal to create new states. The Mid-West could in any event expect to keep its separate identity, either as one of four regions in a confederation or one of the states in a federation. There was some agitation for the sub-division of the West, but the problem was not nearly so acute as in the North and in the East; the West could share the Mid-West's relative indifference to this issue.[75] Colonel Adebayo and Lt-Col Ejoor were therefore in a good position to advocate compromise. They were able to maintain personal contact with Lt-Col Ojukwu and, although neither could command much support within the Army itself, they were

undoubtedly able to bring some pressure to bear in favour of a negotiated settlement.[76]

Secondly, the negotiations appear to have left aside the question of
additional regions (or states), at least for immediate purposes. This is
surprising for not only had Lt-Col Gowon renewed his commitment
on this matter, he had also won more definite support for it in the
North. A meeting of 'leaders of thought' held in Kaduna on 27 January
had recommended that Nigeria should be divided into eleven to
thirteen regions.[77] This was dismissed by Lt-Col Ojukwu as 'camou-
flage', but it was encouragement for Lt-Col Gowon. It was no doubt
pressure from his other colleagues in the Supreme Military Council,
especially Colonel Adebayo and Lt-Col Ejoor, that obliged Lt-Col
Gowon to abandon his own proposals yet a second time. The shelving
of the issue permitted a continuation of negotiations with Lt-Col
Ojukwu on the lines worked out at Aburi. This was still the most
promising and, as far as Lt-Col Ojukwu was concerned, the only
acceptable basis for arriving at some agreement. The negotiations
concentrated therefore on achieving some compromise on the principle
of regional consent to federal action.

Decree No. 8

The outcome of these negotiations was a Decree approved by the
Supreme Military Council meeting without Lt-Col Ojukwu in Benin
on 10 March. The publication of this Decree, known as Decree No. 8,
was notice by all Lt-Col Ojukwu's colleagues that they had made the
maximum possible concessions to Eastern demands for confederation,
and it made public what precisely was still at issue. As such it deserves
some analysis.[78] It confirmed the continuance of the Supreme Military
Council but, as agreed at Aburi, the Head of the Federal Military
Government was no longer described as Supreme Commander and
President of the Supreme Military Council. He became Commander-
in-Chief of the Armed Forces and the Council's Chairman.[79] The
Regional Military Governors were invested with all the legislative and
executive functions possessed by the Regions before 17 January 1966
(instead of exercising them in virtue of a delegation of power from the
Federal Military Government). The legislative and executive functions
of the Federal Military Government were vested in the Supreme
Military Council (instead of in the Head of the Federal Military
Government). Moreover, the Supreme Military Council could not
legislate on certain specified matters without the express consent of the
Head of the Federal Military Government and of all the Regional
Military Governors.[80] The precise extent of this restriction had been

agreed in negotiations with representatives of all the Regions, including the East. It applied to Decrees 'affecting or relating to' any of the following:

(i) external affairs, defence, the naval, military and air forces, the Nigeria Police, arms and ammunition

(ii) maintaining and securing public safety and public order and essential supplies and services

(iii) trade, commerce, industry, transport, communications, labour

(iv) the federal civil service

(v) the federal finances, other than appropriation but including approval of new capital projects

(vi) the legal and medical professions and the various institutions of higher education for which the federation had exclusive responsibility under the 1963 Constitution

(vii) the territorial integrity of a Region

(viii) the administration of the affairs of a Region (subject to an important exception, to be mentioned later)

(ix) Section 4 of the 1963 Constitution which, in its revised form, entrenched the new procedure for Federal-Regional agreement on all the above matters.

Decree No. 8 thus went quite far in implementing the principle of regional consent. Federal law continued, however, to be superior to regional law;[81] moreover, since the Head of the Federal Military Government had also to give his consent to any new Decrees, existing federal law was adequately safeguarded, and presumably also existing administrative practices. Thus, while the veto of the Regional Military Governors gave them power to prevent any proposed increase in federal action, it did not give them power to amend unilaterally existing federal responsibilities. This was a necessary safeguard if the Federal Military Government was to have any real standing *vis-à-vis* the Regions.

The Supreme Military Council also became collectively responsible for various appointments, for example Permanent Secretaries in the Federal Ministries and Ambassadors or High Commissioners, previously appointed by the Head of the Federal Military Government, and senior federal civil servants and police officers, previously appointed by the Federal Public Service Commission and Police Service Commission.[82] Responsibility for appointing the Justices of the Supreme Court reverted very closely to what it had been under the 1963 Constitution: each Region had the right to nominate one judge for appointment by the Supreme Military Council.[83]

Finally, the Decree included a section authorizing the Supreme Military Council, 'acting with the concurrence of the Head of the

Federal Military Government and of at least *three* of the Military Governors', to declare that 'a state of public emergency exists', or that 'democratic institutions in Nigeria are threatened by subversion', or that a Region was so exercising its executive authority as to impede or prejudice the exercise of federal authority or endanger the continuance of federal government.[84] In any such eventuality the Supreme Military Council was given all necessary powers to remedy the situation. The implications of including, or excluding, this kind of reserve power have already been discussed. It put the ultimate responsibility for the government of the Eastern Region into the hands of the other Military Governors. It therefore encountered the resistance of all those Easterners convinced that they had to keep this ultimate responsibility in their own hands. Yet it was, for the rest of the country, an essential safeguard for ensuring 'peace, order and good government' throughout the Federation and respect for federal authority. Deadlock in this point was symptomatic of the degree of mistrust which still prevailed.[85]

The publication of Decree No. 8 was delayed for a week so as to give Lt-Col Ojukwu and his Law Officers time to consider it in its final form. Lt-Col Ejoor received a visit from Lt-Col Ojukwu on 12 March and no doubt gave him an account of the Supreme Military Council's recent meeting; from the 14th to the 16th the Law Officers of all the Governments met in Benin.[86] Meanwhile, representatives of the press, including the foreign press, had been invited to Enugu for a press conference by Lt-Col Ojukwu on the 13th. He condemned unity as a 'foreign coat' that 'will not fit Nigeria' and he reaffirmed his determination to take unilateral action if, at the end of the month, his own proposals for 'association' had not been accepted.[87] Presumably he still hoped to secure Colonel Adebayo's and Lt-Col Ejoor's support for a last-minute revision of the Decree. He claimed that they shared his point of view but were prevented by the presence of Northern troops in the West and by the small size of the Mid-West from giving him their support; he had taken his stand on behalf of the whole of the South against the domination of the North.[88] If this was his aim, he did not express it very diplomatically and he certainly miscalculated, for the Decree was published unaltered on 17 March.

The financial questions were negotiated separately, although obviously as part of a general settlement. With the return of most Easterners to their own Region, many of them refugees requiring rehabilitation, the Government of the Eastern Region was faced with an increase in expenditure both for immediate welfare services and for capital projects to provide future employment.[89] With sufficient revenue-producing resources of its own, notably oil, the East naturally sought greater financial autonomy. At the September Constitutional

Conference it had demanded that all fiscal and taxing powers should be vested in the Regions, with consultative machinery to ensure the necessary uniformity, and that the Federal Government should meet its expenditure out of equal contributions from the Regions. As the end of the financial year drew near the East was obliged, for purely practical reasons, to enter into negotiations on a somewhat different basis. A good half of the Region's revenues were in fact levied and collected by the Federal Government and then paid over to the Region in accordance with various constitutional and statutory provisions.[90] Short of secession, the East could secure an increased share in these revenues (which included the all-important oil revenues) only by agreement with the Governments of the Federation and of the other Regions. The negotiations in March concentrated therefore on obtaining this within the context of existing constitutional and statutory provisions. No agreement was reached, despite protracted meetings of officials at Benin and at Accra.

The negotiations on all these outstanding issues were continued up to the final minute. The Ghanaian Government was particularly active in attempting mediation. Already in the first week of March Lt-Col Gowon had gone to Accra and the Ghanaian General Okran had visited Enugu. With the end of the month in sight another Ghanaian mission was sent to Nigeria and Lt-Col Ojukwu visited Accra. The civilian Advisers to the Regional Governors also met in Benin and there were last-minute visits to Lt-Col Ojukwu by several of his colleagues on the Supreme Military Council.

The Final Phase: April–May 1967

Although Lt-Col Ojukwu decided, contrary to general expectation, not to declare the secession of the Eastern Region on 31 March, and thus kept alive hopes of a negotiated settlement, the crisis undoubtedly entered a new and even more critical phase with his decision to sequestrate all federal revenues collected in the Eastern Region, i.e. by the Customs and Revenue, and the various federal corporations such as the Railways, Airways, Coal and Electricity, the Post Office, and the Ports Authority. As from 1 April the money collected by these bodies was to be paid to the Regional Government.[91] This decision had grave consequences but not because it deprived the Federal authorities of revenue; on balance, the amounts regularly remitted to the Federal authorities in Lagos were in all probability less than the various rebates, transfers, and other payments made to Enugu, for most of the company taxes and the oil revenues were collected in Lagos. Nor was it the first instance of administrative disruption, for movement of traffic on the railways between the Northern and Eastern Regions had ceased in September; and the East was holding not only rolling stock badly needed for the movement of goods in the other parts of the country but also Northern produce sent to Port Harcourt for export. The decision was grave for the obvious reason that it defied the authority of the Federal Government in deliberate and systematic fashion. This was not the kind of action the Federal Government could leave unanswered. It was in fact the start of a whole series of prohibitions and embargoes imposed by both sides, leading to the eventual declaration of secession, which when it came was something of a formality. For example, on 4 April Nigeria Airways, deprived of fares paid in the Eastern Region, suspended flights to the East. An aircraft which the next day flew some stranded passengers to Port Harcourt was seized. Flights between the Eastern Region and Cameroon were suspended by declaring Calabar to be no longer an international airport. A week later, after an alleged purchase of £6 million sterling by the African Continental Bank, a Bank closely connected with the Government of the Eastern Region, strict controls were imposed by the Federal Government on the purchase of foreign exchange. Then in quick succession the East took over all federal statutory bodies, authorized its own Marketing Board to enter into direct contracts with foreign buyers instead of selling via the Nigerian Produce Marketing Company, abolished appeals to the Federal Supreme Court, and called on all those still serving outside the Region in the Nigerian Police and in the Navy to return to the East. Thus within less than a month there was virtual secession, in fact if not in name.

The Supreme Military Council had now to decide what further action to take. Lt-Col Gowon had already outlined in a memorandum his plans for a blockade of the East and for declaring, in the event of secession, the creation of a Calabar-Ogoja-Rivers state, backed by whatever force might be necessary.[92] He had already asserted, on at least two occasions, his readiness to use force and there was little doubt that he meant what he said.[93] However, at least three of his colleagues in the Federal Military Government were opposed to this, namely the Military Governors of the West and of the Mid-West, and the Army Chief of Staff. Lt-Col Ejoor had stated early in March that 'the Mid-West will never accept being used as a base by one Region to fight another',[94] and again at the end of March, on returning from a meeting of the Supreme Military Council, he was reported as saying that the Federal Military Government would not use force on any Region which might wish to secede.[95] The Army Chief of Staff, Lt-Col Akahan, in Ibadan on 5 April, addressing the 3rd Battalion, had also said that force would not be used.[96]

Colonel Adebayo, at a slightly later stage, was the most outspoken. In a broadcast on 4 May he said:

I consider wise and patriotic the solemn pledge signed by the military leaders at Aburi and re-affirmed at the recent meeting of the Supreme Military Council to the effect that force will not be used. I need not tell you what horror, what devastation and what extreme human suffering will attend the use of force. When it is all over and the smoke and dust have lifted, and the dead are buried, we shall find, as other people have found, that it has all been futile, entirely futile, in solving the problem we set out to solve.[97]

Thus some of the support for Lt-Col Gowon's attempt to maintain an effective federal authority had been, in this sense, conditional; once the Eastern Region had virtually seceded it was held that alternative solutions ought to be considered. Obviously this implied some further concessions to Lt-Col Ojukwu's point of view, but this was thought worthwhile if some unity or form of association could be salvaged.

Two alternative ways of proceeding were suggested. The first was to continue negotiations in the belief that the different parts of Nigeria still had sufficient in common to constitute a political community of one kind or another. Colonel Adebayo was the most optimistic and active advocate of this course of action. His meeting with Lt-Col Ojukwu at Onitsha on 27 March had encouraged him to believe that there was still a desire on the latter's part to keep Nigeria together.[98] He took the initiative, early in April, in trying to arrange a meeting of the Supreme Military Council at which all members would be present, and he was in direct communication with the Ghanaian Head of State, General Ankrah.[99] When that failed, and as the crisis deepened, he sought public support for a policy of further negotiation.[100] He held it to be 'well-nigh impossible in the present circumstances of the country to produce an ideal federal constitution with a strong centre or anything like we had prior to the events of 1966', but thought 'an opportunity' existed for arriving at a 'workable formula' provided one avoided the use of terms like 'confederation', which had become 'almost a dirty word'. Each Region had its fears and these needed to be stilled; for example, fears in the West caused by the presence of Northern troops would disappear once there were sufficient Yoruba in the army and in the police to provide the necessary security, and he assured the North that it need not have any fears for its trade and communications with the West and overseas.

The other alternative was based on the assumption that the Eastern Region would in fact secede. In this case, the other Regions should recognize that the Federation no longer existed. Each Region would become a sovereign independent state free to negotiate its own terms of association with the other Regions. This view was held quite strongly both in the West and in the North, but it was never publicly stated in quite such clear terms.[101] Chief Awolowo came nearest to doing so when he spoke at Ibadan on 1 May. He stated it hypothetically:

if the Eastern Region is allowed, by acts of omission or commission, to secede from or opt out of Nigeria ... then the Federation should be considered to be at an end, and the Western Region and Lagos should also opt out of it. It would then be open to Western Nigeria and Lagos, as an independent sovereign state, to enter into association with any of the Nigerian units of its own choosing, and on terms mutually acceptable to them.[102]

This statement was seen by many as itself a move to encourage secession, and as such an advocacy of it. In the same speech Chief Awolowo did indeed say that 'the Eastern Region must be encouraged to remain part of the Federation', expressing the view that while certain of its demands were 'well founded' and 'designed for smooth and healthy association', others were 'excessive' and amounted to a 'complete disintegration of the Federation'. This was, on the face of it, an invitation to further negotiations on the basis of an all-round compromise, but the open recognition of secession as legitimate and acceptable should negotiations prove unsuccessful opened up an alternative, not simply to the use of force but also to the very survival of Nigeria.

Chief Awolowo's proposals—or estimate of the situation—envisaged an outcome which Lt-Col Gowon and his supporters had quite clearly rejected, on the grounds that it left minority demands unsatisfied and so perpetuated a state of unrest destructive of any real peace. The other alternative—a continuation of negotiations—was more acceptable but probably considered by Lt-Col Gowon rather futile, Lt-Col Ojukwu not having shown any disposition to compromise on essential matters. It was for this reason that more forceful measures had now to be used.

Those who favoured a continuation of negotiations hoped, as has already been stated, to arrange a meeting of the whole Supreme Military Council, including Lt-Col Ojukwu. This had proved difficult enough in the past and after 31 March it became even more so. Lt-Col Ojukwu was reported as saying that any such meeting had to be 'on the basis of association as sovereign units'.[103] He proposed a meeting to discuss the terms of association but with African Heads of State present.[104] To Lt-Col Gowon this was unacceptable, for fairly obvious reasons.[105] Thus when the Supreme Military Council did eventually meet, from 20–22 April, it was without Lt-Col Ojukwu. The coercive measures favoured by Lt-Col Gowon were discussed and given at least partial or conditional approval. The communiqué stated that the Council 'authorised certain stern measures to be taken by the Federal Military Government should the Military Governor of the East continue his illegal actions'. The use of armed force was presumably not included by the phrase 'stern measures'. Indeed, Colonel Adebayo stated later that it had been definitely excluded.[106] The meeting also had before it a 'twelve-point' proposal from Lt-Col Hassan Katsina and this seems to have formed the basis of an elaborate 'political and administrative programme of action' which, in the circumstances, was something of a pipe-dream. The communiqué set out a stage by stage return to civilian rule, beginning with the reconvening of the Ad Hoc Constitutional Committee not later than 5 May. It envisaged the appointment of civilians to the Federal Executive Council and to Regional Executive Committees, the summoning of a Constituent Assembly, and the resumption of party political activities and elections. The final transfer of power to civilian government was to be some time in 1969 or later.[107] The constitutional outcome was, however, predetermined; states were to be created by the Supreme Military Council as soon as a special ad hoc committee had made recommendations as to their 'number and identity'. This programme of action was therefore open to the criticism made of General Ironsi's proposals a year earlier: it prejudged one of the main issues in dispute and was on that ground unacceptable. Chief Awolowo had no hesitation in rejecting it. He informed Colonel Adebayo that he was unwilling to continue as Leader of the Region's Delegation to the Ad Hoc Constitutional Committee at least so long as Northern troops remained. These were said to 'constitute an army of occupation', virtually reducing the Western Region and Lagos to the 'status of a protectorate'.[108] His example was followed by others, including Mr Jakande and Sir Ibrahim Kashim, leaders of the Lagos and Northern Region delegations respectively.

Chief Awolowo's decision aroused a storm of debate, heightening still further the already very considerable tension. Meetings were held in all the Regions to test opinion. That held at Ibadan was dominated by supporters of Chief Awolowo and the resolutions followed faithfully the lead he had already given. It was decided to boycott the proposed Conference until such time as Northern troops had been withdrawn and to seek a peaceful settlement with the East 'even if this meant a constitutional arrangement that is looser than hitherto'. The decisions of the meeting were handed to Colonel Adebayo who, in turn, accompanied by all the senior Yoruba officers, communicated them to Lt-Col Gowon on 2 May.[109] The meeting may not have been fully representative and the officers may not have presented a united front in the course of a two-hour discussion with Lt-Col Gowon, but undeniably there was a body of Yoruba opinion that could scarcely be ignored.[110]

In Lagos itself, where the Administrator, Major Johnson, was definitely opposed to the views of Chief Awolowo, there was such a sharp division of opinion that the scheduled meeting was cancelled.[111] The different factions met separately, one endorsing union with the Western Region in a 'loose federation', the other demanding that Lagos should become one of the new states in a strong federation or, in the event of Nigeria's total disintegration, a sovereign state in its own right.[112]

Opinion in the North was less divided but the demand for the creation of states, asserting itself ever more strongly, had to contend with, or at least be combined with, a feeling of regional solidarity. This arose from a deep sense of frustration, exasperation, and suspicion. Many were outraged at the continual rebuffs administered by Lt-Col Ojukwu, first to Lt-Col Gowon personally, then to the conciliatory spirit shown in Decree No. 8, and finally to federal authority. The affront to authority was unforgivable to those brought up in the Fulani-Hausa tradition of government. This feeling of outrage was very evident in Lt-Col Hassan Katsina's opening address to the 'leaders of thought', meeting in Kaduna on 1 May. After referring to the vain attempts made to satisfy Lt-Col Ojukwu's point of view, he compared him to a 'spoilt child' and to 'a man consumed by pride and ambition', who, unable to have his own way, prefers to upset everything. He argued that Lt-Col Ojukwu had, 'by his acts of arrogance, defiance, and ridicule', shown himself to be 'clearly in favour of a settlement by force'.[113] This feeling was echoed in one of the resolutions jointly approved by the 'leaders of thought' and the Emirs and Chiefs; it expressed 'concern and dismay' at 'the failure of the Supreme Military Council to deal effectively with the defiance to its decision by the Governor of the East', a failure which had 'tended to invite public ridicule and contempt of the Council's decisions by the radio, press, and politicians'.[114] At the same time, there was, as is hinted in this reference to 'the politicians', a deep mistrust of Chief Awolowo's intentions. He was widely believed to be in collusion with Lt-Col Ojukwu, and to be using Colonel Adebayo to his own ends.[115] The spectre of a southern coalition, the ever-present fear in the far North, added a note of prudence to the deliberations. These were spread over four days, time being necessary to gain further information about the stand taken in the West and to arrive at some general consensus about the creation of states. On this latter question the meeting eventually made a clear commitment, far more definite than anything which had gone before. It stated:

The North should continue to support a federation with an effective centre as the only form of political association suitable for Nigeria,

and

the North is irrevocably committed to the creation of states whether or not they are created elsewhere as a basis for stability in the North and also in the entire Federation, and urges that the Federal Government should take immediate steps to set in motion the machinery for the creation of these states,

adding

We however would like to see states created simultaneously all over the country . . . a Commission should be appointed on this subject.[116]

The Consultative Committee of the Mid-West was in no position or mood to match the outspoken views of the other Regions. It confined itself to reaffirming 'its belief in the integrity of the Federation of Nigeria' and to mandating its Conference delegates 'to work for a loose Federation'. There was, however, considerable annoyance with the East at the recent hi-jacking of a plane from Benin to Lagos, forced to land at Enugu. Lt-Col Ejoor condemned this as 'a calculated and dangerous affront to the Mid-West'. He went on to describe the measures taken so far by the Federal Military Government as 'precautionary and protective', not at all punitive as some had suggested. He also urged the Easterners to overcome their 'injured pride and wounded feelings'.[117]

Because opinion was so divided, the meeting of the Ad Hoc Constitutional Committee, scheduled for 5 May, never took place, and Lt-Col Gowon was once again forced to retreat. Its cancellation led to renewed pressure to secure a meeting of the Supreme Military Council with Lt-Col Ojukwu, paralleled by a new development—the convening of a National Reconciliation Committee. This was an unofficial gathering of lawyers, chiefs, academics, civil servants, and politicians (including Chief Awolowo) meeting on 4 and 5 May at the invitation of the Federal Chief Justice, Sir Adetokumbo Ademola. His attempts at mediation met with little or no success. It was dismissed by Lt-Col Ojukwu as an 'ill-conceived child', on the grounds that the members from the East were not acceptable to him and that some of the other members could not be considered dispassionate arbiters.[118] He did, however, receive a four-man 'peace-mission', which provided him with an opportunity to meet Chief Awolowo and to state his conditions for resuming negotiations. These included a reconstitution of the Committee. Despite this initial rebuff, the National Reconciliation Committee met again on the 17th and recommended *inter alia* the ending of sanctions against the East. The Federal Government responded by announcing that these would be lifted on the 23rd, but its gesture was said by the East's Director of Information, Cyprian Ekwensi, to have been received in the East with 'contempt, levity and apathy'.[119] These disparaging reactions to the work of the National Reconciliation Committee perhaps go some way to explain Chief Awolowo's subsequent decision to support the Federal Government and to take office as Commissioner for Finance and Vice-Chairman of the Federal Executive Council.[120]

Meanwhile, Lt-Col Ejoor had suggested a meeting of the Supreme Military Council in a 'demilitarized zone'. On the 17th Lt-Col Gowon wrote to all the Military Governors proposing a meeting on or around the 24th, either at Benin, where one or two companies of British troops could provide the necessary security, or on a British warship.[121] This was rejected by Lt-Col Ojukwu. It was also rejected by Colonel Adebayo, who was showing signs of becoming more and more impatient with Lt-Col Gowon's continued refusal to withdraw all non-Yoruba troops from the West; he held that once this was done a meeting of the Supreme Military Council could take place without recourse to any foreign assistance.[122] The National Reconciliation Committee had also made their withdrawal one of its recommendations. Politically, if not militarily, it had clearly become expedient for Lt-Col Gowon to comply with this long-outstanding demand. The decision to withdraw non-Yoruba troops from the West was announced on the 25th, the troops having been given advance warning so as to avoid any misunderstandings. They were to be withdrawn by the 31st, some going to reinforce the Lagos Garrison and the rest to be stationed at Ilorin and Jebba, inside the Northern Region but still quite close to Ibadan.[123]

This belated action may have satisfied the West, but it came far too late as far as the Eastern Regional Government was concerned. The Region's Consultative Assembly met on the 26th, and it was asked by Lt-Col Ojukwu 'to choose from (a) accepting the terms of the North and Gowon and thereby submit to domination by the North, or (b) continuing the present stalemate and drift, or (c) ensuring the survival of our people by asserting our autonomy'.[124] He stated that he had sent a 'final letter' to Lt-Col Gowon, telling him that the East had 'no alternative but to make plans for a separate existence in the interests of self-preservation'. He expressed his readiness to take part in further talks, under certain conditions, but only to discuss the terms of a loose association. There could be no compromise on the basic issue of autonomy for the Eastern Region. The Consultative Assembly, at the end of its meeting on the 27th, authorized Lt-Col Ojukwu to declare, 'at an early practicable date, Eastern Nigeria as a free sovereign and independent state by the name and title of Biafra'.

Lt-Col Gowon decided to forestall the actual declaration of secession. Considering himself 'faced with this final choice between action to save Nigeria and acquiescence in secession and disintegration', he proclaimed 'a state of emergency throughout Nigeria with immediate effect' and stated that he had 'assumed full powers as Commander-in-Chief of the Armed Forces and Head of the Federal Military Government'.[125] He also announced the promulgation of a decree dividing Nigeria into twelve states. The Eastern Region was divided into three: a South Eastern State, a Rivers State, and a Central Eastern State of which Lt-Col Ojukwu was named Military Governor.[126] Lt-Col Gowon concluded his broadcast by repeating the basic argument which had all along been his justification:

If it were possible for us to avoid chaos and civil war merely by drifting apart as some people claim, that easy choice may have been taken. But we know that to take such a course will quickly lead to the disintegration of the existing regions in conditions of chaos, and to disastrous foreign interference.[127]

It was in the name of the minorities that Lt-Col Gowon had acted and to prevent what he anticipated would be a greater evil. This was not how the three largest 'internal nations' had been inclined to assess the situation, but their failure to agree on the terms of their 'drawing apart' had in the end given Lt-Col Gowon a chance of applying his own solution. When, in the early morning of the 30th, the Eastern Region was proclaimed the sovereign independent Republic of Biafra, Lt-Col Gowon was assured of support, even from those who had earlier declared the use of force inexpedient.

The closing stages of the crisis had been played out in an atmosphere of mixed feelings. Secession had seemed the inevitable conclusion of the failure to agree in March on the constitutional and financial issues, but hopes of a negotiated settlement had been rekindled in early May when Chief Awolowo showed himself ready to fall in with most of Lt-Col Ojukwu's demands.

There was still a fair chance, even as late as mid-May, that those in favour of compromise would make their views prevail. But neither Lt-Col Ojukwu nor Lt-Col Gowon was in favour of compromise. This is evident from their words and their actions, and each in taking up his uncompromising stand was representing views which were held very widely and very strongly. The nearest approach to specific agreement was Decree No. 8. It conceded to the East many of the procedural arrangements that Lt-Col Ojukwu had proposed at Aburi, but continued in existence too many of the existing federal responsibilities for it to satisfy Eastern demands for autonomy. Had it been accepted it would no doubt have caused considerable friction in practice and perhaps proved unworkable. The two men really stood for radically different conceptions of government, and the one could prevail only at the expense of the other. Lt-Col Gowon was in the better position tactically. He had control of government at the centre, even if none over government in the East. Control at the centre gave him control over foreign relations, overseas trade, and, above all, federal finance. He could afford, far better than could Lt-Col Ojukwu, to maintain the *status quo* and bide his time. His opponent was much more pressed by the need to act unilaterally in the absence of any satisfactory compromise. He had to make a bid for the oil revenues and this inevitably entailed secession. Secession was no doubt prepared some time in advance, but as a contingency which had to be foreseen, not necessarily as a definite eventuality. But in the end the decision had to be taken.

3

THE NIGERIAN MILITARY:
DISINTEGRATION OR INTEGRATION?

A. R. Luckham

INTRODUCTION

It is my intention to discuss some of the organizational characteristics of the Nigerian army as they have affected military intervention and rule. I am adopting this approach in reaction to the intellectual disarray that has followed the rapid fragmentation of African regimes, both civilian and military, after the first few years of independence; a disarray which is all the more marked because of the tendency of earlier analysts of the African party-state to attribute to the somewhat shadowy political arrangements of the immediately preceding period a degree of institutionalization which did not in reality exist. In these circumstances it is tempting to write off in despair all attempts at structural analysis. Aristide Zolberg, for example, suggests that there is such a wide divergence between organizational models and reality that 'constitutional arrangements' have 'had little reality beyond their physical existence as a set of written symbols deposited in a government archive'; in the civil service 'the usual bureaucratic norms are so rare that it is perhaps better to speak of government employees as a categoric group'; trade unions 'are more by way of a congeries of urban employed and unemployed intermittently mobilised for a temporary purpose, such as a street demonstration'; and the army 'which far from being a model of hierarchical organization tends to be an assemblage of armed men who may or may not obey their officers'.[1] Thus everything, according to Zolberg, is like the smile of the Cheshire cat which may disappear at any moment.

This picture is indeed a persuasive one. Written constitutions and political parties have been cast aside with great ease. Challenges to military discipline have undermined military hierarchies and deformed the Sandhurst image. Sometimes, indeed, these upheavals have taken the form of unplanned, unstructured outbursts of mob behaviour permeating the military organizations themselves, as in the Congo and East African mutinies, the coup which destroyed President Olympio in Togo, or that of July 1966 in Nigeria. Nevertheless, I hope to demonstrate that it is fruitful to seek explanations for this abrupt transformation of organization into anarchy in terms of structural dilemmas that are shared by many modern military organizations. The fragmentation of the Nigerian army's authority system that took place during the coups of January and July 1966, it will be argued, can be understood as the product of the interplay of three groups of factors: the structural weaknesses of the army; cleavages deriving from both organizational and societal (in this case regional and ethnic) roots; and an unstable political environment; though the last of these will not be dealt with in detail.

The generalizations that can be made are necessarily highly tentative and exploratory, because of the difficulties of obtaining data of a kind which would support firm conclusions. The discussion will be confined mainly to the officer corps in the interests of a tightly delimited argument, although it is necessary to point out that the NCOs, too, have played an important role, especially in the events of July 1966.

STRUCTURAL WEAKNESSES

(a) *Size*

A key factor in the Nigerian army's inability to maintain its organizational integrity in a changing and conflict-torn political environment has been its smallness. In January 1966 it was composed of no more than 10,500 men, making up five infantry battalions, a reconnaissance squadron with armoured cars, and a field battery together with the requisite ancillary service units such as the engineers and the medical corps. The officer corps numbered only 518 men, of whom 330 were of combat status.

It used to be thought that the army's small size in most African nations precluded it from intervention in politics. William Gutteridge, for example, argued in reference to Nigeria that 'three to five hundred officers in a country of forty million, based mainly on five military stations, the majority of which are far from the capital, cannot for the time being be regarded as a political factor of the greatest importance'.[2] But such are the organizational and coercive resources of a modern army, compared with those of the weakly articulated civil institutions they confront, that even a relatively small and ineffective force is able to seize power with comparative ease. The superior power of tiny expeditionary forces was, after all, the initial basis of colonial rule, or as Hilaire Belloc put it 'we have got the Maxim gun and they have not'. Although during the period of decolonization the nationalist political parties may have seemed to develop so strong an institutional base as to rule out a military challenge against them, their power subsequently turned out to be rather ephemeral depending as it did on a diffuse and unstable capital of legitimacy which was quickly dissipated in the political squabbles of early independence.

Limitations in size, on the other hand, greatly reduced the capacity of the army to rule after the seizure of power. The small size of the officer corps is perhaps the most crucial consideration here. Inevitably, in any army intervention officers get killed, have to be shuttled off into 'safe' diplomatic or honorary posts, or get absorbed in governmental or administrative tasks. It takes fewer such defections to weaken the authority structure of a small army. This can be well illustrated from the Nigerian case, where rates of attrition amongst senior officers in the course of the events of 1966 were extremely high, even though the absolute number involved was not many. The coup of January 1966 swept away more than half the combat officers who had attained the rank of Lieutenant-Colonel and above. In the process, two of the army's three Brigadiers (the third, Ogundipe, was in Britain at the time of the coup), the Chief of Staff, the Adjutant-General, the Quarter-Master General and the Commandant of the Nigerian Military Training College were all murdered. The July 1966 coup further thinned the upper ranks with only 40 per cent of the officers who had held the rank of Lieutenant-Colonel and none who had held a higher rank remaining militarily effective thereafter. (See Tables I and II.)

It is important to note, moreover, that from July 1966 those officers who were still militarily effective began in practice to make up the nucleus of two armies. All Ibo officers of Eastern origin and a few of the non-Ibo Easterners fled to the Eastern Region to build up what was to become the Biafran army together with the remaining January conspirators who were released from prisons in the Eastern Region in

TABLE I. Effects of January 1966 Coup on Combat Officer Numbers

Rank[a] (in January 1966)	Killed	Imprisoned	Members of Military Government[b]	Remaining in Army	Total	% Remaining in Army
Colonel and above	4	0	1	2	7	29
Lieutenant-Colonel	3	1	3	7	14	50
Major	1	4	1	26	32	81
Captain	0	5	0	47	52	90
Lieutenant	0	5	0	53	58	91
2nd Lieutenant	1	9	0	157	167	94

[a] Gazetted ranks only; a number of officers (especially those in gazetted ranks of Captain and Lieutenant) held higher temporary ranks.

[b] The Head of the National Military Government and the four Regional Military Governors.

Sources for Tables I–IV: *Federation of Nigeria Official Gazette*, 1960–7; *Nigeria 1966* (Lagos, 1967); *January 15th: Before and After* (Enugu, 1967).

TABLE II. Effects of January 1966 and July 1966 Coups on Combat Officer Numbers

Rank (in January 1966)	Killed[a]	Imprisoned	Members of Military Government[b]	Remaining in Army	Total	% Remaining in Army
Colonel and above	5	0	2	0	7	0
Lieutenant-Colonel	4	1	4	5	14	36
Major	6	2	1	23	32	72
Captain	3	5	1	43	52	83
Lieutenant	7	5	0	46	58	79
2nd Lieutenant	13	9	0	145	167	87

[a] Numbers killed include two who had been in the Military Government after January 1966 (General Ironsi and Lt-Col Fajuyi) as well as two of the January conspirators who were assassinated in prison after the July coup (Majors Okafor and Anuforo).

[b] Includes Brigadier Ogundipe and Lt-Col Bassey, both given ambassadorial positions, as well as the Military Governors and the Military Administrator of Lagos.

early 1967. All but one or two of the Mid-Western Ibo sought security in the Mid-West, to become absorbed in administrative duties there until their defection to Biafra when Lt-Col Ojukwu's forces invaded their Region in August 1967. Of the 330 combat officers in the army in early 1966, the Federal army was thus able to muster no more than about 184 for the civil war and the Biafrans some 93. The Federal army, moreover, was virtually bare of officers of any seniority or experience at anything above the company commander level, as Tables III and IV

TABLE III. Disposition in August 1967 of Officers Surviving the Events of 1966

Rank[a] (in January 1966)	Military Government		Militarily Active	
	Federal[b]	Biafran	Federal	Biafran
Colonel and above	2	0	0	0
Lieutenant-Colonel	4	1	0	5
Major	1	0	9	16
Captain	5	0	28	15
Lieutenant	0	0	34	17
2nd Lieutenant	0	0	113	40

[a] Exact numbers for ranks of Major upwards. A small margin of error must be allowed for estimates at lower ranks.

[b] Includes additional Military Governors appointed from the army in 1967, Lt-Col Kurobo, who was appointed Ambassador to Moscow after absconding from the East in mid-1967, and Lt-Col Ejoor whose status in August 1967 after the Mid-West invasion can be regarded as indeterminate until his appointment to the Federal army as Director of Recruitment and Training later in 1967.

TABLE IV. Division of Militarily Active Combat
Officers between Federal and Biafran Armies in August
1967, as a percentage of January 1966 total

Rank (in January 1966)	Federal	Biafran
Colonel and above	—	—
Lieutenant-Colonel	—	36
Major	28	50
Captain	54	29
Lieutenant	59	29
2nd Lieutenant	68	24

indicate. At the beginning of the civil war in 1967 there were no officers in active military roles in the Federal army (as opposed to 'political' roles in the Military Government) who held a rank above that of gazetted Major before 1966 and only four of the militarily effective officers had gained their commissions before 1960. In the light of this shortage of experienced commanders, the shortcomings of both armies in discipline and military effectiveness during the civil war do not seem surprising, the more so given the enormous numerical expansion in the men under arms on both sides in 1967/8. Such a drastic dilution in the pool of experience would be serious in any army; it was even more so in the Nigerian Army because it was superimposed upon a situation in which the military's cohesion was already in doubt.

(b) Age-structure and Discipline

Janowitz and Little suggest that one of the inherent dilemmas of military organization is the tension between the calculus of violence at the point of contact of small unit commands with the enemy and the exacting requirements for military co-ordination and centralization of command. 'The combat soldier', they suggest, 'is hardly the model of Max Weber's ideal bureaucrat following rigid rules and regulations. In certain respects he is the antithesis. The combat fighter is not routinised and self-contained. Rather, his role is one of constant improvision, regardless of his service or weapon. Improvisation is the keynote of the individual fighter or combat group.'[3] One of the most striking features of military intervention in Nigeria is the way in which initiative triumphed over discipline. This was particularly true of the decision by the Ibo Majors to wipe out the whole upper command structure of the army in January 1966, a feat which required both considerable qualities of initiative and a fine disregard of the restraints of military discipline. Much the same could be said of the counter-coup by the Northern Lieutenants in July, except that this took place in a situation in which discipline had already been undermined. The conspirators in both cases combined a good appreciation of the calculus of violence—of the logistics of small-scale operations, of the advantages of surprise and a speedy strike—with an apparent inability or unwillingness to plan or foresee the wider consequences for either the military or the political system. Even the Majors of January, with their relative political and professional sophistication, had no very concrete ideas about how they would rule afterwards nor any appreciation of the dangers of disrupting military discipline. Other examples come readily to mind, such as Lt-Col Banjo's audacious plan to stage a coup within a coup against Lt-Col Ojukwu after the invasion of the Mid-West in August 1967. The most extreme example I can think of comes from the Ghanaian army, which seems to indicate that this may be a pattern that is shared by other newly-created armies in Africa. This is the case of Lieutenant Arthur, the young Ghanaian officer who attempted a coup against the Ghana military regime on 17 April 1967, killed Lieut-General Kotoka, and confessed afterwards that he had wished to become the first Lieutenant ever to seize power and that 'on the formation of the new junta I counted all Colonels and above out. I knew in the coup I would eliminate all of them.'

This does not mean, however, that the constraints of discipline, though frequently violated, were not real and important. During the most uncertain period of all, that between the July 1966 coup and the civil war in 1967, discipline was, as it were, held together by bits of string, Heath Robinson style. It was only with difficulty that Lt-Col Gowon was able to prevent the more adventurous of his subordinates from leading their units unilaterally against the Eastern Region on more than one occasion during this period. Yet the fact remains that he was able to generate sufficient consensus around his objectives and his person to maintain his authority as Commander-in-Chief and prevent army moves in this direction. Patterns of discipline though much weakened, therefore, were not entirely destroyed and the balance struck between the qualities of initiative and discipline at any one time depended very much on the political and organizational context in which they were exercised.

Why were patterns of discipline so poorly institutionalized? This seems to have had much to do with the distorted age structure and promotional pattern, in turn determined by the rapid indigenization of the officer corps which was largely achieved between independence in 1960 and the end of 1964, as shown in Table v.

The age structure of the Nigerian officer corps was as a consequence extremely unbalanced even for a military organization. With the exception of eight or nine ex-NCOs at or near the top, virtually all

TABLE V. Indigenization of the Officer Corps

Date (1 January in each year)	Number of British Officers	Number of Nigerian Officers Combat Commissions	Nigerian Officers Non-Combat Commissions	Nigerian Officers as a percentage of total
1960	228	48	2	18
1962	156	107	50	50
1964	47	240	132	89
1966	0	330	181	100

Note: Approximate numbers only owing to gaps in the Gazettes in estimates of British departures.
Source: Federation of Nigeria Official Gazette, 1960–6.

combat officers fell within the age group 20–35. Rates of promotion were also very high, especially for the small group of officers commissioned before 1960. An officer recruited at the age of nineteen or twenty in 1952/4 could expect to receive his commission after Sandhurst in 1954/6 and attain the rank of Lieutenant-Colonel any time from 1963 to 1965 at the age of thirty-one or thirty-two. Promotion, at least as far as the rank of Major, was even faster for the officers commissioned in the late 1950s (including the Majors who started the January 1966 coup). By 1965, however, promotion was less rapid, though this had its heaviest effect on the young officers at the very bottom of the hierarchy. And though most middle-ranking officers—those in the ranks of Major and Captain—had had an easy ride up the hierarchy so far, they faced at the end of 1965 a distinctly longer wait for promotion than their predecessors.

The implications of this for the disciplinary system were threefold. First, it may have contributed to the feelings of relative deprivation amongst the middle ranks discussed later in the context of peer groups. Second, the unbalanced age structure tended to weaken established patterns of discipline by reinforcing discrepancies in the perception of authority and competence within the military hierarchy. From the time of Weber, writers about bureaucracy have suggested that the conflict between authority based on sheer incumbency in a position of hierarchy, and authority based on expertise, is a recurrent dilemma of organization;[4] this tendency is especially well developed, as Janowitz and Little[5] suggest, in modern military organizations. Circumstances in the Nigerian army tended to increase this dilemma. Because of the very small gap in age, experience, and sometimes even rank between persons in command and those in subordinate positions, the sharp gradations in formal status and prestige that obtained in the army were especially sharply at variance with contributions rendered to the organization.

And although one or two officers at the highest levels before 1966 were clearly superior to their subordinates in age, experience, and probably competence, their authority tended to be undermined by yet another kind of status discrepancy, that deriving from their relative lack of formal education. General Ironsi and eight of his ten most senior officers had come up from the ranks, in contrast to the rest of the officer corps, the greater proportion of whom at all levels had at least a full secondary education (if not more) and direct entry to cadet courses. Although a number of these ex-NCOs, for example Brigadier Ademulegun, were known to be very competent indeed, they were not always greatly respected by their more educated subordinates. This was in part due to the very close link between status and education in West Africa, and it was in part because even those like Ademulegun, whose competence in military matters was widely respected, were felt (especially by politically radical officers) to be too narrowly professional in their outlook. Some of the arrogant contempt one or two of the more intellectual officers felt for their commanders was pungently expressed by one of them who, on being asked to 'listen to his General' at an army banquet presided over by General Ironsi in 1965, was heard to mumble 'General Idiot' at him under his breath.

At the same time officers tended to develop unstable and unrealistic expectations concerning their role. Rapid promotion put many of them in relatively responsible command positions at an early age, tending to develop qualities of initiative to an unusual extent. This obtained even more than the actual rank structure by itself would suggest. Command positions were frequently held by officers more junior than the ranks at which they were established, especially in the period 1962–4: at that time, for example, 50 per cent or more of the posts at Company Commander level were held by Captains or Lieutenants rather than Majors. In addition, transfers were very frequent indeed, tending to inhibit the development of stable lines of authority. In the space of fifteen months in 1960 and 1961, for instance, the 5th Battalion had no less than four different commanders, and this during a time when it was involved in military operations in the Congo. Under these conditions the cavalier attitude of many officers towards authority is hardly surprising.

Such a disorientation of expectations seems to bear a close relationship to the kind of anomie Durkheim suggested might be fostered by an economic boom or a sudden accession to wealth.[6] Speaking of a similar (though rather less disastrous) stage in the evolution of the Pakistan Army shortly after independence, President Ayub Khan says 'there was considerable unrest among the officers caused by a spate of swift promotions from junior to senior ranks. This raised expectations to unwarranted heights. Every officer felt that unless he was made Commander-in-Chief no one would believe he had done well in life. It was a curious phenomenon. Perfectly sensible people, Brigadiers and Generals, would go about bemoaning their lot. Each one of them was a Bonaparte, albeit an unhappy one . . . It was this sudden devaluation of the higher posts which produced fantastic ideas and ambitions in people.'[7]

SOURCES OF CLEAVAGE

(a) *Formation of Peer Groups*

One of the most striking features of the two coups of 1966 was the marked age and rank gradings of the participants, the Majors of January and the Lieutenants of July. It is also interesting to note that a group of Lieutenant-Colonels discussed but rejected the possibility of intervening during the crisis over the Federal Election of December 1964. This reflects a well-developed tendency in the Nigerian army for interaction and friendship to occur within groups of military peers, a tendency which is represented in its strongest form by the solidarity that develops between 'course mates', who have been through the Nigerian Military Training College and Sandhurst, Mons, or other cadet training schools together.

Peer groups are a common feature in many organizations. But as many empirical studies in non-military organizations have shown (for example, Blau's study of County Welfaie Agencies[8]), they are more common at the factory floor or 'other rank' level than at upper supervisory levels. On the other hand military organizations seem quite frequently to generate peer groups at higher levels of the hierarchy, i.e. within the officer corps itself. Cliques formed by groups of peers are, moreover, quite often a factor in the intervention of the military in politics. One thinks, for example, of the Free Officers' Group in Egypt or the '8th Graduating Class' which was prominent in the Korean military revolution of 1961.[9]

This reflects two rather pervasive characteristics of the social structure of the officer corps. First, the high degree of emphasis on internal solidarity. Or, as General Ironsi put it, 'the army is a brotherhood and I cannot emphasise too strongly the need for corporate life among its members'.[10] This is fostered by a number of different institutional devices, the most significant of which is the collegial social life fostered by the officers' mess. There is also the military status system, which creates rather strongly enforced rituals of deference and avoidance modelled on those of the British Army. The interaction of these two factors tends to turn the officer corps into a set of vertically divided fraternities rather than a single solitary brotherhood.

This is illustrated rather well by the manner in which the Majors of January saw their relations with collaborators at other levels of the military hierarchy. Those of a higher rank, though they may, like Lt-Col Ojukwu, have had some knowledge of and sympathy with the conspirators' plans, were excluded from direct participation in the inner circle, for this would have implied either a surrender of control to the superior officers or insoluble status ambiguities. On the other hand, a more direct part could be found for a number of junior officers who could play subordinate roles without violating accepted concepts of military status; with one exception none was in the inner planning group. A further interesting feature is that most of the junior officers brought in by the conspirators were Lieutenants rather than Captains, in the proportion of about three to one.[11] This may suggest a degree of status ambiguity in incorporating officers at this latter rank into the peer category, on the one hand, or the subordinate category, on the other. Lieutenants, however, fitted comfortably into the follower's role.

The importance of peer groups in the social geography of the army might have led one to predict that the issues of conflict would be drawn along inter-generational cleavages. Yet, although peer groups provided a pattern or frame for cleavage in the manner just described, conflicts in the army drew their dynamic from elsewhere and created new conflict groups which transcended the lines between the ranks. The Majors of January did have their grievances against their seniors but these were definitely secondary to their main political objectives; it was the strategy of the coup more than feelings of direct antagonism which dictated the murder of the army's senior officers. As soon as the military were in power the focus of the struggle shifted rapidly towards ethnic and Regional issues. Despite a flavouring of radical populism amongst Northern junior officers and NCOs, the main objects of hostility in July 1966 were officers and men of particular ethnic and Regional origins rather than senior officers or the military high command as such.

How do we account for this lack of overt antagonism between the ranks? It is frequently noted that the cohesion of primary groups at various points of a bureaucratic structure may help to sustain rather than to undermine existing authority relations.[12] Whether or not primary groups of peers in fact help to integrate or tend to fragment the organization will depend on a number of other considerations. There are two such factors that might seem to be important here. The first is the existence (or not) of an adequate system of occupational mobility facilitating the integration of groups at various levels of the hierarchy into the system. Blockages in promotion had only just begun to appear in the Nigerian army by 1965 and were at best a potential threat. On the other hand, adequate provision for upward mobility does not entirely do away with grievances. As the authors of *The American Soldier* first pointed out,[13] men who get left behind when promotions are rapid are all the more likely to experience relative deprivation. This has possibly been a source of discontent for one or two individuals such as Major Nzeogwu, the Kaduna leader of the January coup. But it is difficult to gauge how widespread such feelings were. They may have been more frequent among the more junior field grade officers (like the Majors) whose promotions had been fast, but who lacked the future promotion prospects of their immediate seniors. Nevertheless, discontents of this nature were not among the explicitly stated objectives of the conspirators in either of the 1966 coups although they may have contributed to the underlying rejection of discipline.

The second relevant factor in considering whether peer groups lead to cleavages is the fact that they themselves are a direct product of military norms of solidarity and of the status system within the military. This provides an important set of restraints against overt cleavage on generational lines, restraints deriving from the 'organic solidarity' between peer groups in the chain of command and control. To make a direct attack on senior officers would be to challenge the entire authority system of the army. In contrast, hostilities of other kinds, such as that between different ethnic groups, do not run up against the same kinds of constraints and this may help to explain why antagonisms in the army gravitated during 1966 towards ethnic and Regional conflict in so free-wheeling a manner. Indeed, there is some evidence that this provided a means of attacking the persons in power without directly assaulting the authority system itself, notably during the July 1966 coup when the Ibo who were attacked had dominated the upper sectors of the officer corps and the Military Government.

The tenacity of military norms of authority is illustrated very interestingly in the attempts made during both the coups to maintain the necessary fictions and continuities of command. This was particularly marked during the July coup. As far as it is possible to determine, the greater part of the operational side of the revolt was in the hands of very junior Northern officers. All but one or two of the more senior officers, such as Lt-Col Muritala Mohammed and Major Danjuma, were excluded from direct complicity, and it is not clear how far even these played a direct part in co-ordinating operations. Nevertheless, the top brass were very soon called upon to add their authority when it was felt their legitimation and skills were required. Thus it was Major Danjuma who arrested General Ironsi in Ibadan; and Lt-Col

Mohammed and one or two others who moved up to Ikeja barracks immediately after the revolt in order to take charge of negotiations. In addition, once it was apparent that the coup was successful, the co-operation of the remaining senior officers was enlisted. Lt-Col Gowon, the most senior, was asked, after being sent to parley with the rebels at Ikeja, to assume command himself, although it is fairly clear that he had had no complicity in the planning or execution of the coup.

In January there had been something more like an attempt to attack the military authority system as such, in that the Majors deliberately set out to eliminate most of the holders of key command and staff positions. But it should be noted that political objectives—the ending of Northern hegemony, the removal of corrupt politicians, etc.— were paramount. Senior officers were assassinated for limited and specific reasons, namely to effect a temporary paralysis of the normal channels of command; and to prevent any of them lending support to the old regime. When the hatchet work was over and General Ironsi had succeeded in capturing the initiative in Lagos from the Majors, Major Nzeogwu was prepared to allow authority to return to the established channels of command. As he said in a subsequent interview: 'I was being sensible. The last thing we desired was unnecessary loss of life. If I had stuck to my guns there would have been a civil war and as official head of the army he [Ironsi] would have split the loyalty of my men.'[14]

To sum up, it seems misleading to conclude from the rather sharp rank-grading of the planners in the 1966 coups that conflicts of interest between different generations in the officer corps were a major issue. If peer groups had any significance this probably lies in the conditions they provided of close informal interaction between officers of the same rank within which discontents could be nurtured, developed, and turned into conspiracy. In other words they provided nodal points around which conflicts derived from other sources could develop. It is difficult, however, to provide anything better than circumstantial evidence that this was so. It can be established, for example, that the careers of the main conspirators of January 1966 intersected frequently in the period 1961-5, as can be seen from Table VI. Table VII also shows that four of the coup leaders overlapped at Sandhurst. Yet there is very little evidence as to when and how the clique was established, how it was organized and maintained, or when members of it first discussed political action. The rank structure of the various conspiratorial groups discussed above is thus clearly highly suggestive, but it is difficult to determine its precise significance. Peer grouping is perhaps as much indicative of the integration of the officer corps as it is of cleavage and conflict.

TABLE VI. Military Postings[a] of January Coup Leaders[b] 1961–5

	1961	1962	1963	1964	1965
Kaduna					
Major C. K. Nzeogwu	(5th Bn) ———	(5th Bn) ———		—(1 Bde HQ)—	——(NMTC)——
Major E. A. Ifeajuna					
T/Major[c] T. C. Onwua-tuegwu		(5th Bn) ———	(5th Bn) ———		——(NMTC)——
T/Cptn E. N. Nwobosi				(NMTC) ——	(1 Fld Battery) ——
Zaria					
Major C. K. Nzeogwu	—(NMS)—	—(Depot)—			
Major D. O. Okafor	—(NMS)—	—(Depot)— —(NMS)—			
T/Major I. U. Chukuka		—(Depot)— —(Depot)—			
Lagos					
Major C. K. Nzeogwu			—(GHQ)—		
Major E. A. Ifeajuna			—(GHQ)—	—?—(2 Bde HQ)—	
Major D. O. Okafor				—(Federal Guard)—	
T/Major I. U. Chukuka			—(GHQ)—		? ? ?

[a] Sources for this Table are office and telephone directories for Kaduna, Zaria, and Lagos, with amendments and other details included from other sources where necessary. Allowances have to be made for the fact that the directories are neither wholly accurate nor complete in their coverage of military posts during the period.

[b] The Federal document *Nigeria 1966* designates Majors Nzeogwu, Ifeajuna, Okafor, Onwuatuegwu, and Captain Nwobosi as being the ringleaders. It is not clear whether these are the ones Major Nzeogwu had in mind when he said 'we were five' in his *Africa and the World* interview. In addition to these three other Majors were involved in the coup, namely Major Anuforo and T/Majors Ademoyega and Chukuka. Only for the latter is there sufficient career data to justify inclusion in this Table.

[c] Designation for temporary (effective) rank as opposed to substantive (formerly gazetted) rank.

TABLE VII. Sandhurst Training of January Coup Leaders

	1958	1959	1960	1961	1962	1963
Major Nzeogwu	----	----				
T/Major Chukuka		----	----	----		
Major Anuforo		----	----	----		
T/Major Onwuatuegwu						
Captain Gbulie				----	----	----
Captain Nwobosi					----	----

Source: The Wish Stream: Journal of the Royal Military Academy, Sandhurst, 1958–63.

(b) *Ethnic and Regional Differences*

It is tempting to argue *ex post facto* in the light of the events of 1966 that tribal and Regional ties were the most powerful factor in the patterns of differentiation within the army. I would argue that this was probably not, in fact, the case. It is true that officers were not completely free from contacts with local social structures and tended, like other elites, to become involved in urban networks of kinship and tribe. Cliques like that of the January Majors did tend to be patterned round ethnic groups. Yet the characteristics of the army as a 'total institution', its internal cohesion as well as doctrinal commitment against 'tribalism', counteracted these tendencies quite effectively. This can be seen in the way that cliques shaped by ethnic ties tended to form *within* military peer groups and did not, on the whole, cut across lines of rank and generation. Region is another possible basis for differentiation. Yet it was still less true of the Northerners than of any of the ethnic groups such as the Ibo, Yoruba, or Idoma that they in any sense made up a cohesive bloc within the officer corps. Amongst the bonds linking Northern officers were those deriving from the fact that many of them were contemporaries at the same secondary schools, notably the Nigerian Military School, Zaria, and Government College, Zaria. Sources of differentiation between them, however, such as religion, tribe, and the Middle Belt/dry North cleavage (to the extent that it existed) were about as important as what they had in common.

An attempt has been made by Martin Dent[15] to shift the basis of this argument by suggesting that it is the *combination* of ethnic and Regional cleavages with those deriving from the rank structure that is important. This seems to derive from the hypothesis which is familiar from the work of sociologists such as George Simmel and Lewis Coser[16] that cleavages which are consistent with one another rather than cross-cutting tend to be additive and lead to the polarization and intensification of conflict.

Ethnic and Regional differentiation did to some extent, it is true, follow the lines of cleavage between different ranks and generations in the officer corps. No single group had a dominant position in the topmost group of senior officers. But around 50 per cent of the next layer, the 'Sandhurst generation', commissioned between 1954 and 1960, were Ibo from the East or Mid-West, this being the layer from which the Majors of January were recruited. The third layer, those commissioned from about 1961, was much more heterogeneous in ethnic origin as well as in training, though as a result of the quota system imposed after 1961 slightly less than half of these promotional cohorts were Northerners. In addition, the gap between the officer corps as a whole and the other ranks was marked by a slightly sharper

Regional differentiation, some 65 or 70 per cent of the latter being Northern in origin. Can one, therefore, argue that, though conflict in the army cannot be pinned down to a single source of cleavage, it can be attributed to the combined effects of generation, on the one hand, and tribe and Region, on the other, and that these created in effect a single set of cleavages powerful enough to 'put into question the basic consensual agreement'[17] on which the solidarity of the army rested?

Whether or not one accepts the assumption that these cleavages are in fact additive, this attractive hypothesis must be treated with some caution. The fit between ethnic/Regional and generational boundaries is by no means as impressive as it might be. The only two levels with an appreciable degree of homogeneity are the middle ranking officers and the NCOs, yet these are not positioned at the immediately contiguous levels of the hierarchy where levels of inter-rank tension might be expected to be highest. The imperfection in fit between the two types of cleavage might, on the contrary, be said to be a major factor in the fragmentation of the two coups of 1966. This is evidenced in the failure of the Majors to recruit from among their non-Ibo peers or to elicit genuine support from any of their Ibo seniors. Similarly, military status relations barred all but a few senior Northern officers from direct and overt participation in July and this contributed to the breakdown in discipline which followed the coup.

None the less, it is probably true that the combination of differences in rank and generation with ethnic cleavages sharpened the process of discord without necessarily being its main source. After the elimination of non-Eastern officers at the top in the January coup, Ibo officers appeared to dominate the upper levels of the officer corps more than ever before and became a clearer target for the hostility and suspicion of junior officers and other ranks. Yet it will be recalled that peer group cleavages were hedged with military authority norms, effective enough still to define relations amongst Northern officers and men amid the populistic currents of the July revolt. Even if the military status system reinforced ethnic/Regional cleavages, it also created a sense of solidarity which resisted open conflict along these lines of differentiation in the first seven months of 1966, despite mounting political pressures and the progressive weakening of discipline. The egg broke in the North in May 1966, as Lt-Col Hassan Katsina put it,[18] but it did not break in the army until two months later, after a considerable worsening in the political climate.

Little of the above, however, explains the dynamics of the conflict: how primordial ties became so much more salient after 15 January 1966 than before; or how tensions in the army could become so great as to burst the bounds of the established mechanisms of social control. This calls attention to another facet of the conflict that demands adequate explanation, namely the manner in which it developed into a hostile outburst in which the perceptions of issues and expressions of antagonism were out of all proportion to the issues at stake. In this respect it fits almost perfectly the paradigm for collective or non-institutionalized behaviour put forward by Neil Smelser.[19] The struggle for power was reinterpreted in the light of generalized beliefs defining it in terms of sin and retribution; guilt was assigned by association to ethnic and Regional groups, all Ibo being held responsible for the coup of January and all Northerners for the excesses of July and the massacres of Ibo in Northern cities in the May and September/October riots. Beliefs concerning evil deeds and conspiratorial designs were rapidly diffused and were intermingled with wish-fulfilment beliefs of all varieties. Among Northern soldiers, for example, the belief that the events of January were a sinister plot hatched by Ibo officers was mixed with a singular myth of regeneration according to which Brigadier Maimalari had escaped death like a heroic (and respected) Rasputin, after being shot and stabbed with a bayonet, before being run over by General Ironsi's car. The coup of July 1966, which brought these tensions to a head in the army, was underpinned by the most sketchy planning. Official channels of communication and authority were by-passed and influence gravitated rapidly to charismatic figures such as Lt-Col Muritala Mohammed, only to be routinized back to persons with a more established position in the hierarchy, like Lt-Col Gowon and Lt-Col Akahan, once the immediate crisis within the military had passed. In sum these events can be as fruitfully analysed in terms of mass or collective behaviour within the army as can the riots and massacres of May and September/October 1966 outside it.

It is normal to seek explanations of collective behaviour in terms of ambiguities of expectations and conditions of strain in the social structure. Both factors seem to have been present in an interconnected manner. General Ironsi's Government failed to provide effective leadership in a fluid political situation; it failed to resolve the uncertainties concerning the punishment of the officers who assassinated senior military personnel and politicians in January; and, in publishing in May 1966 Decree No. 34 on the unification of the country, it gave rise to suspicions of its intentions without in practice much increasing central control over the Regions. After these tensions had come to the surface in rioting in the North, it became clearer than ever that they could be resolved only by a realignment of power within the army; and rumours that the Ibo officers were going to 'complete the job' of 15 January,[20] on the one hand, and that the Northerners were going to take their revenge, on the other, gathered momentum.

How did these uncertainties permeate the army? It seems clear that they were only able to do so because of conditions of acute strain within the military organization itself. I have already analysed some of the weaknesses in the disciplinary system which had their roots in rapid promotions and an imbalanced age structure. The sudden destruction of the upper segment of the command structure on 15 January was, under such conditions, a fatal blow to discipline. The charisma of command was tarnished, the hierarchy foreshortened and the social distance between the different ranks reduced.

These conditions of strain were accentuated by the dissonance aroused between military norms of brotherhood and authority and the increasing level of inter-personal fear and suspicion. As George Simmel has pointed out, overt conflict does not easily develop in intimate social relations, but when it does it is far more disruptive: 'It is precisely the keen awareness of dissonance against the prevailing general harmony', he suggests, 'which at once warns the parties to remove the grounds of conflict lest conflict half-consciously creep in and endanger the basis of the relation itself. But where this fundamental intention to get along under all circumstances is lacking, the consciousness of antagonism, sensitized as this consciousness is by similarity in other respects, will sharpen the antagonism itself. People who have many common features often do one another worse, a "wronger" wrong, than complete strangers do.'[21] The army had provided a unique degree of security and predictability in inter-personal relations in a rapidly changing society.[22] This was guaranteed by the relative impermeability of its boundaries as a unitary 'total' institution and by the emphasis on solidarity in the socialization process and the daily rituals of military life. Though tensions did exist before the events of 1966 these could mostly be 'managed' within the established framework of inter-personal relations. These events, however, raised antagonism above the level at which they could be coped with by existing social controls. The most immediate impact of the assassination of senior Northern officers on 15 January was on the NCOs. It violated both their concepts of authority and their personal identification with respected Northern military figures like Maimalari. The reaction of junior Northern officers was less immediate, perhaps because of their lesser commitment to the military authority system and greater sympathy with the conspirators' political beliefs and objectives. Yet after the struggle for power in the army began in earnest following the May riots in the North, they too started to feel extreme mistrust and hostility towards their Ibo confrères. As one of them expressed it, 'Most countries have one or two Judas Iscariots. But ninety per cent of the Ibos are Judases.'

Why did social strains and unstable expectations have such an electric effect on ethnic and Regional differences but leave alternative sources of cleavage almost unaffected? There are a number of reasons why tribe and Region were highly appropriate objects for the projection of anxiety and hostility, including their salience in the political context, the elaboration and diffusion of stereotypes in politicians' speeches and the mass media during the period immediately preceding military rule, and the intimate connection of such ties with self-images and feelings of identity. The only other basis of differentiation within the military that might have been relevant was cleavage between different ranks and peer groups. But, as I pointed out before, to focus hostility against high-ranking officers was to challenge the whole military authority system, whilst ethnic scapegoating permitted aggression to be channelled against the men in power but not their offices.

CONCLUSION

It is rather hard to account for the burgeoning of conflict in the army in 1966 by reference purely to existing sources of cleavage. Ethnic and Regional bonds produced some clustering of interaction and similarities in outlook. They did not have the strength or compulsiveness in and of themselves to stimulate overt expressions of antagonism within the military in the face of the well-enforced and internalized fraternal norms of the officer corps. One can only adequately account for the sudden florescence of animosity in 1966 by viewing this as a contextual effect of instability and strain on tribal and Regional ties which then became the outlets for the expression of a whole range of tensions both within the military organization and outside it in the wider political context.

One major source of tension was political, namely that the accession of soldiers to office also represented a transfer of power between the Regions, away from the North. Not only had the officer corps exposed itself by virtue of its newly acquired political role to unaccustomed political demands and pressures; it had also done so under circumstances which increased the intensity of these pressures, as is evidenced by the urban riots in the North in May and September/October 1966 as well as the July coup itself.

Secondly, there were the purely organizational sources of strain, the relevance of which was argued in the earlier part of this paper. It is somewhat more difficult to conceptualize the precise role of such factors because before 1966 they were largely latent. The speed at which the officer corps was indigenized deprived it of cohesion and made it difficult to balance the contrary requirements of initiative and discipline. But this did not lead to the disintegration of the military organization until unfavourable environmental conditions were superimposed, from the civil violence in the Western Region set off by the Regional Election of October 1965, which provided the immediate stimulus for the January 1966 coup, onwards. Or, as Karl Deutsch has put it, the impact of new information upon a system is related 'to the extent of the instabilities that already exist there'.[23] These instabilities arose not because the army was a 'non-organization' in the sense that Zolberg seems to imply, but from dilemmas common to most military organizations but especially acute in a partially institutionalized one such as existed in Nigeria.

4

THE MILITARY AND THE POLITICIANS

M. J. Dent

THE THEME of the relationship of the military to the politicians might seem at first sight to be somewhat peripheral to the main problem of Nigeria since 1966. In fact, as we shall see, it is itself central and raises most important issues which must be studied if we are to understand the real roots of the conflict in Nigeria.

The relationship of the military to the politicians is not a chance phenomenon, depending primarily on the accidents of individual personality and interest, but rather an illustration of the root cause of that weakness of the military in government in its Nigerian setting which has brought it to its present problems. In the natural revulsion of many of the elite in Nigeria against the misdeeds of the politicians then in power and in the corporate pride of the army, the military for the first vital year of its rule consistently overlooked the vital political functions which the political class had fulfilled and failed either to bring any of the politicians into its system as assistants or middlemen or to find adequate substitute agents for the function. Until bitter experience taught them otherwise, the military did not realize that there was a political function to fulfil. When they finally began to use and to develop political skills and to bring into government those who possessed them it was too late to resolve the major coniflct without war.

In the relations between the soldiers and the politicians, and the groups which those politicians represented, lay a large part of the problems of military rule in 1966, and in the political function and its practitioners on both sides lies a chance to shorten the agony of civil war and replace the battle of blood in the military medium with the more kaleidoscopic battle of the aggregation of interests and the moulding of opinion in the political arena.

The military in most countries dislike the term 'politician' with a peculiar intensity; this dislike was most characteristic of the ethos of the Nigerian military during the early days of their power. They assumed that the whole business of politics was somehow dirty and that the evils in the system could be attributed to the politicians and their ways.[1] At Aburi, for instance, despite their recent experience of mutual murder within their own caste, the army officers managed to

present a fairly common front against the politicians; if they agreed on
nothing else, they agreed on the need to 'keep the politicians out'.
General Ankrah set the tone at the beginning in a speech of peculiar
naïvety: the root cause of conflict among soldiers, he suggested, was
just 'listening to the politicians'. 'It is not difficult', he said, 'for military
people to understand one another. If generals were to meet and discuss
wars there will never be any differences . . . but unity and understanding . . . the two old boys will meet at the frontier and tell each other:
"Old boy, we are not going to commit our boys to die; come LET US
KEEP THE POLITICIANS OUT." '2

Mobolaji Johnson took up the cry, complaining of how in 1966 'the
politicians got what they have been waiting for to come in . . . let
us leave everything that will bring the politicians back into the lime-
light out of the question'.3 Commodore Wey, the most silent of
Nigerian officers and the most contemptuous of the loquaciousness of
the politicians, showed a rare flash of anger when commenting on
politicians. He said that he was behind the desire to keep politicians
out 'One hundred per cent'. 'Candidly,' he remarked, 'if there ever had
been a time in my life when someone had hurt me sufficiently for me
to wish to kill him it was when one of these fellows [politicians—
Awolowo?] opened his mouth too wide. We should let them stay
where they are for the moment [i.e. out of power] . . . It [their coming
back into influence] was simply because we could not get together and
handle our affairs. Now that we have established the basis under which
we can work, please let us leave them where they are.' Only Lt-Col
Gowon and Lt-Col Ojukwu were somewhat muted in their condemna-
tion of politicians, Lt-Col Gowon because of his firm and rather traditional belief that the business of government belongs to 'constitutional',
i.e. civil, government,4 and Lt-Col Ojukwu because he himself possessed some of the articulateness of the politicians.

In general the hostility of the military to the political echelon springs
from a variety of causes. The soldiers believe that the politicians are
too talkative; the military ethos is like that contained in the Hausa
proverb *mai fada ba zai yi surutu ba* (the warrior is not talkative). They
believe that politicians do not speak the truth and that soldiers do, that
politicians concentrate on the things that divide in order to muster
support whereas the military create unity. Perhaps they see in the
politician a larger edition of the bugbear of the military disciplinarian—
the barrack-room lawyer who encourages disobedience and finds for
it a legal ground of support. The military are accustomed to controlling
their lower ranks by a strict chain of command in which obedience and
loyalty are the prime values. Consultation with certain 'opinion leaders',
e.g. the Sergeant-Major, does go on, but discreetly and within a

hierarchical relationship; otherwise, the idea of the leaders taking advice from the led or ordering their course according to the feelings expressed by the lower ranks is repugnant to the idea of command. Politicians, on the other hand, must stand like Anteus with their feet among the people.[5] Although they are adept at tacking and veering and at the use of language to conceal direction, they cannot ignore the winds of popular opinion. In a society where an elite are conscious of their superiority in wisdom to the masses, this attitude of the politicians is often unpopular with those who wish government to be firm and not to demean itself by reflecting popular prejudice or opinion. In fact politicians can lead as well as follow public opinion, but the distance which they keep from popular thinking is not as great as that at which the military tend to stand.

Among the politicians of the old regime, curiously enough, it was the Sardauna who had adopted an hauteur similar to that of the military in regard to reducing oneself to the level of the common man. Part of the anger with which he regarded the challenge of the AG and NEPU was due to the fact that that challenge sought to force the *Manya Manya* (important people) to mount the empty 44-gallon drum and speak in the market-places in the idiom of the *talakawa* (the ordinary people, poor and without governmental office).

This belief in the impropriety of listening too closely to the un-educated or the ignorant masses is common to almost all self-conscious elites, from the members of the communist party in the Soviet Union in the twenties and thirties to the attitudes of civil servants in certain bureaucracies or professors in certain university communities. It is the experts who are to make the decisions, and it is somehow considered to be a loss of standards to be over-attentive to the expression of those at the bottom of the hierarchy. In certain organizations this may be the most efficient method of operation and may not arouse unduly great opposition, but in the body politic as a whole, from the moment that they assume political power, whether they know it or not, the army have a political function to fulfil. Even though there are no longer any formal institutions of representation the function of representation of divergent interests as well as a general desire for unity has to be fulfilled, interests have to be aggregated, uneducated people mobilized not just by orders but by a sense of participation, a sense of legality has to be created, and conflicts have to be reconciled by flexibility within the system. For these tasks the means which have proved adequate for running a regiment are insufficient. Where military regimes have succeeded for any length of time in establishing stable and acceptable governments, it is because they have found means either by themselves or in co-operation with others to fulfil these functions.

The Nigeria in which the military came to power had indeed been largely spoilt by the class of politicians in power. They had usually been able to keep the cleavages from breaking out into violence, although in Tiv areas in 1960 and 1964, and in the West in 1965, the basic conflicts in the political system had resulted in large-scale breakdown of law and order and prolonged conflict between the clients of the major political protagonists. The politicians had been able to retreat from the brink of armed confrontation and to patch up their coalitions, even after bitterness, competitive cheating, and threats as grave as those which occurred at the time of the 1964 election. Parties still possessed substantial cross-regional support. Tarka and Aminu Kano, for instance, now the two most important political figures in the North, were both in alliance with southern-based parties, and ultimately with Enugu; both remained in this alliance until the time of the military coup. None the less the politicians in power failed to avoid regional emphasis and a dependence upon a base of regional patronage. Towards the end of their period of rule there was an increasing alienation of the masses from their evident corruption. The system was thought by most people in the South to contain a numerical bias in favour of a mono-lithic North, which they were not prepared finally to accept. Although there was a widespread admiration among many people for the states-manship and restraint of Sir Abubakar in holding the coalition together and not pressing tribal advantage (as the zealots on his own side would have liked him to do), there was a centralizing and modernizing elite that wished to get rid of the old gang of politicians and make a new beginning towards the creation of a more honest political system, a more unified nation, and a juster distribution of national wealth. This body of opinion was partly able to express itself through the more radical parties in opposition (although some of these had not shown themselves entirely free of fault when they had themselves been in power in the West), and welcomed the coming to power of the military with great intensity. The welcome was more wholehearted in the East than in the West and in the South than in the North, but over the whole country there was a general feeling of relief that the old regime had ended.

This immediate relief concealed a variety of expectation. To some people the coup of January 1966 represented the victory of the UPGA, of its southern emphasis, and its more radical philosophy. It is probable that the original genesis of the January coup, which had been planned for some time before it actually occurred, owed something to certain radical figures in the UPGA and perhaps among Ibo politicians.[6] But once they had control of the coup the Majors declined to make any of the politicians of the old establishment its beneficiaries. The precise political philosophy of Major Nzeogwu is hard to determine. The left has now made him its martyr hero, assuming that his 'new philosophy'[7] corresponded to radical political ideology. From his short record in power it appears that he had a somewhat simplistic view of the political process, assuming that all that was necessary for good government to come to Nigeria was to remove the oppressing political class and to enforce honesty. He was a man of burning sincerity but his ideas were not settled: at one time, for instance, he wished to shoot Ali Akilu, head of the Northern civil service; at another, he was ready to let him continue as head of the civil service and a member of the Northern 'Cabinet'. There is persistent evidence of Nzeogwu having been influenced by radical left-wing views during the years before the coup and some suggestion that he may even have been in contact with certain radical political elements in Ghana. Major Ifeajuna, his coadjutor in Lagos, flew to Ghana immediately after the coup (to Nzeogwu's annoyance). None the less Nzeogwu was not prepared to interpret his radicalism in terms of existing radical political parties and one European observer, who knew Nzeogwu well before the coup and saw him during his three-day period of rule in Kaduna, asserts strongly that Nzeogwu had a profound distrust of all political parties.

The Military Government which finally resulted from the coup was not that of the radical Majors but that of General Ironsi. His ideas were less revolutionary and more pragmatic. The original radical or UPGA orientation of the coup was filtered out and all that remained was a generalized ethos of the need for honesty and for unity, combined with a general attack on all politicians as a class. The military would have been well advised to act as a kind of veto group in the political process, to use their coup to shake up the politicians, to show them the limits which they could not transgress, to sift out the 'old gang', and to encourage a new type of political leader as well as some of those who had been in opposition. These kinds of intermediaries, in the process of consultation and day to day government, would have done much to shield the military from the corrupting process of allowing the divisions of the civilian body politic to creep into their own echelon. If these instruments had proved divisive they could have been discarded in their turn, without injuring the unity of the military itself. The military did make use of an echelon which was partly of political provenance, by appointing the old Regional Governors as advisers to the Military Governors; the valuable role which they filled indicates that the military would have done well to have co-opted other political figures into their system in the same way.

So great was the initial distrust of the political class that in local government affairs the regime dismissed all elected councillors (since,

in their view, election implied politics) and relied solely upon traditional and appointed councillors and upon chiefs. In the sphere of
Central and Regional, Provincial and District Government the military
relied upon the civil service as an intermediary. Initially this co-operation was satisfactory and the day to day business of government was
run by civil servants. This echelon was, however, inert in the process of
mobilization and ineffective in the process of representation. Condi-
tioned to a position of some subservience under the old ministerial
regime, it took civil servants some time to realize that they might have
a function to represent the people to the government as well as the
government to the people. It was hard for them to fulfil the broker
function in the way that politicians could fulfil it.

The one-sided slaughter of the January coup, the treachery to brother
officers involved, and the tribal interpretation given to it by some of
the less educated among the Ibo, soon provided a climate of opinion
in which the displaced political echelons of NPC, and perhaps also of
NNDP, could begin to win back support. General Ironsi had committed
the cardinal error of alienating these elements by excluding them from
all power or patronage and yet leaving them entirely free to go about
and agitate below the surface. They were made more formidable by
possession of the funds of the party. An ex-NPC Minister told me
quite frankly that in his view one of Ironsi's cardinal errors was not to
have locked up people like himself. Furthermore Ironsi failed to avail
himself of the possible support of the old radical politicians; Chief
Awolowo was left in prison—apparently because he would not beg for
release nor accept any particular terms of release, for he regarded his
release not as a favour to be given by Ironsi but as an act of liberation
demanded by the people of Nigeria. In the North, both Tarka and
Aminu Kano soon found themselves making common cause with
Maitama Sule, and Aminu made common cause with Lt-Col Hassan
Katsina against what they regarded as a common threat to their Region
and to Nigeria. Politics, pushed out from the army by its declared anti-
political ethos, found its way back in again through the door of common
Regional interests.

As opposition mounted below the surface the military began to take
more power on themselves. General Ironsi assumed the panoply of
Head of State, living in State House and reducing the nomenclature of
the Regional State Houses to 'Government Lodges', and decided that
the interim period for which he had originally declared that he was
assuming power would last for at least three years. The regime was at
pains to declare that it was to be thought of as a military and not as a
mixed military-civil servant regime. Although it did not in fact use
any large measure of coercion it was quite free with threats. It is

symptomatic of the way the military thought about civilian problems that when a firing exercise with three-inch mortars took place on the range near Kaduna, the blurb or imaginary story invented to explain the hypothetical situation in which such an exercise might occur said that a village had refused to pay taxes and had driven out the District Officer, thus necessitating this punitive action.[8]

The period of military rule under General Ironsi brought many advantages. The level of corruption decreased. Peace came to the West, the Yoruba being determined never again to allow their divisions to bring them to this kind of conflict. Tiv division, which had already seen a remarkable public act of reconciliation between the Tor Tiv and Tarka two weeks before the January coup, became extremely peaceful. With the banning of party activity, relations between party men at almost all levels became much more cordial. The party leaders themselves may well have felt some relief at no longer having to look after their tumultuous and undisciplined organizations. Aminu Kano, whom I met in 1967, told me that he did not wish there to be a return to the old type of politics—flags, marches, symbols, and shouted slogans—but rather what he called 'welfare politics'. The North, apart from the tragic and unnecessary loss of its leaders and the irritation of the boasting of certain Ibo at the local level and of a small number of inquisitional Ibo army officers, who were a nuisance rather than a menace, did not suffer. Colonial experience has, however, shown that good government is no substitute for self-government, and this applies just as much when the colour of the skin of the governors is black and they are native to the country. Self-government may not require at all times formal representative institutions of a parliamentary kind, but it does require a means of producing a sense of participation and of the effective taking of council with the various opinions of the people. This element was peculiarly lacking. The military regime was deaf to the muted 'signals from below'—letters in the paper, murmuring in markets and public places. It did not have the politicians' sensitivity in this respect. The kind of so-called opinion leader on whom it relied was sometimes an efficient civil servant with little political sense, like Dr Okigbo or Mr Nwokedi, sometimes a rather discredited figure from the old regime, like Mr Ikejiani, sometimes a radical centralizing newspaper correspondent with little knowledge of actual difficulties likely to be encountered in areas far from Lagos. Thus Peter Pan (Peter Enahoro) produced a series of articles in the *Daily Times* exhorting Ironsi to push forward without fear, ending with the call 'to the battlements, my General'—a rendezvous with death, to which the journalist did not accompany the soldier.

It is characteristic of revolts on a large scale that they are often caused not so much by actual oppression as by the fear of some future threat which seems to those who rebel to be just taking shape. This was the case with the *Araba* (let us part) killings in the North in May. The exact responsibility of the old echelons of the NPC for these tragic events remains to be fully investigated. The killings appear to have been part spontaneous and part planned. What started as a planned demonstration and a march of university students became a large-scale killing. This killing occurred predominantly in places of former NPC strength. No killing or trouble at all occurred at this time in the Middle Belt areas, such as Jos or Makurdi. Bornu, also, was untouched. Clearly the sole responsibility was not that of the politicians: they could not, for instance, have provoked such an event if they had wished to do so in January or February. Furthermore, the alienation of the intermediaries of the regime—the civil servants—by the assumed threat to their professional interests in Decree No. 34 (see Appendix B, pp. 179–80) and the apparent lack of consultation on the way it had been imposed may have made them less active in restraining trouble.[9] NPC political cadres at the intermediate level had, in my view, a considerable responsibility for the May events. In the African context, as in that of most developing societies, for a riot to occur it is not necessary that all echelons should wish it to begin. The normal state is for there to be certain groups who would provoke ruffians at the lower level to cause violence, were they not themselves restrained by the heads of their own echelons or by civil authority. If that restraint appears to be momentarily lifted violence will often occur.

From May onwards political influence became increasingly important in the army. It was of a Regional and not of an ideological kind. The Nigerian army has never been isolated from civilian contact in the way that certain European armies have been. It was entirely natural for officers and politicians from the same area to associate. Nigeria is a country of opinion leaders and in many areas political figures continued to exercise this function even when excluded from any part in the system of government. In this role they were more dangerous than they had been under the old system. It was the view of the Northerners that the coup of January was not, in fact, a purely military affair; they believed that they had evidence of close connection between the Ibo political leaders, and the army 'mutineers' in the planning of the coup. To the Northerners, the makers of the January coup and the present advisers of General Ironsi were representatives of the Ibo Tribal Union in arms, just as the NCNC had been its representative in politics. The fact that this view was a highly exaggerated estimate of what was a much more tenuous and doubtful link did not diminish its power among those who held it.

Among figures from the old regime Inuwa Wada was in a particularly favourable position to exercise influence on the army by his possession of a considerable private fortune, as well as by his position in the NPC hierarchy and by his ties with officers whose promotion he had assisted in his days as Minister of Defence. He had, also, ties of affinity with Lt-Col Murtala Mohammed. Circumstantial evidence points to a close connection between Inuwa Wada and the army in the period before and immediately after the July coup. Thereafter his influence waned. The return of the 'old gang' was much resented by new elites; the centre of gravity in the army was in the Middle Belt and not in the far North, and lavish distribution of money among soldiers eventually produced a counter-movement among those who would not allow the army to be bought.

In the period immediately before the July coup the morale of the army deteriorated. Deprived of the more sophisticated arbitraments of the power conflict which had cushioned the clash of political and civilian figures, the army units were in a position of classic 'lawless confrontation': whoever struck first with ruthless force would win, the victory of force would be recognized on the government field. The licence to kill and to change the government by killing, which had first been introduced into Nigerian public life in January, worked out its terrible logic in July.[10] The Northerners made a strike which they considered to be preemptive; whether this was a true assumption will need to be investigated by historians of the future, when the archives are open and the collection of evidence can be carried out in a more relaxed atmosphere of peace.

The initial aims of the 'mutineers' reflected those of the old NPC: virtual secession for the North and return to civilian rule. Some of the old NPC figures seem to have seen themselves as likely to emerge as heads of government in the near future. Lt-Col Gowon, originally under the power of these echelons through their supporters in the army, rapidly threw off this yoke and reverted to his natural position— that of a young member of the new elite from a small Plateau tribe, who felt a loyalty to Nigeria and wished to see its unity maintained.

In view of the appalling slaughter of Ibo which had occurred in the army,[11] this was no easy task. Lt-Col Gowon very quickly called upon civilian leaders by co-option to debate the issues of the return to civilian rule and to help him in this task. The meetings of the 'leaders of thought' showed the advantages of the 'mixed' governmental system. Politicians of formerly opposing parties and civil servants debated with vigour but without permanent division. Certain key decisions were made at the Northern 'leaders of thought' conference, including that to accept in principle the division of the Region into States, a decision of principle that many may have wished to see nullified in practice but which was eventually implemented in the 'rough surgery' of military decree in May 1967, after more gentle consultative methods had failed to consummate the decision. The pattern taken for the 'leaders of thought' meetings was that of the British consultations before constitutional conferences, like that of 1951, but the conditions were different. Civilian figures were being asked to do too much, to produce an all-embracing blueprint for the future government of Nigeria at a time when the crying need was for some immediate reconciliation between North and East, for some working agreement on the question of succession to produce acceptance of the Head of Government throughout Nigeria, and for some way to assuage the grief and anger of the Ibo for their losses in May and July. The 120-page document of the proposals of the final constitutional conference reads a little sadly—a collection of Ph.D theses on an ideal constitution made at a time when the chance of any recommendations being implemented was indeed slight (see Appendix A, pp. 154–76). Further massacres broke out in the North, originating from the 4th Battalion and from thugs, some of whom appear to have been mobilized by the echelons at the local level of the old NPC, and the constitutional conference broke up. Whether or not these massacres owed anything to the change of stance forced on the Northern delegation by the Middle Belt army pressure group is not clear.[12]

It would have been advisable to call together some equivalent of the Ghanaian 'political committee', to constitute a permanent committee of all Regions, an embryo representative assembly-in-being, to give advice not just on the distant prospect of the constitution under which to return to civil rule but on the day to day working of the military government. I suggested this to Lt-Col Gowon when I had the privilege of meeting him in September 1966. He replied that he was already preparing such a move. My impression is that he himself would have liked to have called in political advisers long before May 1967 but that with the mood of the army officers, which had not yet lost its corporate hubris, this was not possible.

The release of Chief Awolowo and Chief Enahoro by Lt-Col Gowon on his coming to power brought into the arena political figures with a wide appeal, especially to the radicals. Although they had enemies they were people to be reckoned with and both were immediately chosen as the leaders of their Regions' delegations to the Constitutional Conference.

Unfortunately at the Conference and in its aftermath of drift towards secession the old unity of the AG leaders came under severe strain. Chief Awolowo made a qualified and tactical retreat from his old federal philosophy to one of confederation, and as a 'leader of the Yoruba', one of the three major tribes, gave the impression that he would in the last resort allow Nigeria to be divided up into Regions dominated by these three tribes in a loose confederation, thus sacrificing the interests of the minorities in North and East, which he had so long and so effectively championed. Chief Enahoro and Mr Tarka emerged as firm champions of the cause of preserving and increasing Federal power, while creating States; Chief Awolowo proceeded to explore the possibilities of placating the East by a more confederal approach, putting off the question of the creation of States, which had become unacceptable to the authorities in Enugu at this juncture. From this position, which he expounded quite explicitly in his speech of 1 May, Chief Awolowo came back at the end of the month, partly under military pressure and partly because he realized that the polarization between Lagos and Enugu was so great that he could no longer act as an independent arbiter. From then on he became a firm supporter of the Federal Government, of which he was a member. However, the split between him and his former lieutenants has not entirely healed.

Having failed to achieve reconciliation by the constitution-making exercise, which the military had left largely to the political and civil cadres, the military leaders attempted to do so by personal contact between 'Jack' and 'Emeka' on the telephone. Soon, however, the camaraderie of the former days in the mess turned sour. Lt-Col Gowon was convinced that 'Emeka has not behaved like an officer and a gentleman' and that he was a man driven by personal ambition who behaved more like a politician than a soldier.[13] Lt-Col Ojukwu, on the other hand, regarded Lt-Col Gowon as a weak figure, well meaning himself but in the grip of forces more powerful than himself. Under pressure from a variety of sources, including Britain,[14] the leaders agreed to meet at Aburi. The terms of the meeting were far from clear. To the Federal side this was foreseen as a first get-together to begin to re-establish links; to Lt-Col Ojukwu, it was a venue where a firm constitutional document was to be agreed, loosening the federal ties to give effective power in all important matters to the Regions. From such a position, secession would be an easy step, if he decided upon it. It might, in any case, be unnecessary if he already possessed effective sovereignty at the Regional level to protect his Regional interests. This position he termed 'drawing apart a little in order to come together later'. The Federalists were, however, doubtful if the second part of the process would follow the first.

Aburi demonstrated both the inadequacy of the military's political and constitutional skills and the vulnerable position in which they put themselves if they sought, in their sole capacity, to make generous settlements to each other at the expense of constitutional principles which some considered vital. The extreme bitterness with which Chief Enahoro, for instance, refers to Aburi springs as much from a challenge to the competence of the military to make a final constitutional settlement without consulting the politicians as from the confederal nature of many of the proposals agreed.[15] The Aburi document was, in any case, contradictory. It purported at the same time to effect a drastic reduction in Federal power and to revert to the situation before 17 January 1966.[16] On their return home both military commanders were assailed by the young Turks who disapproved of the concessions they had made. On the Federal side this opposition was crystallized into a document emanating from the senior civil servants, pointing out the inconsistencies of the Aburi document and the destructive effect of its implications on the maintenance of effective Federal power. They defended their right to speak on a constitutional and political matter by quoting Dunnil's manual on public administration,[17] which suggests that senior civil servants possess a general mandate for the defence of the interests of the state and its maintenance. There is some evidence to assume that contacts between certain political figures and the senior civil service were close at this time and that these figures were not without influence in the production of the document.

The main weight of public opinion on either side was pushing towards increasing polarization and confrontation; politicians, deprived of their right to work their magic upon popular opinion by political leadership and alliance building from a position of authority, tended to side with the young Turks. Aminu Kano at this time temporarily adopted an almost chauvinistic pro-Northern position and became associated with certain overstated pamphlets of tribal hatred produced by the Current Issues Society.[18] Tarka and others tried to retain old contacts with Enugu but in the increasingly hostile and hysterical climate of opinion on both sides met with no success. Those who had been in alliance with Enugu in the past had a potentially favourable position for reconciliation in the long run, when the time was ripe, but in the short term they were peculiarly vulnerable to the accusations of witch-hunters, who might try to dub them as pro-Ibo. In any case, the interests of the Middle Belt and the Mid-West politicians were overwhelmingly in favour of the retention of a strong Federal centre for all Nigeria and the creation of more states, several Eastern.

Meanwhile, in the North, at the request of the military and other leaders, Tarka, Aminu Kano, and Makaman Bida carried out extensive joint touring to demonstrate the end of their past ideological conflicts. The real danger of conflict between Middle Belt and Hausa soldiers was averted. Finally, in response to the demands of approaching

Biafran secession and to the clear indication from Middle Belt officers in company with political figures from the same area that their participation in any campaign against Biafra was dependent upon the prior granting of their dream of 'the state',[19] Lt-Col Gowon produced his own 'coup' by the assumption of personal power and by the state creation decree, thus cutting the Gordian knot that the political cadre had for so long been unable to untie. The danger of the division of the North resulting in an immediate breakdown or serious cleavage was avoided by the retention until 1 April 1968 of an interim authority, with a consultative authority of political figures as well as an executive authority composed of Permanent Secretaries and the Chairman of the Interim Council. With the creation of the State Executive Councils, the military government demonstrated its capacity to bring in political figures of different ideological and party allegiance and to produce an ideological truce and in some cases a real reconciliation. In general only the more progressive of the NPC figures were brought into the Executive Councils[20] where they worked in amity with former leaders of the NEPU and non-political figures under military or police chairmanship. Tanko Yakasai, so often imprisoned by the Kano Native Authority courts in the past for his NEPU activities, co-operated on the same executive council with pillars of the Native Authority establishment, such as Sani Gezawa. Abubakar Zukogi, a radical and ascetic NEPU leader, searched his heart with some care before finally agreeing to become a Commissioner in the North East State. It was hard initially for him to overcome the old NEPU attitude, which regarded all government other than a NEPU revolutionary government as somehow oppressive of the people. He faced the same problem as the Austrian socialists in the thirties but came to a different conclusion. The appointments at the Federal level were none the less radical; of the eleven Civil Commissioners appointed, four—Tarka, Aminu Kano, Enahoro, and Awolowo—had been radical politicians for many years and they became from an early stage the most important members of the so-called 'War Cabinet'.

Meanwhile in the West the reconciliation of former AG and former NNDP was not as far-reaching as that between NPC and NEPU or NPC and UMBC in the North. The style of Awolowo was a less forgiving one than that of Tarka and Aminu Kano towards their former opponents; perhaps he thought that a lesson needed to be taught the NNDP for the misdeeds of the past. Prosecutions continued, and no figures of NNDP origin were brought into the Executive Council of the West. For a time before the May volte-face the old AG established its influence to a considerable extent over the Military Governor and asked for the removal of Northern troops from the

West. From June onwards, however, Awolowo became part of the establishment at the Federal level, and important AG figures came into the Western Executive Council, but so unsuccessful had the Governor been at producing unity among the Yoruba people that a recent open letter from a distinguished Yoruba to him suggested that he should resign because of his failure to unite the Yoruba people.

'In politics', Philip Yace of the Ivory Coast once said, 'it is necessary to forget and to forget quickly'—an art in which Tarka, for instance, has excelled. Mr Atedze, the former Tiv Native Authority administrative secretary and NPC leader, who had once sought Tarka's imprisonment, was found a job as private secretary to Gomwalk (the Military Governor of Benue Plateau State); Ayilla Yogh and Ibrahim Imam, who had given evidence for the prosecution against Tarka in the treason trial, were helped by him in the professional and business spheres. Eventually this kind of magnanimity on the part of the political cadre is going to be needed on a larger scale to begin to heal the far deeper wounds of the civil war.

In the Federal Executive Council Lt-Col Gowon remained the centre of unity. All power had been given to him by the wording of the emergency decree and he became more confident than in the past. His leadership is easily accepted in the Executive Council, as much out of personal respect for his integrity and gentleness as out of the power of his military position. His personal style continues to be that of a person who prefers a more gentle solution, if available, to one attained by use of coercion. It was only after some hesitation that he was persuaded to allow the civil war to begin, and he would no doubt, within the terms of the 'one Nigeria' for which he has asked the soldiers to fight, like a generous settlement to it. He is aware that in this desire he has opponents on his own side against whom he must maintain his case.[21]

In the short term the threat to Lt-Col Gowon's position lies not in the political echelon but in the danger of assassination by undisciplined troops or revolt by some ambitious or embittered field commander, protesting against what might be considered a too generous settlement with the Ibo. There was a time in 1966 when one of the army commanders seriously considered trying to arrest Lt-Col Gowon so that the East could be invaded and power then handed back to him after its conquest. Since then, his stature and authority have markedly increased and he is able to impose a measure of generosity on official statements remarkable in a time of war. As regards control of the *Yan Maza* (he-men)—the soldiers at the front—he is less successful. There remains a doubt as to how far they would be controllable in the event of a cease-fire or how far they could be made obedient to the orders of a civilian administration. I believe that they would in fact be controlled, although it would be a near thing, requiring considerable disciplinary sanction and political skill. The mentality of the private soldier is very literalistic. In a situation of war he often assumes a mandate to kill all members of the opposing tribe whom he meets at times of battle; after a declaration of peace his thinking would, I believe, take on a different 'set', for it is in this sense malleable to authority. Furthermore, if a civilian regime were established this of itself would act as a stabilizing factor on military thinking at a lower level. To the untutored legalism of the private soldier 'military government' means power in military hands, including his own, and the rule of the law of the gun. Civil government would be interpreted by them as implying their own subordination to the civil power as in the days before 1966. No one, however, can underestimate the problem of the disarming and resettling of the 80,000 soldiers on the Federal side and of the armed irregulars and soldiers on the Biafran side.

As regards governmental power in non-military spheres on the Federal side, the army have retreated from all positions except those of Head of State and of State Governor. The Ministry of Internal Affairs (including the police) is run directly by Kam Salem. All other aspects of government are controlled directly by political heads, some two-thirds of whom are former politicians. Although they are styled Commissioners to avoid the arrogance and ostentation formally adhering to the office of Minister, their powers are no less than those of the former Ministers with regard to their departments. Liaison between civilian Commissioners and the Governors of their home States is extremely close. Each important political figure in the Federal Executive Council has a kind of power base in his own State. In Lagos personnel from these States of military, of civil servant, of police, and of political provenance discuss State affairs in an informal way and agree on appointments. It is to the credit of this informal consultation that (at least in the Benue Plateau State of which I have the closest knowledge) it has succeeded in warding off the dangers of intertribal conflict or conflict between military and civilian authorities. The figures concerned are aware of the potential danger of this and take great pains to see that it cannot occur.

On the Biafran side the bringing in of politicians took place later than on the Federal side. At least in the early stages several of the major political figures appear to have been opposed to the idea of secession and relations between them and Lt-Col Ojukwu were not cordial. Dr Azikiwe in September 1966 wished to produce a pamphlet in favour of the creation of states and was dissuaded from doing so by the military authority.[22] At the consultative conference preparing for secession in

May he apparently spoke out against secession and was shouted down for his pains.[23] Later, however, as the war escalated and became more bitter, the territorial motive took precedence on either side over the ideological, and political figures were brought into important governmental functions. For a time senior Federal authorities had hopes of bringing in Dr Azikiwe as an intermediary with the Ibo people on the side of one Nigeria. But when he did finally commit himself it was in a sense very close to the Biafran war aims of maintained secession. In a situation where many on the Biafran side considered the very existence of the Ibo people to be at stake, an Ibo who wished to continue to exercise influence could hardly fail to come out as a champion of their right to secession. Dr Azikiwe subsequently further committed himself, in company with Okpara and other former political leaders, by campaigning abroad for the recognition of Biafra (although he later reverted to support of one Nigeria in 1969). These men are, however, seasoned campaigners who know the expedients necessary in political affairs to attain the eventual goal. If a suitable opportunity for a proper place for the Ibo in Nigeria really emerges from peace talks and if it is possible for them to play a part with their old political allies in a joint government, then the slogans of the war aims might be considered as subject to negotiation, bargaining counters for the obtaining of a reasonably satisfactory settlement.

As long as the war continues, it is vain to expect to find effective doves among political figures on either side; the dynamics of their method of operation makes this impossible. But once a cease-fire is obtained with a single political community intact, then they will seek to cross the former battle lines and canvass support among former enemies and I believe they may find it there more quickly than many have forecast.

Tarka said to me recently: 'No one can rule Nigeria without the support of Ibos; they are a major community, of as great an importance to any would-be political ruler as any community in the country.' If Nigeria remains intact it will be through the exercise of political skills, and none can exercise them better than the former political practitioners who have not been discredited by malfeasance in office. Lt-Col Gowon himself may also conceivably develop into a figure of political leadership.[24] If all the people of Nigeria are the potential constituents of a political leader and count in the civilian political process, its politics is sufficiently kaleidoscopic for new alignments to arise quickly to obliterate the old battle lines.

5

WESTERN NIGERIA AND THE NIGERIAN CRISIS

B. J. Dudley

IT IS NOW an accepted commonplace that the individual's behaviour in a given situation is in large measure influenced and shaped by his perception of the situation, from which emerges the crude calculation of gains and losses which issues in an attempt either to minimize losses or to maximize gains. This is the starting-point for game theorists, and federalism, much more than a unitary system of government, makes for such calculations with each unit or component developing a pay-off matrix in its strategy of play. In older federations the stresses generated by such calculations tend to be ameliorated by established rules which limit the permissible boundaries of bargaining. In newer federations such rules are often non-existent since the rules themselves are a product of recent bargaining situations. It is this inability to accommodate the stresses of bargaining in the newer federations which in some measure accounts for the political instability which has characterized them but this is just another way of saying that there are no boundary-determining rules.

As an exemplification of this somewhat simple model one might consider the case of the Nigerian federation, taking as the perspective the point of view of one of the bargaining members, the West, and concentrating on the period 1966 to 1967. But to do this it is necessary first to give a brief description of the politics of the preceding period.

I

The West has often been regarded, not without some justification, as the problem area of the Nigerian federation. It is the most homogeneous of the regions—after the excision of the Mid-West in 1963—its eight million peoples all speaking the Yoruba language. But though homogeneous it has not been easy for the peoples to unite in the same way that the Ibo of the East or the Hausa of the North have done. The explanation for this lies partly in history: the Yoruba were organized into 'kingdoms' and until the end of the nineteenth century fought one another in long internecine conflicts,[1] and attitudes derived from this early history of conflict have been carried over into the present. Part of the explanation also lies in the social structure. They are the most modernized of all Nigerian peoples, having been one of the earliest to come into contact with Western skills and ideas. Traditionally they have always lived in cities. According to the 1952/3 census, 43 per cent lived in towns of 5,000 and above; they are thus the most urbanized and educated, the level of literacy, again according to the 1952 census, being 19 per cent. The area also has the highest *per capita* income, much of which is derived from the cocoa export crop.

Yoruba leaders, such as Chief Awolowo and the late Chief Bode Thomas were the first to espouse the cause of federalism in Nigeria and they were largely instrumental in introducing the extreme regionalism which characterized the decade from 1955 to 1965. The politics of this period can be described easily in terms of Riker's theory of political coalitions.[2] Analytically the politics can be seen as a three-person bargaining situation, the players being the NCNC in the East, the AG in the West, and the NPC in the North. If we assume an equality among the members (a not unreasonable assumption as the 1954 Constitution provided for a Council of Ministers drawn equally from the three Regions), under conditions of rational bargaining stability can only be maintained with a coalition of all three.[3] Although this solution was not adopted after the 1954 elections, the NCNC and the NPC instead forming the Federal coalition, by 1957 sufficient difficulties had arisen to force a coalition of the three, a situation which persisted until 1959.

In 1959 the rules of the game were altered (following the 1958 constitutional conference), the result of which was to alter the relative 'weights' of the three, the players in descending order now being the NPC, the NCNC, and the AG. If we assume unequal 'values' for these three in the same order, with each member seeking to maximize its expectations, then the 'uniquely preferred coalition' would be that between the NCNC and the AG. Overtures by the AG to the NCNC to achieve this proved fruitless;[4] instead there emerged an NCNC/NPC coalition. An NCNC/AG coalition would have meant a bipolarization of the political situation on a North–South axis, which the NPC very much wanted to avoid since it was not unlikely to lead to a dissolution of the federation.[5] The NPC was therefore prepared to accept a coalition with either the NCNC or the AG and in the circumstances surrounding the 1959 elections the former was the most acceptable. The NCNC however soon became disenchanted with its role as junior partner in the federal coalition. In 1961 they invested in NEPU, one of the opposition parties in the North, in an attempt to break the hold of the NPC in the North. The enterprise proved futile, as had the similar attempt by the AG in 1959. Expectations from oil looked extremely promising and they needed a greater control at the centre if any significant change in the revenue allocation system was to be effected. At the same time negotiations over the Six-Year Development Plan suggested that the NPC was prepared to drive a harder bargain than the NCNC would have expected. When the party crisis developed in the West in 1961–2 it therefore came as a timely opportunity to capture the region by filling the vacuum created by the split. The NCNC was in opposition in the West where they had a not inconsiderable following. Were they to win the West, they would be in a position to force a North–South confrontation or, to put it differently, to alter the bargaining structure from a three- to a two-person game situation, something the NPC wanted to avoid. While a three-person, zero-sum game situation made for instability, it had the 'advantage' of leaving open the option of a 'grand coalition' in which, though no member of the coalition gains, none loses either. In a two-person game context, which the NCNC wanted, the NPC feared that whichever 'proto-coalition' became the winning coalition, the other might be tempted to force a break which would mean an end to the federation.[6]

The North was seen by most of the people in the South as essentially feudal and backward, which therefore constituted a drawback to the progress of the federation. An NCNC in control in the West and East would have appeared as the champion of progress. Besides, were they to succeed in having the Mid-West Region carved out of the West, an area where there had been a consistent and persistent demand for a separate Region, this would have given the NCNC an absolute majority in the second chamber, the Senate, in which case they would have been in a strong position to challenge the NPC much more effectively in the play of federal politics. A Senate controlled by the NCNC would have turned the tables on the NPC in the bargaining between the partners in the federal coalition. To this end the NCNC then decided to enter an alliance with Akintola's UPP to form an NCNC/UPP government of the West, once the period of the emergency was over. But for both parties this was a marriage of convenience. For the NCNC the UPP was an expendable item once it could get a toe-hold on the government. Akintola on the other hand was playing for time, time to establish his party and to seek an agreement with the NPC. For him the NCNC was an Ibo party and he was not going to be instrumental in subordinating the Yoruba to the Ibo.

The NPC's calculations were different. The AG party crisis was seen as an opportunity to break the party which the NPC leadership had not forgiven over the 1959 elections. But they had not thought that the NCNC would move in to replace the AG. Once they realized that this was happening it became crucial to forestall it at all costs. The one thing they wanted most desperately to avoid was a North–South confrontation and the only way open to them was to back Akintola's UPP against the NCNC. Since Akintola did not want to be dependent on the NCNC the overtures by the NPC were very welcome. Strengthened in his position he was now able to issue an ultimatum to the NCNC members of the Assembly: either they joined his newly formed NNDP or they would be dismissed from the government. And as none of them wanted to go into opposition they accepted the offer. Having lost in the Assembly, the NCNC then turned to the AG.

In all these moves there was no conception of what was permissible as against the impermissible, what earlier has been termed 'boundary-determining' rules. The dominant motivation was political ascendancy irrespective of the consequences. To both the NCNC and the NPC the AG was little more than a pawn useful only to the extent that it could be used either to protect their own power position or to check the moves made by the other party. The AG itself had conceived of politics in these same terms only to find itself checkmated in the struggle for federal dominance. In the absence of boundary-determining rules— and these would vary from one society to the other, though one would suppose that at the minimum such rules would include some basic conceptions of justice and fair play—politics becomes a self-destructive game. Implicit in any structure of social action is some 'imperative' which cannot be denied. Failure to accept this, or its non-recognition, not infrequently leads to self-defeating ends. In this sense 'pure' power politics is ultimately self-stultifying for the calculus of political gain and loss rarely ever proceeds with mathematical precision. All too often other 'intervening variables' which had not been taken into account intrude to skew the equations of the political power game. Put differently, this is to say that politics by its nature cannot be regarded as a zero-sum game where the 'winner takes all'. Unhappily this is the conception that underlines party strategy in Nigerian politics.

II

By 1964 the society was polarized on a North–South basis and the NPC had ended up with a situation it had always tried to avoid. On the one hand there was the NPC/NNDP alliance which for the purposes of the federal elections of 1964 became known as the Nigerian National Alliance (NNA); on the other there was the NCNC/AG alliance which became the UPGA. It was on this basis that the elections were contested. To say that the elections were 'contested' is perhaps a misdescription of the facts. There were open abuses both in the administrative arrangements for the elections and during the election itself, and the UPGA, dissatisfied with the electoral arrangements, decided to boycott the elections. Only in the East was the boycott complete. There the NCNC-controlled government of the East had instructed the electoral officers not to be present at the polls. In legal and constitutional terms, this was a direct challenge to the executive authority of the federal government but, in the circumstances, it was not in a position to assert its authority. In the end a 'mini-election' was held in the East in March from which an NPC/NCNC/NNDP coalition government at the centre emerged. In a sense UPGA lost the fight but in the process it had succeeded in undermining the legitimacy of the new government.

In the West itself things were becoming more desperate. To win support the NNDP was resorting to increased use of violence. The position deteriorated still further during the regional election of 1965 which was an 'election' only in name, so blatantly were the rules abused. When the NNDP was declared returned this became the signal for open revolt on the part of the electorate. The fillip to revolt came from the announcement of the new cocoa prices which fell from £110 to £60 per ton. Violence broke out in the rural areas among the farmers and gradually spread to the towns where it was joined by the unemployed. By December 1965 it had become almost too much of a risk to travel by car from Ibadan, the capital city of the West, to Lagos, the seat of the Federal Government. It was in this context that a section of the army finally intervened in a coup which led to the overthrow of the civilian government and the death of the Federal Prime Minister, the regional Premiers of the North and West, the Federal Ministers of Finance, and some top army officers from the North and the West. The only Ibo to lose his life was an army officer in charge of the armoury who refused to hand over the keys of the armoury to the rebellious troops. Whatever were the intentions of the leaders of the coup, it is now widely accepted that it failed. General Ironsi, the General Officer Commanding the Nigerian Army, assumed office as Head of State. The Federal and Regional parliaments and executives were suspended and in their place military Governors were appointed to carry out the functions of government.

The significance of the pattern of killings in the coup was at the time lost on the electorate whose immediate reaction was one of relief at the elimination of a hated regime. This was more so in the West where the Akintola NNDP government had lost every vestige of legitimacy, that is if it ever had any. But the relief and the exhilaration did not last long. A series of blunders, if not misguided policies, was soon to make people ask questions and when they did, Nigeria was on the way to a second coup. The first jolt to the mass euphoria which gripped most

Nigerians came with promotions in the army. After the January coup, it had been agreed that there was to be a moratorium on promotions within the army for a period of at least one year. But within four months General Ironsi announced new promotions and the fact that of the 21 promoted 18 turned out to be Ibo, General Ironsi's tribesmen, was not lost on the people. Again, it was noted that the group of men with whom General Ironsi surrounded himself, men who became his close advisers, were Ibo almost to a man. Then came the Nwokedi report suggesting the unification of the administrative and executive classes of the public services of the federation, despite the fact that (a) a constitutional review commission had been appointed which had not reported; (b) both the North and the West were opposed to the inclusion of the executive class; and (c) Nwokedi had not consulted the other members of his committee on the reorganization of the civil service. Finally, there was the decree on unification which abolished the federal nature of the country, the decision to rotate military governors, and the suggestion that the country was to be divided into prefectorial districts to be administered by military prefects. When all this was added to the fact that in the coup only Westerners and Northerners (with the exception of one Ibo officer and the Federal Minister of Finance, an Itsekiri) were killed it did seem as if there was a deliberate attempt to impose an Ibo hegemony over the country.

By June some Yoruba members of the Joint Economic Planning Committee—among others—were walking out of, or deliberately absenting themselves from, meetings of the committee. The Chief Economic Adviser to the 'National' Government (as the Federal Government was called after the decree on unification of 24 May 1966), Dr Pius Okigbo, was felt to be directing the affairs of the committee in such a manner as to give the impression that the demands of the East were primary. In the meantime attempts by the Military Governor of the West, Lt-Col Fajuyi, to investigate the past activities of some of the politicians (many of whom had in fact been detained) alienated the NNDP who thought his regime was out to favour the AG, and by implication, the UPGA. Some of the NNDP, it was alleged, then attempted to undermine the army by creating dissidence within the ranks, largely among the non-Ibo and primarily Northern troops. The culmination of all of this was the second coup in July 1966 when Ibo officers and other ranks were killed and forced to flee to the Eastern region. In the coup the Head of State, General Ironsi, and the Military Governor of the West were also killed. For three days, 29–31 July, Nigeria was without a 'government'. In the end, Lt-Col Gowon was persuaded to assume office as Head of State and Supreme Commander of the Armed Forces. On 9 August, in an attempt to end the killings within the army, representatives of the various regions met in Lagos and suggested that (a) all troops should be repatriated to their 'regions of origin'; (b) the garrisoning of Lagos should be left to the discretion of the Supreme Commander; and (c) a constitutional conference should be summoned to decide the future form of association between the Regions. Before that meeting a significant event took place: Chief Awolowo was released from jail by the new military regime and at a meeting of the 'leaders of thought' of the West in Ibadan in early September he was appointed 'Leader of the Yoruba', in which capacity he later headed the delegation of Western Nigeria to the Ad Hoc Committee on the Constitutional Future of the Federation which met in Lagos on 12 September 1966.

The decision to appoint Chief Awolowo 'Leader of the Yoruba' and his acceptance of that role came as a disappointment to many of his non-Yoruba admirers who had thought that with his release he would help in providing the leadership which most people felt was badly needed if the federation was not to drift into chaos and possible disintegration. But Chief Awolowo, his supporters, and the new military government of the West had other considerations before them. The West, they thought, stood on the threshold of disintegration and therefore needed to be held together first and foremost. With the creation of the NNDP had emerged the *Egbe Omo Olofin* (society of the sons of Olofin, a rival mythical founder of the Yoruba) which like the *Egbe Omo Oduduwa* was also aimed at uniting the Yoruba. Different and conflicting primordial sentiments were therefore aroused which threatened to split the Yoruba 'nation'. It was for this reason that at the 'leaders of thought' meeting Awolowo's supporters felt that if only they could get Awolowo made 'leader' of the Yoruba this would undermine, if it did not actually end, the Olofin appeal. Awolowo obviously acquiesced. That there was a felt need for Yoruba unity could be judged from the Address given by Colonel Adebayo, Military Governor of the Western Region, to the Joint Conference of Obas and Leaders of Western Nigeria in Ibadan on 20 October 1966, when Colonel Adebayo said 'You will, I am sure, be interested to know that my *crusade* for internal UNITY among the Yorubas as a prelude to national unity has gone on apace. One significant development in this connection is the endorsement of the Oba, Chiefs, and representatives of the people of Lagos, of Chief Obafemi Awolowo as Leader of the Yorubas. Nevertheless, we must not relax or slacken our determination to remain united as one people with a common language, common ancestry, common culture, and common destiny. The presence here today of an observer-delegation from Lagos is an eloquent testimony to the spirit of oneness between the people of Lagos and their Yoruba

kiths and kins in Western Nigeria. The Advisory Committee has put
finishing touches to the draft of the *Charter of Yoruba Unity* which we
hope to print shortly for general circulation.'[8] It is important to emphasize the concern for unity for it is central to the position of the West
in much of what followed before the outbreak of war in July 1967.
But unity is always unity for something. And here there was a basic
division among the intelligentsia of the West, for where some saw
unity as a necessary part of ensuring the place of the West and the
Yoruba in the federation others saw it as an end in itself, a unity which
would encompass not only the Yoruba of the West but also those
of Dahomey in a greater Yoruba empire, presumably one in which
the same intelligentsia would wield political power. Political power,
however, has its own dialectics. It forces others to seek the same goal
if only as a self-protective device. This is more the case when the appeal
to power is based on primordial sentiments.[7] In the case of the West,
if the claim to power was to be based on 'Yorubaness', then it was not
unlikely that some would claim to be more Yoruba than others, the
'real Yoruba' as distinguished from the 'Yoruba'. Hence, if some among
the intelligentsia thought in terms of an overall Yoruba 'kingdom', an
'Oduduwa State', others using the same language could argue in favour
of some subdivisions.

The constitutional conference to decide on the political future of
the federation met in early September 1966. The first memorandum to
be presented was that from the North in which the delegates advocated
a confederal system of government based on the East African Common
Services model as the basis of association between the four Regions,
North, East, West, and Mid-West. Each Region was to have a right
to secede unilaterally from the organization. The North was followed
by the East who in their memorandum suggested a form of association
not much different from that advocated by the North. In their own
memorandum, the West came out with a suggestion which advocated
first a federation or, alternatively, a 'Commonwealth of Nigeria' in
which each could secede whenever it so desired. The Mid-West stood
unreservedly for federation, unlike the West who demanded a federation on specified conditions, these being '(a) the creation of more states
including the creation of the state of Lagos; (b) provisions in the
constitution for universal adult suffrage and uniform electoral procedure
throughout the federation; (c) uniform system of penal law; (d) a
National Planning Commission which should be charged with the
responsibility for planning the overall economic development of the
Nation; (e) provision under the constitution for machinery which will
ensure the equitable distribution of resources and amenities; (f) the
establishment and operational control by each state of its own armed

forces and police; and (g) the vesting of residual powers in the states.'
As Chief Awolowo told the delegates, 'our mandate is very clear; we
are not allowed to come here and accept federation at all cost, and we,
in our own good judgment cannot accept federation at all cost. As a
matter of fact, it is our mandate that if these conditions cannot be met
we are prepared to negotiate them, but our mandate is clear that if
some sort of reasonable compromise cannot be reached on these conditions then the Western delegation of Nigeria plus Lagos should opt
out of whatever Federation may be created thereafter.'[9]

But if the West were prepared to negotiate the stipulated preconditions for federation—that is even ignoring the incompatibility of
the preconditions themselves, for example (d) and (e), and (d) and (f)—
why, one might ask, the ambivalence in their stance? Chief Awolowo
might be taken to have suggested an answer when he said 'My delegation, as delegates to this Conference, have adopted an ambivalent attitude towards the work of this Conference for an important reason', this
being that 'knowing the circumstances which prevailed in the country
at present and knowing also a good deal of the firm attitudes which had
been taken by two units within the federation we felt that in addition
to our first preference [i.e. federation] we should be prepared to meet
the other delegations to this conference if they wanted something
different from our first preference'.[10] In real fact the West was indifferent
between the two options they put forward as they were equally
prepared to accept confederation and federation.

It is even plausible to argue that their preference was for a 'Commonwealth of States' for when Chief Enahoro, the Mid-West chief delegate, said 'I do not think that any one will pretend that we can come
together if some of us can go back and set up dictatorships, some can go
back and become democracies, and some of us can go back and become
monarchies, and yet pretend that we are going to come together later.
There will be no basis to come together; on the contrary it will all end
in conflict'[11] he was reminded by Professor Oluwasanmi, another
Western delegate, that 'the fact that a federal system or a common
services organisation failed in East Africa is not an argument that it
might fail in leading us to the path of a federal system in the future'.
He added that 'if one looks again at history one would look at the
American system when they were at cross roads where we are now.
They created an organisation which through time grew into a federal
system. Swiss example is another system which grew into a coherent
whole.'[12] To think of a federal system, under the circumstances, was to
daydream[13] for as Professor Oluwasanmi had earlier told the Conference delegates 'I should like to say that some 22 years ago, the
Leader of our delegation looked [in Awolowo's *Path to Nigerian*

Freedom] at the realities and he came to the conclusion that this country at that time and I think now, is a geographical expression. I reminded him a few days ago that, at the time that book came out, I was a student and when I reached that section of the book, I closed the book for three years because to many of us who yearned in an *idealistic* sort of way for a united Nigeria, Nigeria is not in fact a geographical expression. But I think we have come to face the realities which 20 years ago we lacked or swept under the carpet and proceed from the understanding of these realities to fashion out a new nation, a new society and if you look at our memorandum, we started with these realities because it is no longer a sacrilege, it is no longer a sin to state now that in fact this country is comprised of a large number of peoples of different cultures, different languages, different social environs and so forth.'[14] Realism therefore dictated, to use the then fashionable euphemism, a 'moving apart' in a confederal system of government, but with Lagos, the capital territory, as part of the West (and possibly the areas of Ilorin and Kabba, Yoruba-speaking areas of the North). At the start of the Conference, the West had in fact manœuvred the Lagos delegation into joining them in presenting a common memorandum.

After four days the Committee adjourned for the weekend to permit delegates to consult their regional governments. When it was resumed, the North came with a changed stand, now demanding an 'effective central government'. Protracted negotiations led to some agreement being reached.[15] On 30 September the delegates adjourned promising to reassemble to discuss points of disagreement in three weeks' time. But before the conference adjourned the terrible massacres in the North occurred (supposedly in retaliation against reported killings of Northerners in the East). As a result the East felt they could not attend the resumed conference because they thought their safety could not be guaranteed by the Federal Government. To ensure their safety they then demanded the withdrawal of Federal troops from the West in conformity with the agreement reached on 9 August 1966. At this point Chief Awolowo also announced that he would not be able to lead the Western delegation and would therefore withdraw. Though he had earlier not opposed the presence of troops in the West, he now came out protesting at their presence, claiming that the troops were in fact a 'Northern army of occupation' and that no meaningful talks or negotiations could be held when they, the Yoruba, were not free to express themselves freely, being always conscious of the threat posed by the 'army of occupation'. With the position taken by the East and the West, the Head of State, Lt-Col Gowon, felt he had no alternative but to adjourn, or rather suspend, the conference indefinitely. A stalemate was thus created, during which period it was generally believed that the West went ahead with arrangements for holding elections in the West, to be supervised by UN experts, as a preliminary to a return to civilian rule. Whatever the Federal Government wanted to do, it would seem that the West under the leadership of Chief Awolowo and the Military Governor, Colonel Adebayo, was determined to have its own way. For all practical purposes, Chief Awolowo had given up the idea of federation. His concern now was with the possibility of an independent West. There were two main reasons for this. The first was the suspicion that the Federal Government had no intention of withdrawing what by this time had come to be known as 'Northern troops' from the West, that in fact there was some sort of a conspiracy to subordinate the West to the North which needed an outlet to the sea; the second was Lt-Col Ojukwu's expulsion of all non-Easterners from the East. There was in fact a threat that the East would secede from the federation at the beginning of October 1966. This did not happen but with the expulsions it seemed that secession was eventually inevitable; it was a question of time, and if the East went the West did not want to be caught out. Besides, to some among the Western intelligentsia an independent West which included Lagos stood as much chance and was just as viable outside as within the federation. If the federation broke up the bulk of federal investment would be in the proposed West and, as Chief Awolowo reminded one of the meetings of the 'leaders of thought', the burden of external debt which would fall to the West would be negligible. The attitude was not unlike that of 1954 when the West threatened to secede from the federation if Lagos was excised from the West. Militarily, although the Yoruba in the army were only about 10 per cent of the total (that is, after the exodus of Eastern members of the armed forces), the majority of the top officer corps were Yoruba-speaking. Whatever the deficiency in men, this, it was thought, could easily be remedied by a system of rapid recruitment and training. It was in this spirit that the demand to remove 'Northern' troops was made. When it was suggested that this was not really practicable, as the Yoruba in the army would be inadequate for the defence of the West, the retort was that more efforts should be made to recruit Yoruba into the army. To summarize, the following was the position as Chief Awolowo and his followers saw it:[16]

East

    i. their men had been killed in the July coup and in the September/October massacres in the North;

    ii. the Ibo attempt at domination had failed;

    iii. they had been denied the room for 'expansion' which they needed;

iv. in order to ensure their own survival, they were opposed to the creation of states;

v. they resented the 'injustice' in the siting of federal projects in the 1962/68 Development Plan;

North

i. there was lack of direction following the loss of their leaders in the January coup;

ii. there had been a setback in their bid to dominate the federation;

iii. there was strong opposition to the creation of states on the part of the Hausa/Fulani and top civil servants for fear of losing their privileged status;

iv. they feared that the Ibo might take their revenge and that the South might dominate the North, and they were despondent about the failure of regional projects;

Mid-West

i. they lacked cohesion and were in constant fear of disintegration;

ii. they were open to assault by the East and therefore threatened with subjugation;

iii. they would be insolvent as an 'independent' state and hence depended for their survival on the continuance of federation;

West and Lagos

i. they were the victims of injustice—the dismemberment of Yoruba territory, the excision of Lagos, Ilorin and Kabba, and Akoko-Edo from the Yoruba homeland;

ii. they were subordinate to other Regions in governmental matters;

iii. they were the victims of the misuse and abuse of power in the First Republic and had suffered loss of life and property;

iv. they were envied by other groups in the federation for their human and natural resources;

v. other groups in the federation feared that the West and Lagos might come to dominate the federation in the future.

From Awolowo's point of view then the East, suffering from past and recent grievances and having failed in their attempt at domination, was not likely to support federation. Nor was the North which was afraid of being dominated by the South, the more so since the North had lost its leaders and there was no force other than the bureaucracy to hold it together. The Mid-West lacked cohesion and might be overrun by the East. (Awolowo obviously envisaged the prospect of war.) The West was the only cohesive unit in the federation though it had suffered from the 'dismemberment' of its peoples, had been used as a 'battle ground' in the struggle for federal power, and, being the envy of all other groups, there was a fear that it might dominate the federation if federation continued.

With these considerations Chief Awolowo thought the strategy dictated for the West was some arrangement which would guarantee and preserve the interest of the Yoruba as a collectivity. Structurally, this was seen to be a form of association in which there would be a unicameral legislature composed of equal members from all Regions— Nigeria was to be divided into some eighteen 'regions' or states based on linguistic homogeneity; a Cabinet composed on the same pattern; a rotating Head of State and an equal grant by each Region to maintain whatever services might be left to a central coordinating authority. Under the direction of Chief Awolowo and the Military Governor of the West, committees were then set up to examine the details of such an arrangement and to make recommendations as to how these should be implemented.

While one might doubt the realism of Chief Awolowo's perception of the political situation, it is hardly questionable that he thought a break-up of the federation was inescapable and possibly imminent. Thus, though he had had no objections to the presence of the army in the West (it is even believed that in early October he had actually approached Lt-Col Gowon and requested that the troops should not be moved away from the West), in November he headed a twenty-four-man delegation to Lt-Col Gowon to demand the withdrawal from the region of 'Northern troops', which he saw as an 'army of occupation'. A number of the Chief's supporters thought as he did and as some of them put it, it was customary in the local tradition when a husband and wife quarrelled for them to separate, the wife returning to her parental home until such time as a reconciliation could be effected.[17] On the supposition that a break was imminent, Chief Awolowo had promised his audience when he toured the Region in November that the government of the 'reconstituted' West would ensure full employment, which he thought could be achieved within five years, and free education from primary to university level.

It would be a mistake, however, to suppose that everyone saw the situation in the same terms as Chief Awolowo or accepted his prescriptions. In fact it can be argued that the political leadership underestimated the division of opinion that existed among the Yoruba. Even within Chief Awolowo's own camp there were differences of opinion. A description of the varying strands of opinion that existed will make clear the extent of these differences. First, there were those who like Chief Awolowo thought in terms of a 'moving apart' of the Regions, the euphemism for a break-up of the federation. This category, which formed a large part of the political leadership, was in fact an amalgam of three separate groups, (a) the *pragmatists*, supporters of the 'greater Yoruba' idea, composed in the main of the higher echelons of the regional civil service (including some Yoruba federal civil servants), a significant proportion of the intellectuals (university dons), and the bulk of the Action Group activists; (b) the *progressives*, led by men like the writer Wole Soyinka (Lt-Col Banjo who later led Biafran troops into the Mid-West in the bid to make a break for Lagos also belonged to this group), who accepted the 'moving apart' theory but only as a preliminary to a 'Southern alliance' to oppose the North, the aim being to split the country into two, a 'North' and a 'South'; (c) the *radicals*, sections of the urban working class and a sprinkling of intellectuals, the self-avowed Marxists and socialists who saw in 'moving apart' the only possibility of converting the component units into 'socialist' states through an overthrow of the civil-military 'bourgeois' elite, and who were led by men such as the Editors of the *Socialist Vanguard*, a newspaper which appeared sporadically and was dedicated to the propagation of 'scientific socialism'.

If we call the *pragmatists*, *progressives*, and *radicals* collectively the *confederalists*, then we could entitle the second category the *federalists*, who were again made up of two sub-groups, (a) the *statists* who thought the continuation of federation was the only possibility of their getting a separate state of their own and were made up of Yoruba from *outside* the boundaries of the Western Region. They were led in Lagos by the Oba, Chiefs, and elders (the traditional elite) and by the professional and business (modern) elite which included the Military Governor of Lagos, Major (later Colonel) Johnson. In Ilorin/Kabba the group was led by former politicians such as J. S. Olawoyin and the Native Authority functionaries; (b) the *'real' Yoruba* or *insurance buyers* who, unlike the *statists*, were Yoruba from within the Western Region but, like the *statists*, wanted a separate state carved out of the existing Region. They have been styled *insurance buyers* because in supporting federalism they saw the federal authority as an insurance against possible 'persecution' by a government which they felt was as likely as not to be controlled by the AG. Being in the main supporters of the late Akintola's NNDP, they saw Chief Awolowo as 'a man who never forgot and who did not forgive' and in the Piper Commission (set up to investigate the behaviour of officials involved in the 1965 regional elections) and the Shomolu Commission (investigating the assets of politicians who held office from 1960 to 1965 they thought they discerned the start of the vendetta. Similarly, if segments of the West were going to demand a 'Yoruba' state, then they, as the 'real' Yorubas, were entitled to a separate state. The problem was that the boundaries of what was to be the new state were not clearly defined but, at a minimum, it was to include both Ibadan and Oshun divisions.

There is, it seems, a 'bandwagon effect' in the demand for states, for no sooner did the peoples of Ibadan and Oshun give notice of their claim than those of Ekiti and Ilesha felt they also should have a separate state. The call for separate states then became intertwined with other felt and imagined grievances. The Ekiti/Ijesha argued that although their area produced much of the wealth of the Region, being the main cocoa-producing area, they had been denied essential services such as hospitals, roads, and pipe-borne water to be found in other parts of the Region. Besides, not only had industrial developments been concentrated in areas other than Ekiti or Ilesha, but also they had been discriminated against in the civil service, the Ijebus (Chief Awolowo's section of the Yoruba), who monopolized the top ranks of the service, preferring to employ—and to promote—peoples from their own part of the Region. Thus underlying the demand for a greater Yoruba 'kingdom' were strong centrifugal tendencies which threatened even the stability of the region as it then existed. Just as the civilian population was divided into two broadly opposed sections so were the Yoruba personnel of the armed forces. Representative of this division is the contrast between Major Johnson, Military Administrator (later Governor) of Lagos and a Lagos Yoruba, and Colonel Adebayo, the Governor of the West, an Ekiti Yoruba, a contrast which is clearly shown in the respective stands which each took at the meeting of the military leaders at Aburi.[18]

Each group naturally saw the political situation differently. Chief Awolowo's position and that of his 'greater Yoruba' group has already been described in detail because he was the official spokesman—and leader—of the Yoruba. But whereas he saw it as a conflict between the Hausa and the Ibo, or put differently, between the North and the East, a conflict in which the Yoruba became the innocent victims, the *progressives* as one would expect saw the conflict as one between the forces of 'reactionary' feudalism and those of progress and enlightenment. In this respect therefore they were willing to co-operate with the East which they saw as an ally. The *radicals*, *statists*, and the *real Yoruba* saw the conflict as arising from the inordinate ambition and corruption of the politicians but, where the *statists* supported the efforts of the federal authorities towards reconciliation, the *real Yoruba* found an ally in the North and particularly in the politicians from the Emirates of the far North.

Because of these divisions of opinion and loyalties it became accepted practice for the supporters of the 'greater Yoruba' conception to exclude from meetings of the 'leaders of thought' all those known to be opposed to that idea. In this respect they had the active support of the Military Governor. It ought to be pointed out that Colonel Adebayo had his own ambitions. As the most senior Nigerian officer in the army[19] (after the departure of Brigadier Ogundipe to be Nigerian High Commissioner in London) he felt he ought to have been Head of State. Alienated by this sense of 'deprivation'—he is reported to have walked out of a meeting of the Supreme Military Council on at least one occasion—he readily threw his support behind the 'greater Yoruba' group. By March 1967 this group was therefore in the ascendant in the West though the undercurrents of opposition remained. At a meeting of the 'leaders of thought' in the same month Chief Awolowo came out with the statement that were the East to secede from the Federation the West would also follow and proclaim its sovereignty.

On 30 May 1967 the East seceded from the Federation but the West did not follow suit. Indeed Chief Awolowo accepted office as Vice-Chairman and Commissioner for Finance in a new civil-military Federal Executive Council in a federation which was now composed of twelve States. The States were created by decree on 27 May but, instead of the creation of a larger West, the Region actually suffered a loss of territory, territory which was excised and merged with the State of Lagos.

It would be interesting to speculate why the West did not follow the East in seceding but whatever the reasons it would seem that the following factors contributed to preventing the West from carrying out its threat. First, the declaration of emergency in the Federation at the same time as the States were created; second, the presence of Federal troops in the West—at Abeokuta and Ibadan—in sufficient numbers to enforce Federal will in the face of any opposition; third, the demand for separate States within the West itself, a demand which by April 1967 had become sufficiently articulated to warrant the intervention of the Federal Government to remind those concerned that the ban on 'party' political activity was still in force; fourth, lack of support from the peoples of Lagos and Ilorin/Kabba; and, fifth, a factor which cannot be ignored, though its precise importance cannot be specified, the offer of office in the Federal Government, an office virtually equivalent to that of Prime Minister, to Chief Awolowo.[20]

III

The declaration of war, and over two years of fighting in which the Yoruba have taken part as an equal partner with the other peoples of the federation, cannot but alter the nature of the demands of the West. With the exodus of the Ibo from the federal civil service, the places they filled have in the main been taken over by the Yoruba. Lagos and Kwara (Ilorin/Kabba) States have assumed a separate existence with distinct interests since their creation. With the excision of the coastal areas, the 'region' no longer has any direct access or outlet to the sea. The combination of all this makes unlikely that the 'greater Yoruba' idea can be revived. What is not so certain, however, is the result of the demand for states to be created within the existing Western State. How successful this demand will be will depend in part on the ability of the present Government of the West to conciliate dissident factions, in part on the demand for states in other areas (if, for instance, there should be a demand for the creation of another state from the present North-Eastern State, it is not unlikely that the 'real Yoruba' might use this opportunity to bring up the question of splitting the West). But all this depends on the success which attends the efforts of the federal authority to hold the federation together.

Unlike the old, basically tripartite, structure the new twelve-State system provides greater safeguards for group interests because by extending the basis of coalition formation it creates, for the first time, the opportunities for more genuine n-person games, a more realistic recipe for stability than the ill-fated attempt at unitary government.

6

ENUGU: THE PSYCHOLOGY OF SECESSION
20 JULY 1966 TO 30 MAY 1967

K. Whiteman

To be furious is to be frightened out of fear; and in such mood the dove will peck the estridge.
Shakespeare, *Antony and Cleopatra*

What matters to me is the powers, not how you describe them.
Lt-Col Ojukwu [1]

I HAVE deliberately chosen 29 July as the starting-point rather than any other date, such as 15 January 1966 or 29 May 1966, or even 11 October 1965,[2] because it seems to be the point at which the Nigeria crisis crystallized, the point at which the course of events leading to secession and war really started. The January coup is equally critical perhaps, but the period between January and July was of a different nature. The crisis at that time was at once more subterranean (erupting only at the time of the May riots and the July mutiny) and more fluid. After 29 July it was out in the open; from then on relations between Eastern Nigeria and the rest of the country dominated the political scene: the reformist themes heard stridently after January now became intermittent noises and the corrosive ethnic arguments began to dominate.

In Enugu the effect of 29 July, the overthrow of Ironsi, the killing of as many as thirty-three Eastern army officers and the reversal of the power situation at the centre, was deeply traumatic.[3] There were many, both inside and outside Nigeria, who openly said 'the East will surely secede now'. Dr Graham Douglas has related how, during the three days when Nigeria had no government at the centre and Northern troops in Lagos seemed to wish the North to secede, the country could well have been split into four sovereign units.[4] The name 'Republic of Biafra' was suggested for the Eastern Region. He says that on 30 July he was entirely in agreement with his Cabinet colleagues; if secession of the North and splitting the country into four was the solution to 'the pestilence of periodic *coups d'état*' it had his support but he repeated his warning that the support of the minorities would have to be secured. With the emergence of Lt-Col Gowon as leader in Lagos, however, those who favoured secession found themselves faced with opposition not only from Dr Graham Douglas, who saw things from the 'minorities' viewpoint, but also from those who, while sympathetic to eventual secession, believed that the operation could be planned as a gradual exercise. Although others were less sure that a complete breakaway was the answer, a monolithic front was presented to the outside world and the visitor. There were, after all, many points of agreement, and fear for their own security, with the apparent breakdown of discipline in the Nigerian army in Lagos, the West, and the North, was widespread among Easterners. Many of those with misgivings about secession were to the forefront on the security question, absolutely convinced of the rightness of the East's case.

Dr Graham Douglas records a meeting of the Executive Council on 3 August, at which he was the only speaker 'except for the Military Governor putting a long series of questions to me', after which Lt-Col Ojukwu 'appeared persuaded of the futility of his design', which, according to Dr Graham Douglas, had still been to secede there and then. It had been planned for 1 August, the day Lt-Col Gowon took over, but Dr Graham Douglas was not available to advise on the instrument of secession, although this had already been drawn up. He does not name those advisers pressing for secession, but it is clear that the Solicitor-General, C. C. Mojekwu, was a principal advocate. He cites as moderating influences the Commander of the 1st Battalion, Lt-Col David Ogunewe, the Commissioner of Police in Enugu, Chief Patrick Okeke, and all the members of the Executive Committee, who congratulated him after he had raised objections to secession on 3 August. To these should be added Mr N. U. Akpan, Secretary to the Military Government, and the Chief Justice, Sir Louis Mbanefo, and possibly the Vice-Chancellor of Nsukka University, Dr Eni Njoku. Moreover, at that stage the presence of so many Easterners outside the East meant that any unilateral attempt to secede would be extremely difficult, leaving them as hostages. There were many other administrative, financial, and economic ties which reinforced the case for a slow unscrambling.

Dr Graham Douglas also mentions the facts that Lt-Col Ojukwu did not then know if General Ironsi was dead and that there was a garrison of largely Northern soldiers in Enugu, disarmed, it is true, but still a source of tension.[5] They did not leave until the middle of the month, after the 9 August recommendation that troops should return to their Region of origin.

For commentators, whether the East would secede or not remained a riddle. On the one hand, there was a very strong rumour in Lagos that secession was planned for 1 October; on the other, a visitor to Enugu early in September said that although secession might have been a natural reaction after the events of July he could find no responsible support for it.[6] The fact that the East was prepared to send delegates to the Ad Hoc Constitutional Committee was taken as an encouraging sign. Admittedly, the East's confederal stand at the conference, shared to some extent by other delegations, would have created a situation in which each Region was virtually sovereign: it was not a surprising stand in the circumstances, and there should be no illusions about what it was. There was, however, still some fluidity in the situation and conciliation might not have been impossible. The blowing up of the Ore bridge and the Agu bomb incident in Lagos may have been intended as an attempt to foul any 'compromise' settlement.

Papers dating from this period captured by the Federal troops in Enugu, while reportedly making no mention of secession, nor initially of confederation, underline above all that the Ibo would no longer trust any group or set of groups to wield political power over them and that the East had to have control of its own finances. An account of the actual mechanics of the movement towards secession will have to await the publication of these papers, personal memoirs and other documents. In the meantime, accounts written from the outside are of necessity impressionistic and open to revision.

One element in the situation which became more and more important after July was the question of the minorities in the East. Now that (at the time of writing) Biafra has been reduced very much to what is usually called the Ibo heartland it is hard to recall that, after July 1966, people on both sides of the Niger avoided direct public reference to the Ibo as such, even though a great deal was being said in private. Whereas in Lagos the phrase 'a certain part of the country' and other such euphemisms were used, in Enugu the talk was very definitely of 'the East', and it was maintained strongly that the non-Ibo minorities of Ogoja, Calabar, and the Rivers areas (generally said in mid-1966 to be about 5 million of the 12 million people in the Region) were one with the Ibo.

It was easy in Lagos at the time to find people from the minority areas to dispute this; all the most devoted champions of minority rights concentrated on the Federal capital from August 1966 onwards,[7] especially as they saw the opportunity, with the setting up of the Ad Hoc Constitutional Committee, of a 'second chance' to establish minority states. The creation of more states was one of the key issues when the Committee met in September. In the East at the time the situation was more opaque although the minorities, if asked, would undoubtedly have chosen to have their own state. This was a major weakness of the Eastern delegation's stand at the September talks. In Enugu it was felt, however, that the 'States' card was being played as a gambit to secure the division of the East, and that the sudden switch of the Northern delegation in mid-conference was due to this rather than to a genuine concern for the rights of the minorities.

The massacres of the end of September gave the Enugu authorities ammunition in their bid for 'one East' in that Easterners generally had been attacked and killed. There had already been the case of Major Ekanem, the Ibibio Provost-Marshal of the Nigerian army, gunned down on Carter Bridge shortly after 29 July, which was used as evidence that the Northerners did not have the interests of minorities at heart.[8] The return of wounded and mutilated minorities citizens alongside the Ibo at least meant that public clamour for states was considered 'bad taste' for the time being. Conversely, there were those who felt further aggrieved that their people were paying for the sins of the Ibo.

Some Ibo accepted that the minorities were a problem, although one admitted to me that 'for every Ibo who understands the minorities there are nine who don't'. Lt-Col Ojukwu showed himself aware of this and tried to rally support by creating a new provincial system. He felt that in return the minorities should support him in the 'struggle for survival'. Moreover, while the minorities people in Lagos were strongly and genuinely militant for their own states, the people on the spot could afford no such luxury; realistically they had come to terms with the actual power in the area and with their close neighbours and seldom admitted their preferences for a state of their own, even though they may have felt it. In Enugu it was also pointed out that there were bitter clan feuds in the Rivers, and tensions between Ibibio and Efik in Calabar. The appointment of the Ibibio Mr N. U. Akpan as Secretary to the Military Government in Enugu and of other non-Ibo to high positions in the civil service and military command were often cited as examples of Lt-Col Ojukwu's new deal for minorities.[9] Their continuance in those jobs later, after having been divorced from their communities, increasingly came to look like window-dressing.

There is little doubt that there was more opposition to secession among the minorities than among the Ibo, although Lt-Col Ojukwu claimed that he had more trouble from the Ibo than from minorities people. The unwillingness of Calabar and Rivers people in Lagos to follow the Ibo on the great trek homeward was solid evidence of their lack of enthusiasm for secession; events since secession have shown that, although the minorities never rose against Lt-Col Ojukwu, for the most part they welcomed the Federal troops and co-operated with them. Some communities, Ikot-Ekpene for example,[10] have had a fairly raw deal from both sides, but the anti-subversion scares in Biafra were often violently directed against minorities, which increased the sense of bitterness, as has the feeling that the starving in Biafra's camps are largely from minority areas. In addition, the establishment of States caused a rallying to the anti-Biafran cause among the minorities.

The basic cause of minorities' frustration in the East was the neglect from which they had suffered over the years, first at the hands of the British, then from the NCNC. This was particularly so in the Rivers, which has suffered especially from lack of communications and a corresponding lack of organization for the airing of grievances. The Willink Report had found feelings in the Delta particularly high,[11] as a result of which the federally controlled Niger Delta Development Board had been set up, but it was largely frustrated in its work by the Regional Government.

Resentment at neglect was compounded in the Rivers area by the particular argument over Port Harcourt, whose commercial success had eclipsed the decaying Rivers ports of Bonny, Opobo, and Brass. Willink referred to Port Harcourt as an Ibo town but the original inhabitants of the area, the Edwerri, are what has been described as 'marginal Ibo', speaking the Ibo tongue but sometimes claiming separate identity (the most celebrated marginal Ibo are the Onitsha and the Aro).[12]

At the moment, with the foundation of the new States, the emphasis is on the difference between Ibo and minorities, but the solidarity of the Ibo and their awareness of what President Senghor has chosen to call 'Iboïté' is a fairly recent phenomenon. The name Ibo was originally derogatory, used apparently on the coast and the river to describe the people of the interior of Iboland,[13] and only became widespread in the colonial period, especially as the colonial power was trying to standardize language and the Ibo were, above all, distinguishable as a language group, although there are even now wide differences of dialect. The Ibo, we are told, share with the other peoples of the former Eastern region features of a segmentary society with no overall ruler—a population 'distributed in a very large number of relatively small local communities each strongly attached to its land and in active rivalry with its nearest neighbours'.[14] It was not until the Second World War and the advent of Dr Azikiwe that Pan-Ibo sentiment caught on in a big way, and then it was an external development, or in the main towns; Ahoada or Abakaliki Ibo were outside the mainstream. U. A. Asika records that 'wandering round the liberated parts of Iboland . . . without exception and in all cases I have been told: We didn't start this trouble; it was the Ibo who caused the trouble. And these were all Ibo-speaking people.'[15] I can add to this that in Aba, the day after it was captured by Federal troops in 1968, I met people wandering in the town who told me they were not Ibo but

Ngwa. This is not to deny the existence of the Ibo, merely to point out that such ethnic identity is elusive and was often a phenomenon which developed in the colonial period. It is, paradoxically, an argument that might have been used in the early days in favour of Biafra.

After the worst round of massacres of all, at the end of September, which precipitated the massive exodus of Easterners from the North, the expectation of secession was inevitably intensified. The main point about the September killings was that they affected the mass of the people and created the sort of emotional climate in which secession was possible. The argument about numbers (whether it was 5,000 or 30,000 killed or whether there were 700,000 or 2 million refugees) is irrelevant. Whatever the number, it was sufficiently large to create a trauma of considerable proportions, because it affected so many families and stretched right down through society. It was also on a very much larger scale than the killing of Hausa in Port Harcourt and elsewhere, killings which are sometimes taken as cancelling out those in the North. All those in Enugu who went to the station to see the refugees arriving, some bandaged and maimed, were horrified, as I was when visiting hospitals there a month later. If it had been possible to avoid the September massacres it is hard to see how secession could have been staged, in spite of the existence of elements in favour of it among the elite. The massacres have provided the weightiest moral argument in the Biafran case and it is still difficult to find satisfactory excuses for them in Lagos.

Visiting Nigeria in November 1966 I was conscious of the extreme gulf between the attitude towards the massacres in the East and that in the rest of Nigeria. It was astonishing how many people, not only in Kano and Kaduna but in Ibadan and Lagos, merely commented that, while it was very sad, 'the Ibos had it coming to them', and that, despite evidence that the massacres were planned by political groups for political ends, they were somehow 'God's will'. I was told in Kaduna that several expatriates had had to threaten to resign before the Northern Government laid on a modest airlift to help evacuate Easterners. There were also many gravely troubled by the events, including those who had helped Ibo to escape, who seldom voiced their concern publicly, and it too often seemed to the East as if they were faced with callous indifference, if not murderous hostility.

This was reinforced by the Ibos' own psychological condition before these events, which sprang, in particular, from their view of their role in the history, indeed in the making, of Nigeria. If the Ibo collectivity only developed in the colonial period, the exploitation of this sense of tribe came with the expansion of the Easterners, above all the Ibo, into the rest of colonial Nigeria, with the development of welfare unions and, most important, with the advent of politics. The NCNC, in its time one of the most remarkable political parties in Africa and the pioneer of modern Nigeria nationalism, was the symbol of what the Ibo saw as their place in Nigeria. Although the NCNC attracted many political stars from all over Nigeria into its galaxy, its motive force was undeniably Ibo. At its best it was the nearest to a national political party Nigeria ever had, and at its worst it was a 'jobs for the boys' machine, seen by many people outside it as a front for the Ibo State Union, which existed legitimately to protect and help the interests of the Ibo. It was an example of the paradox of which the Ibo have been so conscious: they could not forget how much Nigerian nationalism owed to their efforts. James Coleman, analysing the reasons why they became such ardent Nigerian nationalists, notes resentment of European glorification of the past of the Hausa and Yoruba kingdoms, the 'cruel economic realities' of overcrowded and infertile Iboland, and the fact that regional separatism might have affected 'the careers and future opportunities of large numbers of Easterners'.[16] They came to believe that they had built up the country but had been deprived of the main prizes—a case of 'monkey work, baboon chop'.

After July, and more especially after the September massacres, there was a reaction from being the most Nigerian of Nigerians to completely writing off Nigeria, yet at the same time justifying their past actions. Incomprehension and fury that the killings should have been taken to the level of the masses was a contributory factor and was made much worse from the psychological point of view because something which had been feared for some time—so much so that the fears had been dismissed as paranoia, arising from a talent for self-pity—actually happened and was far worse than had been imagined.

One vice of the NCNC had been a certain desire to have their cake and eat it; to be at one and the same time the voice of reasonable government and of militant opposition. A feature of the Eastern case after July was the willingness to continue justifying the actions of the NCNC in the political disputes of the 1950s, especially their coalition with the NPC after the Federal elections of 1959, an alliance which seemed to betray their radical commitment.[17] The devotion of the Ibo to Nigerian unity, it was further argued, was demonstrated by the self-sacrificing lack of federal projects in the Region and by the 1962–4 census affair, in which the NCNC, as part of the federal coalition, helped to 'do down' the Action Group, not unaware that they might be the next to suffer. By 1965 the concealed struggle for power at the centre between North and East was engaged once more with a vengeance, using the Western Region as a battle ground. The blatantly rigged election of

October 1965 and the subsequent violence formed the prelude to the coup of January 1966 in which the ambiguity of the Eastern stand came to a head. To understand the let-down of July it is essential to recall the widespread justification which had greeted 15 January throughout southern Nigeria. Later the Easterners bitterly printed the editorials of Lagos newspapers welcoming the January coup. For although there were Ibo central to the planning of it, Major Nzeogwu himself seems to have been genuinely Nigerian in outlook, and Major Ifeajuna died, with his Yoruba colleague Lt-Col Banjo, because of a 'One Nigeria' plot against Lt-Col Ojukwu.

I found extreme resentment in Enugu after July that in Lagos there were efforts to brand 15 January as a tribal coup. The point was, I was told, that it was not fully successful, and General Ironsi was the wrong man to take over, alternating between doing nothing and acting in a manner which first offended then appeased the North, depending on who was the last person to advise him. General Ironsi had few enough champions in office, but late in 1966 there were none, even though, or perhaps because, it was well known that he was dead, despite the lack of an official announcement. Decree No. 34, it was felt, might have worked had it been introduced immediately after 15 January as part of a general programme for unity. As it was, there is ground for thinking that the East's dream of unity was shattered by the May riots. Mr Asika has claimed that, as early as April 1966, Ibo colleagues of his at Ibadan were planning secession on the ground that unity was non-existent, and that they had prepared a memorandum in June calling for secession.[18] He blamed oil (the possibility of Eastern secession from 1964 onwards was always associated with the develop- ment of oil in the East), and refused to join them when in July they left Ibadan to go to Nsukka. There they formed part of an articulate group influencing opinion in Enugu, where likewise, after May, talk of the possibility of secession had re-emerged. He has also seriously questioned the extent of mass support for Lt-Col Ojukwu's policies of 'defiance' and 'survival' and for secession itself. He has said: 'My friends must know that they represent, and the views they hold and articulate form, at best, one per cent of opinion of Ibo society.' This is to say that Biafran secession is that of the elite, a class Asika categorizes as 'struc- turally irresponsible', who in Eastern Nigeria, to a greater extent than elsewhere in Nigeria, constitute a veritable *Who's Who* in terms of academic degrees and so forth, and that the Ibo masses were led by the nose in 'the exercise of purely elitist power'.[19] This is a questionable assumption.

The elite attitudes which are said to have played such a key part in the psychology of the impulse to secede could be found above all in

the 'returnees' who had left Lagos and the West. Some, who had been
closely associated with the Ironsi regime or who were well-known Ibo
figures,[20] would have been marked men in Lagos, no matter what
assurance the authorities might have given. Even Sir Louis Mbanefo
was molested at Lagos airport. There was sufficient uncertainty in
Lagos in August, September, and October to make anybody who
fancied he might be a marked man flee 'for his life'. The tales of the
killings of 29 July and of indiscipline thereafter were repeated again
and again in Enugu, particularly the incident of Colonel Tony Eze[21]
and the case of Stephen Achilefu, the personnel manager of Nigeria
Airways, who was taken out by soldiers and shot.

The returnees swelled the civil service: Lt-Col Ojukwu, in his
April 1967 budget speech, said that £3m had been allocated to the
absorption of refugee civil servants and £1m for extra charges ensuing
from that absorption. Everyone who had been a civil servant before
was taken on, creating a Dahomey-style[22] top-heavy civil service.
While not denying that, up to November at least, there was definite
danger, there was no doubt that there was tremendous corporate
pressure brought to bear on those outside the Region to return home.
After 31 December the pressure took more extreme forms; it was often
said in Enugu that those who stayed behind were subversives, and had
'only themselves to blame'. Some people I met in Enugu who had
worked in Lagos seemed to have returned because it was the thing to do,
because all their friends had returned, or because secession was expected
and they wanted to be sure to be on the right side of the Niger when it
came. There was also the simple fact that they believed promotion
prospects had been drastically reduced, quoting, for example, the
replacement of Lawrence Anionwa by Brigadier Ogundipe as High
Commissioner in London.

Another element contributing to the build-up towards secession was
the controversial role of Eastern propaganda. This has been blamed
in Lagos as one of the main factors holding the people of the East in
thrall, making their intransigence much worse by playing on and
exaggerating horror stories, and in some cases deliberately producing
fabrications to make things seem worse than they were, thus preparing
the climate for secession.[23] At the time one could see what they meant:
papers and broadcasts were militantly partisan, sometimes to the
extent of fantasy. This was no new phenomenon; the Eastern Nigeria
Broadcasting Service, for example, had played a pioneeringly active
role in the Western Region election crisis in 1965. Now they had their
own cause to exploit and they did so with a vengeance. But the
undeniable excesses of the various information media were as much a
symptom as a cause of the state of mind in the East. What appeared

in the papers and was said on the radio was a reflection of a certain prevalent opinion articulated, with bitterness, by influential voices, which would have been difficult to contradict.

The drive to gather in the clans and the propaganda campaign both fit into a master-plan for eventual secession. So does the expulsion of all non-Easterners from the East at the end of September. Although for the Northerners such a move was essential, for Westerners and Mid-Westerners it was more a manœuvre to help solve the undeniably difficult job problem that arose in the East from refugees and returnees. As such, it was one of the main obstacles to the achievement of that 'Southern solidarity' which was still preached in Enugu intermittently throughout this period. To unite the 'progressive South' of Nigeria against the 'conservative North', thus ultimately aiding the 'progressives' in the North, had been the ideal of Nigerian radicals for years. It was a notion that had seen fulfilment at the time of the formation of the UPGA in 1964 and could be seen in the motivation of the 15 January coup, although it withered away in the Ironsi period. The Yoruba had been disillusioned by the unwillingness of General Ironsi to liberate Chief Awolowo (according to one Eastern publication of early 1967, Major Nzeogwu had wanted to make him Prime Minister) and had welcomed Lt-Col Gowon's release of the majority of the Action Group detainees in early August. But in the East they remembered only the original welcome given by the Yoruba to 15 January and the fact that it had been of major benefit to the West, in that it had brought peace to that Region after a period of acute political strife.

One prominent Easterner I met in Enugu that autumn told me that the question one should always ask in the West was 'what happened to Lt-Col Fajuyi', the forgotten man of the 'Nigerian revolution' whose killing alongside General Ironsi in July, unannounced for several months, was a symbol of the shreds of solidarity which remained across the Niger. There was interest in the development of 'confederal' views on the part of Chief Awolowo,[24] but only in so far as it would help the East to achieve what it wanted, and there was special admiration for an article by Wole Soyinka[25] in which he criticized the mealy-mouthed attitudes of some Westerners to the crisis—for example, the Yoruba community of Zaria who only rejoiced that they had been spared in the massacre. This typecast the Yoruba as two-faced, and there was a widespread desire to typecast in Enugu. (Paradoxically, it was possible to meet people who still preferred Northerners, in spite of what had happened. There was a peculiar love–hate relationship arising, perhaps, from the attraction of opposites. It is important to remember that for every arrogant domination-conscious Ibo there were many who had extremely cordial relations. There are, in fact, a

fair number of 'assimilated' third-generation Ibo with Hausa names
and culture still living in the North.)

The East after the massacres was too absorbed in itself to have much
heart for actively playing the Nigerian political game any more. Communications with the rest of Nigeria up to early 1967 were fairly
reasonable, in spite of road blocks and searches, but there was a gulf
in spiritual communication which meant that resentments usually out-
weighed a genuinely constructive policy, and where some communication did exist it was of an unreal kind. Because of the great
damage that had been done to the East, other regions, even those
friendly to them, such as the Mid-West, were expected to give their all.
The Mid-West, especially, was too often thought of in old 'NCNC'
terms as bound to go along with the East. Hence Lt-Col Ejoor's alarm
at an incident like the Benin plane hijacking in April 1967, which
seemed to compromise the Mid-West as much as the celebrated raid
on Benin prison by Northern soldiers in August 1966. The culmination
of this insensitivity to the thoughts of others was the invasion of the
Mid-West in August 1967 which boomeranged badly.[26] Another
example was the total unwillingness to differentiate between different
sections in the North but merely to lump them together as Hausa-
Fulani dictators. The Middle Belt peoples, extremely influential in Lagos
after 29 July, were abused as 'Munshies' for their part in the killings.

There is a case for arguing that, had the Easterners cared to settle
with Lagos at the end of October or in early November, they could
have had very good terms indeed, because there was so much sympathy
for them in the wake of the massacres, and the situation was still fluid
in Lagos. But the refusal to send a delegation to the resumption of
constitutional talks on 24 October, however understandable, resulted
in the indefinite postponement of the talks, and eventually in Lt-Col
Gowon's speech of 30 November, in which he not only promised that
more states would be created but said for the first time, albeit in very
discreet language, that force would have to be used to defend the
'territorial integrity of Nigeria'.

Coming at a time when the Easterners were looking for signs of
regret and apology, this dramatically deepened the suspicions in Enugu
of the intentions of the Government in Lagos. After the trauma of the
massacres there was need, above all, for reassurance, and Lt-Col
Gowon's statements had been sufficiently ambivalent to cause doubt,
even if unwittingly, as when he said the killing had gone 'beyond
reason' (as if to say there had been 'reasonable' killing). One remark
by Lt-Col Hassan Katsina (which, as Wole Soyinka pointed out, was
greatly to his credit), that 'whatever may have been the motives
or reasons behind them [the killings] they deserve to be severely

condemned', was not given the publicity it needed, and the image of Nigerian reactions to the massacres received in Enugu was one of sanctimonious indifference ('The Ibos brought it on themselves').

The major event of the period between the September massacres and secession the following May was the strange meeting of Lt-Col Ojukwu and his military colleagues at Aburi, Ghana, early in January. From the Eastern point of view Aburi seemed to produce a recognition of their demands—Lt-Col Ojukwu certainly presented it as such—and the more it was criticized in Lagos the more they nailed their banner to the Aburi mast: 'On Aburi we stand' became a favourite slogan in the months before secession. Yet Lt-Col Ojukwu has spoken several times of the reluctance of his people to let him go to Aburi. The solicitude arose partly from a desire that nothing should happen to him while out of the Region[27] but also from a fear that he might be persuaded to sell out. There was a 'several times bitten' element, going back to Mr Okpara's ineffective handling of the census crisis and the Western Region election crisis, and, above all, the miserable failure of Dr Azikiwe's attempt to move into the seat of power in the election crisis of 1964/5. I was made acutely aware of the contempt in the East for the 'compromises' of the old regime in which they had always lost and it may well have been a factor in the decision to secede and in any subsequent rigidity of attitudes.

One issue which seemed to rankle in the East after Aburi and was seen as a betrayal by Lagos was the apparent going back on the pledge not to use force,[28] which seemed to have been agreed unequivocally on the first day of the meeting. In fact, the transcripts of Aburi make it clear that Lt-Col Ojukwu seized the initiative right at the beginning to propose 'no force' and other participants raised no significant objection. No attempt was made to define how far the pledge should go—whether it meant that, should they be unable to agree and the East left the Federation, no force would be used to bring her back. Had this been put to them nobody on the Federal side would have accepted it, while it was clearly Lt-Col Ojukwu's intention in raising it so early in the proceedings. It was almost a protection for peaceful secession, and if interpreted in this way conflicted with Lt-Col Gowon's 30 November speech, which implied that force might have to be used. The issues subsequently became confused still further by two enlargements on what 'force' meant—Lt-Col Ojukwu's famous phrase that the East was being 'forced out of the federation', and the Federal view that the secession itself was an act of force. But it was important in Enugu as a factor that might have rebuilt confidence. For there was widespread belief, hardly surprising in the circumstances, that force would be used to 'finish the job' and bring the East back into line.

The rapid deterioration in relations that followed the meeting at Aburi started with Lt-Col Ojukwu's declarations to the press on his return to Enugu the next day, portraying what had happened, with some justification, as a victory.[29] It continued through the publication of the pamphlet *Nigeria 1966*, which Lt-Col Gowon subsequently denied having authorized,[30] and Lt-Col Gowon's own press conference, at which his interpretation of Aburi was very different from that of Lt-Col Ojukwu, and through the series of unsuccessful meetings of 'legal and financial boys', in which the Eastern demands seemed to be continually hardening, to the decision made by both sides, more or less at the same time early in March, to publish the Aburi proceedings virtually in full.[31] Through all this period the question of an ultimate use of force remained in the background. It was now clear that the creation, expansion, and arming of an army had been continuing in the East for some time. Hard evidence for this at the time was hard to come by, as the operation by its very nature had to be highly secret. Even at Aburi Lt-Col Ojukwu denied buying arms,[32] but it had been established that the aircraft which crashed in Cameroon in September 1966 had been carrying arms for Enugu. Dr Graham Douglas says that Lt-Col Ojukwu took him aside after the 3 August meeting which rejected secession to show him plans for raising an army with Israeli assistance.[33] By March it was possible to see recruits marching in the streets of Enugu singing 'If you've never never been a soldier you will never ever be happy' and trenches had been dug by the roadside. There was also a poster campaign to prepare the population against imminent invasion and the establishment of Vigilance Committees, although the way society was organized produced ready-made civil defence groups.

The fear that force would be used against them came to the surface again with the publication of Decree No. 8. The point in the decree that was seized on in Enugu was the provision for a declaration of a state of emergency if all but one of the Military Governors agreed. They had the precedent of the 1962 State of Emergency in the West very much in mind.[34] It can be argued that it was so certain that the decree would be rejected in Enugu that the Federal Government may have made concessions in it to Aburi which they would have been reluctant to implement, in the full knowledge that they would never have to implement them. This was a war of nerves which two could play, and in this case the Federal Government outmanœuvred Lt-Col Ojukwu, as he had outmanœuvred them at Aburi itself. There is evidence that there was an attempt at financial horse-trading at several meetings from November to March, ending in a meeting in Ghana, at which it was apparent that the amount of compensation for refugees the East felt was owed to it as of right was far beyond anything the Federal Government was prepared to give.

In the collapse of confidence after Aburi reconciliation was much more difficult and although there was no shortage of candidates for the role of intermediary—notably Ghana at the end of March and in early April,[35] and Chief Awolowo and the National Conciliation Committee in May—all attempts at mediation proved abortive. In the meantime Lt-Col Ojukwu was engaged in a slow unscrambling of the East's remaining ties with the Federation—the public corporations, the police and the multitude of financial links. By the time secession came it had been half expected for so long it was an anti-climax.[36] Had it not happened then the idea might have begun to lose credibility. The circumstances surrounding the timing of the actual declaration are still obscure. Once Lt-Col Gowon had decreed the creation of States the challenge could not be avoided although even then some sources indicate that the decision to secede was still in the balance. But what brought on the Constituent Assembly meeting which gave Lt-Col Ojukwu a mandate to secede? This seems to have been the factor which precipitated Lt-Col Gowon's action. Was there really any increased popular pressure for secession? Was the demand to withdraw Northern troops from the Western Region, which became notably more marked in May, completely ignored, or was it taken in Enugu as evidence that the West was more on their side than in fact it proved to be? Chief Awolowo's statements at the beginning of May implying acceptance of the breakaway of the East had been received with rejoicing in Enugu[37] but there was an undercurrent of bitterness at his ambiguity, which came out again when they heard the compromise proposals his mission put, and when the mission went back empty-handed. In Enugu 'concessions' had become a word they did not want to hear, and, although they were capable of switching on to the old Nigerian political wavelengths, a desire to opt out of the game had become increasingly evident. This phenomenon of opting out, of giving up the struggle (the unkind would say because they had lost), was particularly strong on the part of the returnees, the people who had surrendered hard-won entrenched positions at the centre, especially at the top of the professions, the universities, the civil service; they, particularly, had made a profound emotional commitment to some kind of secession the moment they left Lagos or Ibadan.

What was the role of Lt-Col Ojukwu himself? In Lagos from January onwards increasing emphasis was being placed on his personality as the main cause of the crisis and visitors were provided with convincing details.[38] The case against him was that he was ambitious to be a head of state at all costs and if he could not achieve it in Lagos then he was going to try in Enugu. Of his ambition and his liking for power there is no doubt. From an early stage the cries of 'power, power', which have traditionally accompanied the more pushful and flamboyant of Nigeria's politicians,[39] attended his movements and he is reported to have held views on the political role of the military from an early stage in his career. His performance at Aburi, and his subsequent arrogance about it ('I ran rings round them at Aburi'),[40] encouraged his too-clever-by-half image. Moreover, within the officer corps there was resentment of his Oxford degree and contempt for his book-learning. Lt-Col Hassan Katsina, for example, was once quoted as saying of one of Lt-Col Ojukwu's press conferences that it was 'only a repetition of his effort to display what English he knows'. There was also suspicion of his known love of acting, and it is not hard to detect an innate theatricality in his make-up.[41] The measured tones, the studied pauses, the statesmanlike air, all indicate the skilled, if slightly hammy, acting style that characterizes nature's politicians. He reveals more of himself than perhaps he realizes when, in his official biography,[42] it is recorded that his philosophy is 'knowledge of oneself; truth to oneself', evoking Polonius' advice to Hamlet. The showmanship, and the playing of what Senghor calls *la politique politicienne*, served to irritate rather than lubricate links with Lagos and his personal relations with Lt-Col Gowon seem to have deteriorated badly after Aburi. There are several examples at Aburi of Lt-Col Gowon attempting to be friendly with Lt-Col Ojukwu, only to be repulsed by the Eastern Governor. And some of the scurrilous abuse of Lt-Col Gowon from the radio stations in Enugu, which must have shocked someone of the latter's patent, if unworldly, sincerity, can only have made things worse. Lt-Col Ojukwu also reportedly had a personal feud with Lt-Col Mohammed Murtala, going back to their time together in the Congo.

The attempt to single out Lt-Col Ojukwu as the source of the trouble served only to increase solidarity in Enugu. Lt-Col Ojukwu knew this very well and played on it ('they want to get their hands on Ojukwu') but it would be fair to say he came to represent the stubborn spirit of resistance which so many were expressing at that time. As with the propaganda, cause and effect are entwined, but he was as much the symbol of defiance as its mentor.

One factor to remember is that before 29 July Lt-Col Ojukwu had probably been the most unpopular of the Military Governors. On the one hand he was criticized for giving a job to his father[43] and for his unwillingness to conduct probes in spite of the anti-corruption atmosphere prevalent in Lagos. On the other hand he ran up against political figures such as Dr Azikiwe, whose interests at Nsukka were harassed and whose companies were pressed to pay their debts by the Eastern

Government-controlled African Continental Bank, and more especially Dr Michael Okpara, the former regional Premier, who still had much support but was detained from March until after the July coup.

The bickering ended abruptly with the changed circumstances in Lagos and Lt-Col Ojukwu became the man of the hour. He grew a beard (the symbol of mourning) and made grave and solemn speeches and, in the prevalent atmosphere of insecurity, seemed to represent at that stage a continued guarantee of survival. In a kind of Toynbeean 'challenge and response' during the terrible days between July and November, the support and sympathy he rallied to his side were tremendous. And by November a collective psychosis had set in which seemed at times almost to take over events and to render personalities of secondary importance.

It is sometimes argued that if Lt-Col Ojukwu had shown more moderation and restraint he could easily have stopped the slide towards secession, that in the end it happened because he wanted it to happen to satisfy his own ambition. Being an instinctive politician, however, he knew the political state of mind of those on whom he depended for power and what he would have to do to survive. It is true that the large-scale backing he commanded meant that he might have been in a position to dictate any settlement arrived at with Lagos but if it was one that was unacceptable[44] in Enugu even he might well have been in trouble. 'Governing the East is like riding a pack of wild horses' he once wrote in a private letter, and his own relations with the 15 January men were sufficiently ambiguous to cause him concern, especially as some of them still retained 'One Nigeria' ideals.[45] Subsequent postsecession events attendant on the Mid-West episode and the 'Ifeajuna plot'[46] showed that solidarity could be broken.

There were other important but obscure developments in this period. What were the pressures caused by the frustrations of the vast numbers of jobless refugees, only temporarily absorbed by the extended family? What was the role, for example, of Philip Alale's[47] Eastern Nigeria Youth Movement, which rose to prominence in late 1966 and seemed to be trying to take over all the regional trade unions? Trade unionists in Enugu in April were extremely worried about Alale's activities, and there was no doubt that some of the 'militant' meetings, calling for secession at that time, were held under the auspices of Alale, who had certain talents as a demagogue. Again, one could meet people who were concerned at the way a traditionally most disputatious region had been transformed into a police state with very little resistance; as it was part of 'the emergency' in Enugu it was accepted for the most part as an inevitable limitation.

The misgivings about secession were more widespread than seemed

apparent at the time; there was certainly little or no preparation for
the idea in Enugu. There were plenty of rumours as to possible dates
but the word Biafra was seldom publicly uttered, at any rate in the
presence of outsiders. All was geared, rather, to possible violence,
which it was widely assumed was coming; 'The Northerners will
try to finish it off', I was told, and every piece of evidence that fitted
this theory was dwelt on. I even felt, and wrote,[48] that some people
might even try to provoke a fight 'to settle things once and for all',
and if secession was the surest way of provoking a fight, they would
secede. There seemed to be a disastrous impulse to tempt fate and bring
on themselves the very disaster they feared. It was disturbing to find
the extent of unreason by April on the part of people who had earlier
been able to take part in rational discussion, even in the aftermath of
pogrom, and it is ingenuous merely to put it down to their having
been influenced by propaganda. Communal pressures, the siege mentality, and an increased sense of insecurity had all made their mark.
I wrote at the time: 'I feel a machine is in motion it will be difficult
to stop. Many believed that the East would carry out an emotional
secession last autumn, but were persuaded by the disciplined and cool
reaction that this was not uppermost in Eastern minds. But it seems
clear that the frightful experience of massacre and pogrom is only now
beginning to work its psychological toll. Bottled up fury is in the end
more explosive.'[49]

7

THE CREATION OF NEW STATES
IN THE NORTH*

S. K. Panter-Brick and P. F. Dawson

OVERSHADOWED by the conflict between the Federal Government and Biafra, important constitutional developments have taken place within the old Northern Region. Although subordinate to the main issue of Nigerian unity or Biafran secession they constitute an important element in the general pattern of events. Indeed most Northern Nigerians have probably attached as much, if not more, importance to these local developments as to the progress of military operations against Biafra. By the creation of six new States in the territory previously known as the Northern Region, each with extensive autonomous powers, and by the distribution of the assets and liabilities of the former Regional Government, major changes have been effected in the potential balance of power within the Federation, as in the position and powers of the Native Authorities and of the many ethnic groups, especially the 'minorities'. The full significance of these changes will probably not be apparent until an element of competitive, electoral, party politics is reintroduced into the governmental processes of Nigeria, but after two years of operation evidence of the tendencies inherent in the new system begins to accumulate.

The six States were set up by Decree No. 9 of 27 May 1967, and the Table shows the area, population, number of Native Authorities, and Administrative Divisions of each State and Province.

There was, it must be admitted, something bizarre about the way in which the former Northern Region set the pace along a road which hitherto it had always refused to travel or had said it would travel only in the company of others. The dominant view had always been that the Region must be maintained intact; any contrary point of view, as expressed by people of the Middle Belt, was firmly overruled. Indeed, the motto of the NPC, 'One North: One People irrespective of Religion, Rank or Tribe', aroused great pride both as an ideal and as a partial achievement, at least among Fulani, Kanuri, Nupe, and other smaller groups, and even among the Yoruba of Ilorin and Kabba

* This account concentrates on the North for obvious reasons. The establishment of the three States in the former Eastern Region has been hampered and complicated by the civil war.

States and Provinces	Area (Square Miles)	Population	Native Authorities	Divisions
Benue/Plateau State:				
Benue	28,018	2,641,960	7	5
Plateau	11,253	1,367,448	8	4
	39,271	4,009,408	15	9
Kano State:				
Kano	16,630	5,774,842	4	2
Kwara State:				
Ilorin	17,719	1,119,222	4	3
Kabba	10,953	1,287,143	8	4
	28,672	2,406,365	12	7
North Central State:				
Katsina	9,466	2,545,005	2	1
Zaria	17,243	1,403,390	3	2
Kaduna N.A.	45	149,910	1	-
	26,754	4,098,305	6	3
North Eastern State:				
Adamawa	20,821	1,585,200	3	3
Bauchi	26,120	2,496,329	8	3
Bornu	44,804	2,853,553	5	5
Sardauna	13,197	878,271	5	3
	104,942	7,813,353	21	14
North Western State:				
Niger	28,666	1,404,567	9	3
Sokoto	36,338	4,334,769	4	3
	65,004	5,739,336	13	6
Total	281,273	29,841,609	71	41

Note: The population figures are those of the 1963/4 Census and are generally considered to have been inflated by about 25 per cent. They provide, however, a fairly accurate picture of comparative size of population.
Source: Northern States of Nigeria, *Local Government Yearbook 1968*, p. 6.

provinces who found in the Northern Region no lack of opportunity for good employment. This remained the dominant view throughout most of 1966, although some account had to be taken of minority demands. It was certainly the official policy of the Northern Nigerian Military Government, as can be seen from the appointment of the Committee on Provincial Authorities and the nature of the proposals to the Ad Hoc Constitutional Committee. Both the appointment of the Committee and the proposals reflected the same basic decision to preserve the unity of the Region while conceding considerable internal devolution of authority.

The Committee on Provincial Authorities was appointed in September 1966 to make recommendations 'in the light of the decision of the Military Governor to reorganize Provincial Administration

along the lines suggested in the Hudson Report . . .' The Hudson
Report[1] had been commissioned in 1957 in circumstances not dissimilar
to those of 1966. A constitutional review was taking place and there
was a strong division of opinion between those seeking to preserve the
unity of the Region and those demanding States. Hudson had recommended the creation of Provincial Authorities which would have given
the Provinces a measure of self-government at the expense of the
Regional Government and Native Authorities. The proposal to set up
such authorities was used in 1957 to oppose the demands of Middle
Belt spokesmen for the creation of States. The Hudson proposals were
never in fact fully implemented and it was the task of the 1966 Committee to take a fresh look at the problem and to make further recommendations. Its work really made sense only on the assumption that
States would not be created, and it was no doubt for this reason that the
leading Middle Belt spokesman, Mr Tarka, refused to serve.[2]

The stand taken by the Northern delegation to the Ad Hoc Constitutional Committee made some concession to the demand for States,
especially in its revised proposals.[3] The original proposals had envisaged
a Confederation of the existing Regions. The possibility of subdividing
Regions and of holding plebiscites was recognized, but as a Regional
responsibility. No indication was given as to how such plebiscites
were to be organized, and since under these proposals each Region would
have been a law unto itself, with its own armed forces, police, and
courts of law, they may be said to have provided clear guarantees for
Regional sovereignty but only a doubtful safeguard for those in favour
of more States.

The revised proposals—made under pressure from the minorities—
envisaged a federation, not necessarily of the existing Regions. The
principle of creating additional Regions (or States) was admitted as an
immediate issue. It was however to be applied simultaneously in all
Regions (except the Mid-West) as part of a general agreement.

During the ensuing months the two opposing views in favour of
Regional unity or of creating States were more or less openly contested
among Northerners.[4] The mass killings at the end of September 1966
had a double effect. They strengthened the movement in favour of
confederation, by widening the gulf between the peoples of the various
Regions, but also made the peoples of the Middle Belt more than ever
determined to secure their own separate State(s). 'It would be better to
agree on separation now, without violence, than to run the risk of
sharing the fate of the Ibo and enforced separation at some future date'
was a common argument.

Lt-Col Gowon's speech of 30 November 1966, in which he rejected
the idea of a 'temporary confederation' as 'unworkable', and favoured a

Federation of eight to fourteen States, brought the issue into the open and considerably strengthened Middle Belt opinion.

One unmistakable sign that the advocates of additional States were beginning to carry more weight was the decision to discontinue the work of the Committee on Provincial Authorities. It had produced an interim report early in December and had planned to tour the Region in order to discuss it with Native Authorities, beginning in mid-January. This tour never took place. The members of the Committee from the Middle Belt (four out of twelve) would almost certainly have resigned had its work not been discontinued.

This open confrontation of views in the North was gradually over-shadowed by, and made subordinate to, that between Lt-Col Gowon and Lt-Col Ojukwu. In the long run this had the effect of weakening still further the upholders of 'One North'. Involved in the process of forestalling the probable Biafran secession, they were committed gradually to supporting a Federation of States rather than a Confedera-tion of Regions. Although the eventual outcome of the war or of negotiations may not necessarily be a Federation of twelve States, it is hard to imagine the peoples of the Middle Belt accepting a reconstitu-tion of the old Northern Region. The idea of 'One North' is dead. Its ghost no doubt lingers on but it is no longer practical politics.

None the less, even if the principle of a Federation of States itself came to be more generally accepted, there remained divergent views as to the precise number of states to be created and as to whether existing provincial and Native Authority boundaries were to be respected in the process of fixing state boundaries.[5] As J. H. Smith has observed '. . . the states issue had long been a political talking point . . . [but] . . . in the event, the signing of the Decree [which created them] was not the culmination of lengthy preparation and detailed negotiations'.[6] The urgency and haste which accompanied the creation of the twelve States imposed its own necessities. In the North at least, it was almost overnight that the newly appointed Military Governors installed them-selves in their new capitals. There was no time for the second thoughts, compromises, and boundary adjustments which might have occurred had a more leisurely pace been possible. The present structure, both within and between States, is regarded by few as unalterable and changes are bound to occur,[7] but survival tends to breed permanence, as interests develop within the new territorial nexus. The merging of two or more States under a unified internal administration or the transfer of large areas and populations from one State to another is less probable than the further subdivision of existing States. The North Eastern State is the one most likely to be split on the alleged grounds of its administrative unwieldiness and the ethnic incompatibility of its people.[8] The apparent ease and success with which the new States were created has tended to encourage some critical observers of the Nigerian scene to advocate similar piecemeal tinkering with the remaining constitutional arrangements as a feasible solution to long-term political and social problems.

The necessity to build anew has created opportunities for reform which have often been gladly seized, not least by many of the younger civil servants newly elevated to influential posts in State administrations. The creation of entirely new jurisdictions has made apparent a need for fundamental reappraisals in many fields, especially those of local government and the machinery of administration. Arrangements which were suitable when Northern Nigeria—more than 264,000 square miles in area—was governed from Kaduna are no longer appropriate to States much smaller in size and population

The maintenance of the Provinces as an intermediate level of administration under the direction of a Provincial Secretary became a cumbersome arrangement in each of the four States comprising only two provinces, especially as one of the two provincial headquarters was designated the State capital. In both Benue-Plateau and Kwara, the Provinces have been abolished and the powers of Provincial Secretaries over Native Authorities have been re-allocated, partly to a newly-created Ministry of Local Government and partly to divisional officers. This is a process which seems certain to enhance the responsibilities and status of divisional officers, while increasing the degree of supervision and control over Native Authorities. In North Central State it is proposed to replace the three previous divisions with eight new 'Administrative Areas' each manned by a District Officer with a direct radio link with the State headquarters in Kaduna, the objective being closer and more detailed supervision.

Similarly the Native Authorities are likely to be affected now that they have State Governments on their doorstep. In the vast administrative space of the Region there was perhaps an important place for the Native Authorities. In the shrunken administrative space of the States this is much less certain. One hesitates to say that there is no room for both State Governments and Native Authorities, especially as many of the latter are quite small in size. But a graphic illustration of the kind of confrontation that is now taking place is provided by Kano. There are four Native Authorities in Kano State but three of these are relatively small. The fourth, Kano Native Authority, is three-quarters the size of Kano State and has 85 per cent of the taxpayers. It provides a wide range of services and employs a large staff. It is the tax-collector. It spends a large amount not only on recurrent account but also on development projects. It is conceivable that the State Government will confine itself to providing those services and exercising those powers which it has inherited from the Regional Government.[9] But it is also conceivable that the State Government will want to play a more prominent role by claiming a more exclusive authority for certain administrative services and by instituting a more rigorous control over the Native Authority.

Recent changes, brought into effect on 1 April 1969 in North Central State, suggest that this will indeed be the tendency. The Government has reorganized the Native Authority Councils, now renamed Local Authority Councils.[10] Two-thirds of the members are to be elected (in this first instance they have been nominated by the Military Governor). Traditional authority as such is retained only in the person of the Emir, acting as Chairman, and a small number of traditional office-holders. The remaining members are nominated *ex officio* and are either district heads or heads of departments. It has also been decided to appoint a council for each of the eight new administrative areas which have replaced the three divisions; the State's own field administration is thus being carried down to a more local level and presumably strengthened. Similar changes have been introduced in Kano State, where five administrative areas with councils have been established, four of them within Kano Emirate.

Such innovations are not merely administrative in nature. They are substantially political. Any adjustment in the status and functions of Native Authorities is likely to modify the social and political balance which has hitherto tended to preserve traditional authority. Important changes have taken place in recent years in the social structure and outlook of the North but at a much less rapid rate than in the other Regions. It has also varied considerably within the North itself. Control over the rate of social change and its particular effects is the key political issue. It has been slowest in the areas of the well-established Emirates where much of the administration, and thereby control of the electorate, has been in conservative hands. It has been slow generally because of the close political links between these traditional authorities and the ruling political party in the North. The Native Authority system operated as an unofficial electoral machine for sustaining modern-type but conservative-minded political leaders in office at Kaduna and Lagos.

The Native Authorities have in fact already lost some of their powers and precisely those powers which they valued the most, namely the maintenance of law and order, and the administration of justice. One of the first measures taken by the Federal Military Government after the January 1966 coup was to put the Native Authority Police under the operational control of the Nigerian Police. It also planned to bring the Native Authority Courts under the authority of the Chief Justice, but for various reasons no action was taken until a year later, in February 1967. Coming so late, it was all the more significant. The effect of the blow struck in January 1966 had largely worn off and the traditional authorities had recovered their accustomed prestige by appearing to be almost indispensable. Such at least was the impression created, for instance, by the regularity with which the Military Government at Kaduna formally consulted not only the so-called 'leaders of thought' but also the Emirs and Chiefs. These met as a separate body, a reconvened House of Chiefs, coequal with the 'leaders of thought', who for their part were seen as a reconstituted House of Representatives. This apparant recovery in status was rudely checked by the decision of the Regional Military Government to take over Native Authority Courts. It undermined traditional authority in one of its most vital aspects. The Native Authority Courts, headed in each Emirate by the Emir's own court, were, together with the Native Authority Police, one of the principal signs of that authority. There was practically no aspect of daily life which did not come within their original jurisdiction, and the decision to take them out of the hands of the Native Authorities was bound then to be seen as a real diminution of authority.

Simultaneously with the take-over of the Native Authority Courts, changes were made in the Staff Regulations for Native Authority employees, making them subject to the same restrictions with regard to political activities as Regional Government employees. This was of no immediate importance, since all political activities were in any case banned by the Military Government, but it was a further indication of what the future held in store. Like the take-over of Native Authority Courts, it was a reform which had long been advocated. The very extensive participation of Native Authority officials in party politics— and invariably on behalf of the dominant party, the NPC, produced in the minds of electors an identification between the Native Authority system and the NPC. Loyalties and long habits of obedience to the Native Authority were transferred to the party. The reform gave notice that in future no party could expect to enjoy this advantage.

These reforms, with regard to police, courts, and political activities, are likely to modify fundamentally the place of the Native Authority in Nigerian administration and politics. Instead of functioning as traditional authorities with wide general responsibilities to which administrative policy and the style of administration has to be adjusted, they will become clearly subordinate, instrumental—but no more—in carrying out prescribed policies in certain restricted fields. The announcement in February 1967 of the last two reforms caused considerable concern and unrest, so much so that the Military Governor convened a meeting of Emirs and Chiefs. His address[11] sums up very

well the general situation. It is also the voice of someone in a position
to understand the problem of adjustment.

The extent to which any of the State Governments will assert their
authority at the expense of the Native Authorities will depend, however, on at least four factors:

(i) *The administrative reputation of the Native Authorities*

Where this is low there will be little difficulty. The two Middle Belt
States are faced with mostly small, impecunious, and inefficient Native
Authorities. Elsewhere, for example in the North Eastern State, there
are several large, prosperous, and remarkably efficient Native Authorities.

(ii) *The political orientation of members of the State Governments*

All the Military Governors have appointed Commissioners to head
the different Ministries who are in every case indigenes of their States.
Although it is difficult to obtain detailed information from which to
assess the political make-up of the six Governments, it can be said that,
while most of the Executive Councils contain members who were
prominent in the NPC before 1966, they are not of a uniformly 'conservative' temperament. Some had sat unhappily in the old NPC
regarding it at that time as the only feasible vehicle for political action
in the North. Others are of an obviously 'radical' disposition, while
several appear to be 'men of straw' capable of being pressed by younger,
reform-minded civil servants.

(iii) *Financial resources*

In this respect the State Governments may find themselves in
difficulty. The Regional Government had derived most of its revenue
from taxes collected by other authorities and from external loans. Over
three-quarters of revenue on current account came from taxes collected
by the Federal Government. The States are in a similar position for in
the financial year 1968/9 they budgeted to receive the following proportion of their revenue through Federal Government channels:

	%
Benue/Plateau	75
Kano	66
Kwara	68
North Central	66
North Eastern	64
North Western	68

Such revenue was statutorily allocated to the Regional Government and the States are likewise assured of their share, but the arbitrary manner in which the Distributable Pool was reallocated under the Decree of 27 May 1967 left most States in considerable deficit.[12] In 1968/9 only Kano State, of the six in the North, budgeted for a surplus (of £1.4m.) while the other five had estimated deficits ranging from £1.3m. (31 per cent of recurrent revenue) in Benue Plateau to £2.9m. (116 per cent of recurrent revenue) in Kwara. Budget statements speak repeatedly of the necessity to maximize local revenue both by making collection more efficient and by seeking new sources, but a realistic appraisal suggests that neither method is likely to lead to a substantial improvement. One alternative source of revenue is the Cattle Tax and Community Tax collected by Native Authorities. In 1966/7 their estimated yield was more than £12m. (compared with an estimated Regional Government revenue, for the same year, from all sources, of £39m.). The Regional Government received 12½ per cent of these taxes but already several State Governments have increased their share to 20 per cent (although this in part might be considered only a financial rectification consequent on the transfer of local courts, police, and prison services from Native Authority control). As revenue collectors, the Native Authorities are regarded as being comparatively efficient and there is a strong possibility that State governments may come to regard them as 'milch cows'—a tendency which would undoubtedly arouse considerable opposition.

A change in the allocation of revenue imposed and collected by the Federal Government is clearly necessary. A Revenue Allocation Review Commission was appointed to make recommendations but these proved unacceptable to several States and were rejected at a meeting of Finance Commissioners held in April 1969.[13] Subsequent negotiations have resulted in a measure of agreement more favourable to States' interests. This should increase very considerably the amount of revenue accruing to the Distributable Pool and provide all States with sufficient revenue to meet present levels of expenditure. Half the Pool is to be divided among the twelve States equally; the other half is to be distributed on the basis of their population. The Federal Government hopes however to take over all revenue from off-shore oil, as was proposed by the Revenue Allocation Review Commission.[14]

(iv) Staff

The staff of the Regional Government has been transferred to the States, apart from a small number employed by the Interim Common Services Agency,[15] and in some instances State administrations have attracted officers from Federal Government employment. Some of the

States are in difficulty, however, for several reasons. First, the staff available is less effectively deployed. Each State has at least seven ministries making a total of more than forty, whereas the Regional Government was organized into fifteen ministries; even so, the Regional Government was understaffed in many of the more important grades. A small number of officers with particular skills and experience now feel their talents are under-utilized in the newly created secretariats. This feeling, coupled with their recognition of the very limited opportunities for promotion, has led to a partial diminution of morale. In other States there is an acute shortage of officers with experience in key fields. Kano State, for example, was launched in April 1968 with at least three ministries (one being that of Finance) headed by civil servants with no previous senior experience in that ministry's area of specialism. 'Surplus' experience in one State is largely inaccessible to the administrations of other States although the Permanent Secretaries of the Ministries of Finance meeting monthly as Directors of the Northern Development Corporation have been able to pool experience and discuss a wide range of matters beyond the scope of their formal agenda, and to a certain extent meetings of the Military Governors and their Secretaries (who in every case act as heads of the State civil services) on the Board of the Interim Common Services Agency have provided another informal channel of liaison and advice.

There is a marked imbalance between States in both the quantity and quality of staff available. On the one hand Kwara, although poor in natural resources and minerals and in a precarious financial position, was not able to absorb all the civil servants indigenous to that State who were available; its administration is now widely regarded as the most competent of the six Northern States. Kano, on the other hand, ostensibly the richest of the six, suffers from major staff shortages and a dearth of experience. The inequalities in the intensity of education over the past two decades and longer have now exacted their toll and since preference in each State in employment and promotion is given to persons of local origin it is the more northerly States which experience the greatest staff weakness. These are precisely the States which contain the most powerful Emirates. They comprise areas which supplied the former Regional Government with few of its more highly trained administrators and there are not many in Native Authority employment suitable for transfer. The greatest shortage is in the higher technical grades, without which the State Governments can scarcely hope to establish any important services of their own or closely control Native Authority administration.

Another effect of the preference given to persons of local origin in employment and promotion is that it will in future be difficult to prevent a situation in which civil servants will be responsible for control and supervision in their own home areas. Hitherto it was a principle in the deployment of all officers, other than the more junior, that this situation must be avoided. Many civil servants now find that their work brings them into close contact with kinsmen and others to whom they owe respect and loyalty. They are more susceptible to pressures and commitments which must derogate from those notions of objectivity and detachment which had in any case gained only limited acceptance amongst many Northern officers. It should be noted that nearly all the new permanent secretaries of ministries are indigenes of their States and that many began their careers in the employment of their own Native Authorities. Nor is this their only area of vulnerability. The absence of any differentiated political structure in the new States, as D. J. Murray has pointed out, has aggravated other difficulties. 'Without a representative system and without politically responsible ministers, the administration has come to occupy an exposed position at the heart of politics.'[16] If competitive electoral politics return, the Native Authorities could provide the foundation for a substantial representative faction, which might even come to form a State Government. In the meantime it would not be surprising if civil servants, faced by a conflict between a State administration and the Native Authorities under its control, should choose to hedge their bets.

It would appear, therefore, that the balance of forces is by no means on the side of the State Governments. The more powerful Emirates may still prove administratively indispensable and politically influential. We are left wondering whether the traditional authorities in the North did not in the end come to the conclusion that the creation of States would perhaps be a lesser evil than the maintenance of 'one North'. They could no longer tame the Regional Government and might have felt confident of being able to tame a State Government nearer home. Was it calculated that, with powers over police, courts, and prisons in State hands, change might be minimized? It is possible that traditional authority in the North has once again embraced change in order to survive.

NOTES

1. THE ETHNIC BACKGROUND TO THE NIGERIAN CRISIS

1. O. Arikpo, 'Who are the Nigerians?', 1957 Lugard Lectures (Lagos, 1958).
2. R. A. Levine, *Dreams and Deeds* (Chicago, 1964), pp. 92–3.
3. M. G. Smith, *Government in Zazzau* (London, 1960), p. 273.
4. P. C. Lloyd, *Africa in Social Change* (Harmondsworth, Middlesex, 1967), Chapter 12.
5. J. S. Coleman, *Nigeria, Background to Nationalism* (Berkeley and Los Angeles, 1958).

2. FROM MILITARY COUP TO CIVIL WAR

1. For an account of pre-1966 political developments see J. P. Mackintosh *et al.*, *Nigerian Government and Politics* (London, 1966).
2. For an account of the coup see W. Schwarz, *Nigeria* (London, 1968), pp. 193–8.
3. Constitution (Suspension and Modification) Decree 1966. See Appendix B, pp. 177–9. It was the Acting President who 'formally invested' General Ironsi. The expression is his own, used in his broadcast of 16 January. There was a meeting on the evening of the 16th of General Ironsi, Commodore Wey of the Navy, Alhaji Kam Salem, the Deputy Inspector General of Police, and seventeen Federal Ministers, which agreed to a military take-over, this being regarded as inevitable. See T. O. Elias, *Nigeria. The Development of Its Laws and Constitution* (London, 1967), p. 457. Text of broadcast is given in Appendix C, pp. 186–7.
4. See Constitution (Suspension and Modification) Decree 1966.
5. The main changes related to the right to legislate on those matters over which the Federal Government and the Regional Governments had had concurrent legislative powers. The Military Governors could not now legislate on these matters except with the prior consent of the Federal Government. Since existing Regional legislation remained in force and since prior consent was not needed for incurring expenditure in such matters, this change did not in practice constitute much of a limitation.
6. The official death roll in the three months October to December was 153. (Federal Parliament *Debates*, 13 January 1966.) It is widely believed that the number killed far exceeded this figure. General Ironsi seemed to expect to have to deal with disturbances in the Tiv Division of Northern Nigeria. The army had already been used to restore order there in February 1964, but the 1964 elections had passed off fairly quietly and a more conciliatory attitude on the part of the Regional Government had made its authority more acceptable. The only area outside the Western Region requiring pacification (before the May disturbances in the Northern Region) was the Yenagoa province of the Eastern Region, where Isaac Boro led a minor insurrection on behalf of the peoples of that area (mainly Ijaw). He was arrested in early March, charged with levying war against the state, and sentenced to death. He was said to have proclaimed that 'the Niger Delta area had been created into a new Peoples Republic distinct from the Federal Republic of

Nigeria'. (*West Africa* [London], 16 April 1966.) He was later reprieved (by Lt-Col Gowon), became a captain in the federal army, and died in action in October 1967.

7. This question is discussed by Mr Luckham in Chapter 3. He also draws attention to the small number of experienced senior officers available for effective military duties.

8. *Daily Times*, 29 January 1966.

9. Ibid.

10. *Morning Post*, 31 January 1966.

11. *Sunday Times*, 13 February 1966.

12. *Daily Times*, 17 February 1966.

13. In the same article criticism was made of Lt-Col Ojukwu, Military Governor of Eastern Nigeria, for appointing his father as chairman of two state corporations. 'The past is too recent for Nigerians to appreciate the choice.'

14. *New Nigerian*, 23 February 1966.

15. *West Africa*, 2 April 1966, p. 391.

16. *West Africa*, 12 March 1966, p. 303.

17. *Official Gazette*, 28 April 1966, p. 730.

18. *West Africa*, 9 April 1966, p. 417.

19. *West Africa*, 16 April 1966, p. 440.

20. *West Africa* commented 'The key group is that responsible for constitutional review since, to a greater or lesser degree, all the recommendations of the other groups must reflect and be affected by the type of constitution it is to have. Yet the constitutional group . . . has an enormous task—it even has to examine the merits of the one-party system. Would this task not be easier if the military government, as it is entitled to do, stated plainly that Nigeria is to be a unitary state, and all discussion should proceed from that?' (2 April 1966, p. 369.) The assumption that the Military Government was entitled to decide such a vital question in this arbitrary manner was not one shared by all Nigerians. This was precisely the difficulty.

21. The Federal Government already had control over the major sources of revenue but a large part of this revenue was redistributed to the Regional Governments on the basis of derivation. The Regional Governments prepared their own Estimates.

22. The Estimates for 1966/7 underline the financial importance of the Regional Governments.

Recurrent account		£m
Federal Government expenditure on own account		107
Federal Government payments to Regional Governments under various constitutional and statutory provisions	£m	
East	22	
North	29	
West	17	
Mid-West	10	
	—	78
Regional Government expenditure		
East	30	
North	37	
West	22	
Mid-West	8	
	—	97

Capital Account		£m
Federal Government expenditure		81
Federal Government capital grants to Regions		16
Regional Government expenditure	£m	
East	19	
North	21	
West	18	
Mid-West	7	
	—	65

23. *West Africa*, 9 April 1966, p. 417. As far as I can discover only one minor change resulted from this meeting. This was the centralization of responsibility for labour questions—a very insignificant part of government activity.

24. See Appendix B, pp. 179–80.

25. In General Ironsi's broadcast, 28 January 1966.

26. Federal Ministry of Information, Press Release, 3 March 1966.

27. See *Daily Times* and *New Nigerian*, 18 and 19 March 1966.

28. A member of the committee has confirmed this. It was common knowledge at the time.

29. This opinion is based on personal observations in Zaria. A detachment of police at first tried to prevent the mob crossing over into the *sabon gari* where most of the southerners lived and traded. They withdrew after about half an hour, and for the next twenty-four hours the mob virtually controlled all traffic. It was only later that the army appeared in the streets. The official death roll in Zaria was 92. The number actually killed is, no doubt, higher and many more were seriously wounded.

30. *Morning Post*, 10 June 1966. The Military Governor in the North, Lt-Col Hassan Katsina, gave his own specific assurances: '. . . no soldier wants to rule . . . the unification Decree is not intended to give advantage to any section of the community. Its aim is to treat all Nigerians alike. But we do realise that it is difficult to treat everybody alike. Some areas are more advanced than others. It is our intention that the National Government should give massive assistance to the less developed areas so that they can catch up as soon as possible with the more developed areas. In this way all fears of domination can be ended and all Nigerians will be able to compete with one another on an honest, competitive basis . . . the Supreme Commander has made it perfectly clear that the measures introduced are interim and temporary until Civilian Administration is once again restored. We in the Army have got a unified command and it is the method we are used to. We believe that if we are to carry on this holding operation, until the return of civilian rule, we have got to work with the methods we are used to. The Supreme Commander has said that this is an interim arrangement merely for the Army to work under methods it is used to. The permanent arrangements for the Government of Nigeria cannot be made without the fullest consultation with the people. As you all know the Government has appointed a number of Study Groups to make recommendations on various aspects of Government. These Study Groups are still working and our decisions on the future of Government and its institutions will depend on the recommendations of these bodies, if they are found to be acceptable to the people. We will not for one moment impose a permanent system which is not acceptable to the majority of the people . . . the National Government intends to give special consideration to the more backward areas. We shall continue special training programmes and introduce new ones so that all areas of the country will continue to be fairly represented in Government Service, Industry and Commerce. More important, the National Government will

pay special attention to the rapid development of education in areas lagging behind. I have pressed this in Lagos and I am glad to say that I have got the support of the Supreme Commander and my colleagues, the other Military Governors . . . neither I nor my colleagues will support any proposal that is aimed against any section of Nigeria. We are working for the country as a whole and we shall not allow sectional interest to deviate us from our task. We shall support merit, but we shall also protect the weak.' *New Nigerian.*

31. *West Africa*, 25 June 1966, p. 728.

32. *West Africa*, 23 July, p. 839, and 30 July 1966, p. 868.

33. One noble gesture deserves mention. The Military Governor of the West, Lt-Col Fajuyi, gallantly regarded himself as host to General Ironsi and in honour bound to share his fate.

34. For example, by Peter Enahoro in *Transition* (Kampala), no. 36, vol. vii (July 1968).

35. There is an important minority of Ibo in the Mid-West and most of the army officers of Mid-West origin were, in fact, Ibo.

36. There were similar but more limited movements on the part of the police.

37. Lt-Col Ojukwu's refusal to recognize Lt-Col Gowon as Supreme Commander was discussed at the only meeting of the Supreme Military Council which Lt-Col Ojukwu attended after July. This was held at Aburi, Ghana, on 4–5 January 1967. There are two verbatim accounts of the Aburi meeting which differ only in minor respects, one published in Lagos by the Federal Ministry of Information, the other in Enugu by the Government Printer. The former will be cited as *Aburi Report* (Lagos), the latter as *Aburi Report* (Enugu).

38. *Aburi Report* (Enugu), p. 20.

39. Ibid., pp. 19–20.

40. Ibid., p. 36.

41. Ibid., pp. 22, 24, 35. The position of Lt-Col Ejoor, the Military Governor in the Mid-West, was not quite so clear. Lt-Col Ojukwu's view of the situation resulting from the July coup was that 'Nigeria resolved itself into three areas— the Lagos, West, North area; the Mid-West area; and the East area'. Ibid., p. 21.

42. See Chapter 5, p. 108–9.

43. No such body existed at the Federal level. Lt-Col Gowon announced in his broadcast of 8 August his intention of appointing a civilian advisory committee. The Mid-West nominated two representatives, but the East flatly refused to do so and the idea was dropped.

44. The terms 'confederation' and 'federation' came to be used very freely, and often without much precision. This needs to be borne in mind when referring to any of the documents. For instance, Switzerland was cited as a confederation, which it is in name but not in practice. I myself define these terms as follows. By *confederation* is to be understood a union of states which expresses the desire to act jointly in certain matters but leaves them with the right to act independently. It is in the logic of a confederation to require unanimous decisions for all joint action, to admit the right to secede, and to meet the costs of the confederation by equal *ad hoc* contributions from member states. A *federation*, on the other hand, assigns an agreed set of powers to a central authority. The right to exercise these powers or to raise the necessary finance does not depend upon the unanimous decision of state representatives and there is no recognized right to secede. Both a federation and a confederation need to be sustained by a continuing desire to act in unison on matters which are of common concern, but in a federation the central authority has an independent right to act in matters previously agreed to

be of common concern, and the exercise of this right is not so strictly dependent on an expression of unanimity.

45. The quotations in this paragraph are from the introductory statements to the proposals submitted by delegates from the Northern and Eastern Regions to the Ad Hoc Constitutional Committee held in the second half of September.

46. I have coined this term for want of a better. It means any group aspiring to assert its cultural and political autonomy.

47. For a more detailed analysis, see Chapter 6.

48. An editorial in *New Nigerian*, 24 April 1967, commented in retrospect that the conference proceedings had been like *Hamlet* without the Prince.

49. The proposals of the various delegations are summarized in Appendix A.

50. In the North a Committee had been set up to make recommendations on these lines, and in the East provincial authorities were established under the Provincial Administration Edict, 1966 (summarized in Appendix B, pp. 180–2).

51. See Appendix A.

52. For text, see Appendix C, pp. 190–5.

53. The third time this had been proposed. The previous occasions were Lt-Col Gowon's statement of 8 August and the communiqué issued by the Supreme Military Council on 15 October—a meeting not attended by Lt-Col Ojukwu.

54. *Nigeria 1966* (Lagos, Federal Ministry of Information, 1967), p. 17.

55. See Appendix D for the draft minutes of the meeting.

56. *Aburi Report* (Enugu), pp. 17–18, 23, 36, 43, 47, 49–50.

57. Lt-Col Ojukwu, for example, declared his belief that Lt-Col Hassan Katsina had 'never ordered anybody to do anything to an Easterner'. *Aburi Report* (Enugu), p. 65.

58. *Aburi Report* (Enugu), p. 45.

59. Draft Minutes of the meeting. See Appendix D.

60. *West Africa*, 21 January 1967, p. 93.

61. *West Africa*, 11 March 1967, p. 357.

62. *Aburi Report* (Enugu), pp. 50–1.

63. Ibid., p. 28.

64. Only five senior officials attended, one from the Federal Cabinet Office, the others from the offices of the four Military Governors, as secretaries, not as advisers.

65. See Appendix D, especially the statement that 'the Council reaffirmed its belief in the workability of the existing institutions, subject to necessary safeguards'.

66. *The Meeting of the Supreme Military Council, Aburi* (Enugu, 1967), p. 38.

67. The Supreme Military Council was asked to decide:

'(a) whether . . . a meeting . . . will not be properly constituted and so cannot be held unless all the Military Governors are present

(b) whether where all the Military Governors are present . . . decisions . . . can properly be taken only with the concurrence or unanimity of all the Military Governors, or by a majority of the Military Governors present or else by a majority of all members present

(c) whether where one or more Military Governors are not present . . . their concurrence in decisions taken at such a meeting will still be necessary before such decisions can be implemented

(d) whether all decrees (whether affecting the whole country or not) are to be formally approved by the Supreme Military Council before they are signed by the Head of the Federal Military Government

(e) in what manner should the concurrence of the Military Governors in the making of Decrees ... be signified, that is ... orally in the course of a meeting ... or by writing ... or ... the appending of their signatures.' Ibid., pp. 47–8.

68. Ibid., pp. 56–64.
69. Ibid., p. 62.
70. Reported in *West Africa*, 14 February 1967, p. 189.
71. *Aburi Report* (Lagos), p. 38. The Enugu version omits Colonel Adebayo's question.
72. *West Africa*, 28 January 1967, p. 126. See also Appendix C, Lt-Col Ojukwu's speech of 26 May 1967, pp. 216 and 220.
73. *West Africa*, 28 January 1967, p. 126.
74. *New Nigerian*, 27 February 1967.
75. See Chapter 5 and Appendix F.
76. Lt-Col Ojukwu visited Lt-Col Ejoor at Benin on 12 March 1967 and met Colonel Adebayo and Lt-Col Ejoor separately on 27 March 1967. *West Africa*, 18 March, p. 361, 1 April, p. 449.
77. *West Africa*, 14 February 1967, p. 189.
78. The Constitution (Suspension and Modification) Decree 1967. *Supplement to Official Gazette Extraordinary*, no. 16, vol. 54, 17 March, A 55–92. It repealed all the earlier Constitution (Suspension and Modification) Decrees issued since 17 January 1966.
79. Section 14.
80. Schedule 2 Section 69 (6), and Section 4 (1), of the 1963 Constitution as modified by Decree No. 8.
81. Section 69 of the 1963 Constitution as modified by Decree No. 8. The Federal Military Government had issued a few Decrees which went beyond federal jurisdiction as laid down in the 1963 Constitution (e.g. the Rent Control Decrees). The Regions were now free, if they so wished, to repeal these Decrees. Their relatively minor importance underlines how little the Federal Military Government had legislated in matters reserved to the Regions before 17 January 1966.
82. Sections 147–50 of the 1963 Constitution as modified by Decree No. 8.
83. Section 111 of the 1963 Constitution as modified by Decree No. 8.
84. Sections 70 and 71 and 86 of the Constitution as modified by Decree No. 8 (italics added).
85. For a statement of Lt-Col Ojukwu's reasons why Decree No. 8 was rejected, see his speech of 26 May 1967, Appendix C, pp. 218–20.
86. *Daily Times*, 13 and 16 March 1967.
87. *West Africa*, 18 March 1967, pp. 361–3 and 389.
88. *New Nigerian*, 14 March 1967.
89. The Eastern Region's Budget for 1967/8 provided for an expenditure of £39m, an increase of £9m over the previous year.
90. See note 22.
91. Revenue Collection Edict, No. 14 of 1967.
92. Another memorandum which came into Lt-Col Ojukwu's hands. *Sunday Times*, 23 April 1967.
93. In his 30 November broadcast, already quoted (p. 34), and in his meeting with the Heads of all foreign missions on 1 March.
94. *West Africa*, 4 March 1967, p. 357.
95. Ibid., 8 April 1967, p. 456.
96. *New Nigerian*, 7 April 1967.
97. *Daily Times*, 5 May 1967. One can only regret such words were not given the weight they deserve.

98. *West Africa*, 1 April 1967, p. 449.

99. *Daily Times*, 14 April 1967.

100. For text of his speech, see Appendix C, pp. 205–10.

101. That is, not since the September 1966 Constitutional Conference.

102. Full text of speech is given in Appendix C, pp. 200–5.

103. *Daily Times*, 3 April 1967.

104. *West Africa*, 15 April 1967.

105. Set out in his address to heads of diplomatic missions on 25 April. See *West Africa*, 29 April 1967, p. 573.

106. See quotation, p. 50.

107. *West Africa*, 29 April 1967, p. 573.

108. Ibid., 6 May 1967, p. 609.

109. *New Nigerian*, 3 May 1967.

110. One of the officers, Lt-Col Olutoye, Area Commander for the West, had earlier made a very strong statement opposing 'regionalization' of the army and expressing his loyalty to Lt-Col Gowon (*West Africa*, 11 February 1967, p. 221).

111. See Major Johnson's letter accepting Mr Jakande's resignation, *Daily Times*, 3 May 1967.

112. *New Nigerian*, 9 May 1967.

113. *New Nigerian*, 2 May 1967.

114. *Daily Times*, 6 May 1967.

115. Chief Awolowo, in his letter of resignation, had denied being in collusion with Lt-Col Ojukwu.

116. *Daily Times*, 6 May 1967.

117. *New Nigerian*, 4 May 1967.

118. *West Africa*, 20 May 1967, p. 673. The Easterners in question were Okoi Arikpo and S. J. Amachree, both from minority tribes and resident in Lagos; invitations had been sent to Sir Francis Ibiam, formerly Governor of the Eastern Region, and to Sir Louis Mbanefo, the Region's Chief Justice, but neither had been able to attend because, it was reported, of the short notice and lack of 'clearance' from the Regional Government (*New Nigerian*, 5 May 1967). See also Lt-Col Ojukwu's speech of 26 May, Appendix C, p. 225.

119. *West Africa*, 3 June 1967, p. 715.

120. For other possible explanations, see p. 109.

121. *Daily Sketch*, 19 May 1967.

122. *West Africa*, 27 May 1967, p. 709.

123. *West Africa*, 3 June 1967, p. 715.

124. For text of speech, see Appendix C, pp. 210–34.

125. For the text of the broadcast, see Appendix C, pp. 234–9. It would seem that the emergency was declared in accordance with Section 70 of the 1963 Constitution as modified by Decree No. 8. This required a declaration of the Supreme Military Council, acting with the concurrence of the Head of the Federal Military Government and of at least three of the Military Governors. The Military Governors of the West, Mid-West, and North had presumably given their assent.

126. States (Appointment of Military Governors) Order 1967. Legal Notice 48 of 1967. He was dismissed on 1 July 1967.

127. *West Africa*, 3 June 1967, p. 716.

3. THE NIGERIAN MILITARY: DISINTEGRATION OR INTEGRATION?

[I wish to thank Professor Morris Janowitz, Professor Edward Shils, and members of the Committee for the Comparative Study of New Nations, the Centre for Social Organization Studies, and the Committee on African Studies of the University of Chicago, as well as Ahmadu Bello University, and the Department of Government, University of Manchester, for assistance in the completion of a longer study of the Nigerian military on which this paper is based.]

1. A. R. Zolberg, 'The Structure of Political Conflict in the New States of Tropical Africa', *American Political Science Review*, vol. lxii, no. 1 (March 1968), p. 72.

2. W. F. Gutteridge, *Military Institutions and Power in the New States* (London, 1964), p. 105.

3. Morris Janowitz and Roger Little, *Sociology and the Military Establishment* (New York, 1965), p. 42.

4. See H. H. Gerth and C. Wright Mills (eds), *From Max Weber: Essays in Sociology* (London, 1948), Chapter 8, and A. W. Gouldner, 'Organizational Analysis', in R. K. Merton *et al.*, *Sociology Today* (New York, 1959).

5. Janowitz and Little, op. cit., pp. 28–38.

6. Emile Durkheim, *Suicide* (New York, 1961), Chapter 5, especially pp. 241–6.

7. M. Ayub Khan, *Friends Not Masters: A Political Autobiography* (London, 1967), pp. 37–8.

8. Peter Blau and W. R. Scott, *Formal Organizations* (San Francisco, 1962), Chapter 6.

9. See C. I. E. Kim, 'The South Korean Military Coup of May, 1961' in J. Van Doorn (ed.), *Armed Forces and Society* (The Hague, 1968), pp. 298–316.

10. Foreword by Major-General Ironsi to *Nigerian Army Magazine*, vol. 3 (December 1965).

11. Temporary (or effective) ranks rather than formally gazetted substantive ranks.

12. See, for example, E. A. Shils and M. Janowitz, 'Cohesion and Disintegration in the Wehrmacht in World War II', *Public Opinion Quarterly*, vol. 12 (1948), pp. 280–315.

13. S. A. Stouffer *et al.*, *The American Soldier* (Princeton, N.J., 1949).

14. Interview of Major Nzeogwu by Dennis D. Ejindu in *Africa and the World*, vol. iii, no. 1 (May 1967).

15. M. J. Dent, 'The Military and Politics: A Study of the Relation between the Army and the Political Process', unpublished paper given to the postgraduate seminar on 'Nigeria: The Politics of Disintegration' at the Institute of Commonwealth Studies, University of London, on 7 June 1967.

16. For elaboration of the concept of cross-cutting ties and the way in which such ties reduce social conflict, see L. Coser, *The Functions of Social Conflict* (New York, 1964), and J. S. Coleman, *Community Conflict* (New York, 1957).

17. Coser, op. cit., p. 77.

18. Lt-Col Hassan Katsina was reported by the *New Nigerian* on 24 May 1966, after coming back from the meeting of the central Executive Council which decided on Decree No. 34 centralizing the country, as saying 'Tell the nation that the egg will be broken on Tuesday. Two important announcements will be made by the Supreme Commander.'

19. For a definition of 'collective behaviour' see N. J. Smelser, *Theory of Collective Behaviour* (New York, 1963). My discussion is heavily influenced by Smelser's most perceptive analysis.

20. *The Struggle for Nigeria* (Lagos, 1967), p. 11.

21. G. Simmel, *Conflict and the Web of Group Affiliations*, trans. K. Wolff and R. Bendix (New York, 1964), p. 43.

22. L. W. Pye in 'Armies in the Process of Political Modernization' in J. J.

Johnson (ed.), *The Role of the Military in Under-developed Countries* (Princeton, N.J., 1962), suggests that the socialization process in military organizations in general is likely to be less traumatic than the processes that are to be found in the unstructured interaction of urban areas. It cannot be said that there is any adequate data to support this hypothesis but the high degree of commitment to military life and values that is encountered among officers (even after the events of 1966) is one possible indicator.

23. K. W. Deutsch, *The Nerves of Government* (New York, 1963), p. 147.

4. THE MILITARY AND THE POLITICIANS

1. A slight but typical example of this attitude was a sentence in a letter which I recently received from a senior figure in the military administration, who wrote that in his younger days he had taken no interest in politics, which he had regarded as 'horrible'—perhaps an attitude towards a fact of life as unrealistic as that of a Victorian spinster towards sex.

2. *Aburi Report* (Lagos, 1967), p. 1.

3. Ibid., p. 12.

4. Lt-Col Gowon disapproved not only of the way in which the military came to power in January 1966 but of the fact that they did so at all. When I mentioned to him rumours that I had heard in Freetown in August 1966 of a possible military coup by younger officers, he expressed vehemently his disapproval of the military taking over civil power. His attitude of total disapproval of the January coup may be motivated partly by the fact that he himself was an intended victim of it and partly by the fact that he was absent from Nigeria during the last disastrous months of civil rule, so that he had no personal experience of the degree of breakdown which the old politicians had produced in the Western Region.

5. The analogy is that applied by Stalin to the Communist Party where its applicability to current practice was not always clear; it is more than ever true of the popular politician in a liberal democracy.

6. Such a link is clearly suggested in both Lt-Col Gowon's speech on coming to power and the Federal pamphlet *Nigeria 1966* (Lagos, 1967). There is clear evidence of a close connection between Ifeajuna and radical UPGA figures, e.g. Ikoku in Ghana.

7. Attitudes towards Nzeogwu among supporters of the Federal cause differ widely; he remains anathema to the old NPC echelons and by 1967 he had become very unpopular with Northern troops at the private and NCO level. On the other hand, many radicals regard his memory with great veneration. Lt-Col Gowon courageously referred to him after his death as a 'gallant but misguided officer' who would be given a military funeral in his native Kaduna— a speech that was not popular with some NPC figures in high places.

8. I quote this not as an example of any supposed 'plot' but of the incorrigible clumsiness of the military mind in delicate matters on the borderline of the political and the administrative.

9. Thus in Gboko in September, when a pogrom of the Ibo did occur and all were killed or driven out, the action was the responsibility of the newly arrived unit of the 4th Battalion and of a motley collection of thugs partly collected by X a former NPC leader at the local level.

10. The light-hearted phrase 'the return match' has often been used in military circles to describe this far from sportive massacre.

11. The estimate of the Easterners, which I published in *The Observer* (London), 9 October 1966, was 'about 200'. The nominal roll of the dead published by the

Eastern Regional Authorities in *January 15th: Before and After* (Enugu, 1967) totals 260, though it is mentioned that there are several more dead whose names cannot be traced.

12. This is the suggestion made in the Eastern Regional publication, *Crisis 1966* (Enugu, 1966), vol. IV, *The Ad Hoc Conference on the Nigerian Constitution*.

13. This is very much the impression that I acquired from an interview with Lt-Col Gowon, which I had the privilege of enjoying in October 1967.

14. British High Commission sources.

15. This came out extremely clearly at a press conference he gave in Ghana which I attended.

16. Paragraph 12 of the Minutes suggests a reversion to the situation prior to 15 January 1966 although perhaps in the sense of the dismantling of excessive measures of centralization adopted since then. (See Appendix D, p. 244.) To the Federal side it also implied the retention of the right of the central government to intervene in a Region during a 'State of Emergency' as provided for under the 1963 Constitution.

17. *West Africa*, 1 April 1967.

18. I am told by a distinguished academic in Zambia that Dr Okpara was particularly bitter about this attitude of Aminu, his old ally.

19. There was some trouble in the barracks in Kaduna in the autumn of 1966. This was rapidly stopped by Lt-Col Hassan Katsina. There was quarrelling between Far North and Middle Belt soldiers about who should be promoted to the post of Chief of Staff; this was ended by the promotion of Lt-Col Akaahan to the post.

20. Iuwa Wada, for instance, has no post in Kano State; he has the courtesy Native Administration title of *Magajin Gari*.

21. Interview with Lt-Col Gowon in October 1967.

22. Information from Chief Morphy, who was at this time in the East and was informed by Dr Azikiwe.

23. Information from H, a senior British civil servant who was in the East until a week before this event.

24. Lt-Col Gowon does, however, appear to be genuinely unwilling to remain in power longer than necessary to complete his job of repairing the land and handing back to civil rule. If he were to continue after that it would have to be as a civilian and not as a military figure and in response to genuine and wide public pressure, operating perhaps on the principle of government once enunciated by Shehu Dan Fodiyo that 'power should only be given to those who do not seek it'.

5. WESTERN NIGERIA AND THE NIGERIAN CRISIS

1. See J. F. A. Ajayi and R. Smith, *Yoruba Warfare in the Nineteenth Century* (Cambridge, 1964).

2. W. H. Riker, *The Theory of Political Coalitions* (New Haven, 1962).

3. A. Rapoport, *Fights, Games and Debates* (Ann Arbor, 1960).

4. See K. W. J. Post, 'The National Council of Nigeria and the Cameroons, the Decision of December 1959' in J. P. Mackintosh *et al.*, *Nigerian Government and Politics* (London, 1966), pp. 405-26.

5. See Alhaji Sir Ahmadu Bello, *My Life* (Cambridge, 1962).

6. Mackintosh, op. cit., *passim*.

7. G. Geertz, 'The Integrative Revolution: Primordial Sentiments and Civil Politics in New States' in C. Geertz (ed.), *Old Societies and New States* (New York, 1963).

8. *Address by His Excellency Colonel R. Adeyinka Adebayo, Military Governor, Western Region, to the Joint Conference of Obas and Leaders of Western Nigeria,* Ibadan, 20 October 1966 (mimeo, 1966).

9. *Ad Hoc Committee on Constitutional Proposals for Nigeria, Verbatim Report,* 21 September 1966 (mimeo, 1966), pp. 13–14.

10. Ibid., 20 September 1966, p. 5.

11. Ibid., 16 September 1966, p. 12.

12. Ibid., 16 September 1966, p. 7.

13. Professors Mabogunje and Ogunsheye, two of Awolowo's supporters, used the analogy of the star-gazing astrologer with reference to those still talking of federation.

14. *Ad Hoc Committee on Constitutional Proposals,* 14 September 1966, p. 5.

15. *Memoranda submitted by the Delegations to the Ad Hoc Committee on Constitutional Proposals for Nigeria* (Lagos, n.d.), pp. 86–96.

16. From notes and directives given by Chief Awolowo to the meeting of the 'leaders of thought' meeting at Ibadan in November 1966.

17. It is not clear from this analogy who was the husband or who the wife, but the reference was clearly to the North and East.

18. *Aburi Report* (Enugu) Appendix F reproduces some of the petitions.

19. This is a claim made by Colonel Adebayo in a number of public statements.

20. See for example Chief Awolowo's 'Flashes of Inspiration' reprinted in L. K. Jakande, *The Trial of Obafemi Awolowo* (London, 1966), p. 354. In Item 6 Awolowo writes 'I thank God Almighty, in advance, for granting the object of my desire' (i.e. the Prime Ministership). The 'Flashes' was a prayer said daily by Chief Awolowo before the 1959 federal election.

6. ENUGU: THE PSYCHOLOGY OF SECESSION

1. *West Africa,* 3 February 1967.

2. The date of the Western Region election.

3. See *January 15th: Before and After* (Enugu, 1967) for a usefully detailed and in many ways accurate account of who was killed and how on 29 July.

4. N. B. Graham Douglas, *Ojukwu's Rebellion and World Opinion* (London, 1967), published by Galitzine, Chant and Russell, public relations consultants to the Federal Government. Although written very much from a Federal Government and Rivers point of view, this contains useful information, especially on the period during which the author was still Attorney-General of the Eastern Region, that is, up to mid-September 1966. 'I did not know whether the name "Biafra" was the original creation of that member of the Executive Committee by whom the suggestion was made or a name adopted by the former politicians when they first threatened secession.'

5. I was subsequently told in Enugu that the 'Young Men' had wanted to attack the barracks to take revenge on the Northerners stationed there.

6. 'Matchet's Diary', *West Africa,* 17 September 1966.

7. Some, such as Wenike Briggs and Harold Biriye, were based in Lagos anyway; others, such as the former Deputy Leader of the Action Group in the East, E. O. Eyo, had been released with others under the general amnesty.

8. I attended a rally in May 1967 at Uyo at which Lt-Col Ojukwu told the story of Major Ekanem's death with great effect on his Ibibio audience (see *West Africa,* 11 May 1967).

9. Mr Akpan himself had a civil servant's distaste for some of the politicians who had emerged in Lagos.

10. A Commissioner in South-East State told me recently that the Annangs, the people of the Ikot Ekpene area, divided fairly evenly into pro- and anti-Biafran camps. Notable sons of Annang, such as Colonel Effiong, commander of the Biafran army, and Mr A. E. Bassey, the politician, sided with Biafra.

11. Great Britain, Cmnd 505 (1958), *Report of the Commission appointed to enquire into the fears of minorities and the means of allaying them.*

12. See Daryll Forde and G. I. Jones, *The Ibo and Ibibio-speaking Peoples of South-Eastern Nigeria* (International African Institute, London, 1950). 'Today the name is used by the people primarily for the language, secondarily for Ibo-speaking groups other than one's own, but with reference to oneself only when speaking to a European.'

13. P. Aumary Talbot, in *Tribes of the Niger Delta* (London, 1932), records of Degema Division that 'the name Ibo has indeed only lately penetrated to this region, the inhabitants of which, although undoubtedly of the same stock as those dwelling further northward, are known among themselves as Ihura-Onhia . . . the Ibo are known to the Kalabrari as Biri'.

14. G. I. Jones, *Chiefs Report* (1957). The report notes, however, along with a certain cultural and social homogeneity, some important differentiations, notably 'a more aggressively democratic temper of the people' among the Ibo (p. 83).

15. U. A. Asika, 'Why I am a federalist', *Transition* (Kampala), no. 36, vol. vii (July 1968), pp. 39–44.

16. J. S. Coleman, *Nigeria: Background to Nationalism* (Berkeley and Los Angeles, 1958). He also stresses the charismatic influence of Dr Azikwe and the influence of American negro ideas of Pan-Africanism.

17. *The Problem of Nigerian Unity* (Enugu, 1966) referred to this: 'Again the NCNC proceeded to allay the fears of the North and to negotiate an entente with the NPC; by so doing it was once more demonstrating to the Action Group that sacrifices had to be made for the accession to independence and for the maintenance of national unity. It was this saving gesture on the part of the NCNC, perhaps more than any single factor, which gave Nigeria a new lease of life.'

18. *Transition*, no. 36.

19. Ibid. Asika argues that a new power group based on traders within the East, as opposed to those who had won success outside the East, was just beginning to find its feet at the time of the January 1966 coup. He also states that from around November and December refugees from the North were in some cases prevented from returning.

20. Cyprian Ekwensi, Chinua Achebe, Francis Nwokedi, Pius Okigbo, Kenneth Dike, to name only a few.

21. Recounted by Peter Enahoro in *Transition*, no. 36, p. 29.

22. Those who harp on ethnic stereotypes should remember that the Southern Dahomeyans (the Yoruba and related Fon and Mina) were the 'Ibo' staffing the civil service of the old French West African Federation (AOF).

23. Lt-Col Gowon said at Aburi: 'Sometimes I feel that my quarrel is not with anyone but the blooming *Outlook* because it has done a lot, honestly . . .' *Aburi Report* (Enugu), p. 95.

24. First shown in the suggestion for a 'temporary confederation' in the foreword of *Thoughts on Nigerian Constitution* (Ibadan, 1966) but expressed more emphatically in his statement of 1 May 1967.

25. Appeared in truncated form in *Daily Times*, 10 November 1966, and in full in *Nigerian Outlook* the same month.

26. There is a curious document, claimed to have been captured in Enugu and shown to the first press party to visit Enugu after its capture by Federal troops,

which purports to describe a conversation between Lt-Col Ojukwu and Philip Alale, one of those shot with Ifeajuna, in which alternative expansionist plans are discussed. In this Alale comes out as favouring broadly speaking a 'Greater South' and Lt-Col Ojukwu a 'fortress Biafra' but stretching to the Benue, which would have meant the conquest of Tiv country. Lt-Col Ojukwu is quoted as saying: 'I cannot see myself offering heaven to the West in order to maintain friendship', and again 'A free Biafra but not at the expense of creating another potentially big West.'

27. The assassination of General Ironsi had made both sides acutely aware of the importance of the person of the ruler. All parties at Aburi returned to Nigeria for the night. Lt-Col Gowon had never spent a night out of Lagos since coming to power. The security in Enugu during Lt-Col Ojukwu's absence was intense.

28. At first seen in continued recruiting, then in declarations, especially those to foreign diplomats in March and April.

29. Criticisms of Lt-Col Ojukwu's saying so much and slanting what he said so strongly in his press conference were widespread on the Federal side.

30. Colonel Adebayo later defended Lt-Col Gowon's failure to make an immediate statement on Aburi on the grounds that he was ill.

31. In Enugu it was even issued as a set of long-playing records.

32. *Aburi Report* (Enugu), p. 12.

33. Rumours of Israeli assistance were current in both Lagos and Enugu at the time, but faded out curiously after secession and the ill-timed and hastily denied claim of the radio that Israel (and five African countries) had recognized Biafra.

34. The NCNC was part of the Federal coalition at that time and the party's complicity in cracking down on the West and in furthering the carving out of the Mid-West from it was considerable. Dr Elias, an old NCNC man, was Federal Attorney-General in 1962 and as such was legal architect of the State of Emergency. In 1967 when he was still Federal Attorney-General his former party colleagues, now in Enugu, thought they recognized his hand in both the memorandum of the Permanent Secretaries and in Decree No. 8.

35. The abortive 'Guitar Boy' coup in Ghana on 17 April put an end to Ghanaian efforts at a vital time.

36. I was myself sent to Enugu in the middle of April so that I should be there when secession was declared. I stayed until the first week of May when I left amid rumours that secession would take place on 15 May.

37. *The Daily Sketch*, containing Chief Awolowo's April statement in full, was selling in Enugu at a shilling a copy.

38. A good example was an article by Michael Wolfers in *The Times* (London), 21 March 1967.

39. Notably Chief R. A. Fani-Kayode, former Deputy Premier of Western Nigeria, author of *Blackism*.

40. *West Africa*, 6 May 1967.

41. 'I respected his intellect and liked him as a man, except of course that he read too much Shakespeare than was good for a Pan-Africanist.' Obi Egbuna on Lt-Col Ojukwu in the pamphlet *The Murder of Nigeria*.

42. Handout issued by the Ministry of Information, Enugu, 1966.

43. Pressure was so great that Sir Louis Ojukwu was forced to resign.

44. Unacceptable to whom? it might well be asked; for this one has to go back to the old argument that it was at the very least the bulk of the Ibo elite, defiance of whose wishes would have been extraordinarily difficult, given, or perhaps because of, the confidence they had in what he was doing.

45. Major Nzeogwu in his interview in *Africa and the World*, vol. iii, no. 1 (May 1967), said he had been against secession. One plan he had repeatedly tried to sell to Lt-Col Ojukwu was for an attack on Kano.

46. The document referred to above—the conversation between Lt-Col Ojukwu and Alale—includes a reference to 'Victor's hidden motives' (an allusion to Lt-Col Banjo who was allegedly involved with Ifeajuna and Alale in the plot which led to their execution).

47. Philip Alale was a Rivers man, trained in Moscow and at Winneba Ideological College, married to a distant relation of Ojukwu. After secession he emerged as 'Political Commissar of the revolutionary wing of Biafra's armed forces' and was eventually shot for treachery in September 1967 with Ifeajuna.

48. *West Africa*, 13 May 1967.

49. Ibid.

7. THE CREATION OF NEW STATES IN THE NORTH

1. *Provincial Authorities: Report by the Commissioner, Mr R. S. Hudson CMG*, (Kaduna, 1957).

2. *West Africa*, 15 October 1966, reports Mr Tarka as one of the members. Benue Province was in fact represented by Mr E. T. Orodi. Most Provinces were represented, as was the Regional Government. Mr S. K. Panter-Brick served as an outside expert.

3. See Chapter 2, p. 32 and Appendix A.

4. *New Nigerian* invited its readers to air their views and several articles were published as a contribution to the debate.

5. Views ranged from the creation of 13 States (there being 13 Provinces) (see *New Nigerian*, 30 December 1966) to the creation of only 3 States (see *New Nigerian*, 7 December 1966). There was some agitation in the southern districts of Zaria Province for a State boundary which would put an end to their administration by Fulani district heads appointed by Zaria Native Authority.

6. J. H. Smith, 'The Creation of State Administrations in the Former Northern Region of Nigeria', *Administration* (Ibadan), vol. ii, no. 3 (April 1968), p. 121.

7. A Delimitation Commission was envisaged by the Decree establishing the States but it has not so far met.

8. The administrative capital of the North Eastern State was at first Bauchi, much to the discontent of the Kanuri, the majority tribe, but was later shifted to Maiduguri.

9. Services provided by the Regional Government tended to be complementary to those provided by the Native Authority, e.g. the hospital service (taken over from the Native Authority in 1962), demonstration farms, secondary education (administered by a separate Education Authority on which the Native Authority is heavily represented). The powers exercised by the Regional Government over Native Authorities were mainly supervisory, default powers, the prescribing of standards and procedures. They were not always effective.

10. Local Authority Law (Amendment) Edict No. 1 of 1969.

11. See Appendix C, pp. 196-200.

12. For details of the Decree see Appendix B, p. 183.

13. *West Africa*, 19 April 1969, p. 453.

14. *West Africa*, 8 November 1969, p. 1327, reports part of this agreement. It is not certain whether the increase in size of the Distributable Pool depends for its implementation upon an agreement on the re-allocation of royalties derived from *off-shore* oil.

15. The Agency, governed by a committee of the six Military Governors of

the States, was established to administer those services which could not immediately be allocated to States or which have been allocated to the Federal Government and could not immediately be taken over. It is interim in concept, its expected life being about five years. It is therefore not responsible for any service with a long-term future. See *Report by the Special Duties Officers' Committee on the Division of Assets and Liabilities of the former Government of the Northern Region and the future of Kaduna Capital Territory* (Kaduna, 1968), Part I, Section III.

16. D. J. Murray, 'Kwara State and its Administration', *Administration* (Ibadan), vol. ii, no. 3 (April 1968), p. 137.

APPENDIX A

THE AD HOC CONSTITUTIONAL COMMITTEE: AN ANALYSIS OF PROPOSALS AND PROGRESS

The Committee met 12–28 September and again 24 October to 1 November. No delegation from the East attended the second session. The Committee adopted as its agenda
(i) consideration of the form of association best suited for Nigeria in the future
(ii) interim arrangements.
Each Region (the West and Lagos jointly) submitted proposals. The North introduced new proposals on 20 September. The Committee sought expert advice on the questions of banking and monetary policy.

After submitting a Progress Report to Lt-Col Gowon on 29 September, the Committee adjourned (officially not until 3 October) to enable delegates to report back to their Regions. In the course of the second session revised proposals were tabled by all delegations.

The views of the various Regions on all major issues are summarized under the following headings:
1. Form of government and component units
2. Head of state
3. Central government
4. Central legislature
5. Judiciary
6. Central civil service
7. Finance (power to raise revenue, the allocation of revenue and national debt)
8. Defence
9. Police
10. External affairs
11. Immigration and emigration
12. Banking, currency, monetary policy, external loans
13. Transport and communications
14. Higher education
15. Concurrent powers
16. Planning (including the equitable distribution of capital investment)

Under each heading will be found:

1. Extracts from the Progress Report (if any)
2. The proposals made by the Regions, distinguishing where necessary (i) original proposal(s) (ii) revised proposal(s)

N.B. The West and Lagos, in their original proposals, set out two alternatives shown here as: (a) first alternative: Federation; (b) second alternative: Commonwealth.

1. *Form of Government and Component Units*

EAST: An Association of the existing Regions, with a right to secede. Opposed to the creation of new states on three grounds: (a) inadequate time: 'will involve a long-drawn-out process of inquiries, commissions and plebiscites, taking up many months or even some years which we cannot afford under the present crises' (b) entails a strong central government: 'not in the interest of harmony and peace of the country to have a strong central government. The splitting up of the country into new states will automatically have the effect of transferring functions which the smaller states cannot be expected to execute with their limited resources. This would, once again, engender inter-regional rivalry and political warfare to control the Centre' (c) fails to satisfy all minorities: 'it is impossible to devise any political arrangement which will be devoid of minority problems . . . these problems can best be contained and satisfied within larger regional units'. 'The points raised above notwithstanding, it should be provided in the future constitution of the country that any Region can agree to split into more States which may be accepted into the future Nigerian association on equal terms as the existing Region if the people of such an existing Region and the areas concerned so desire . . . the initiative for the creation must come from the Region within which the State is to be created.'

MID-WEST: A Federation of the existing Regions, Lagos continuing as Federal Territory or becoming a Region.

N.B. The Memorandum considered a redrawing of the constituent units desirable and set out the following criteria:

(a) ethnic, linguistic, and cultural affinity or homogeneity
(b) historical association (e.g. Hausa/Fulani, Ejik/Ibibio)
(c) viability of states both absolutely and relatively
(d) geographical contiguity
(e) comparability in size
(f) reciprocal self-determination (i.e. not only should each minority group be given the opportunity to determine its future but also a majority group must be given the opportunity to determine whether it is willing to associate with a minority seeking such association).

On the basis of these criteria, twelve states might be created (4 in the North, 2 in the West, 4 in the East, the Mid-West, and Lagos). Although desirable, such a rearrangement was considered impracticable in the prevailing circumstances.

NORTH: (i) *Original proposal.* A Union or Association of the existing Regions, 'and such other States as may be formed subsequently', with a 'right to secede completely and unilaterally'.

The 'right of self-determination of all people in the country must be accepted and a referendum or plebiscite shall be the method through which the wishes of the people concerned shall be ascertained. These rights include the right of any State within the country to secede. But the implementation of these principles shall not delay the determination of the future of Nigeria. All necessary guarantees shall, however, be written in the future constitution to establish the right of self-determination by any section.'

(ii) *Revised proposal.* A Federation with an 'effective Federal government'. The above-mentioned method of creating new states was to be 'discussed and formally adopted'. 'Grave doubts about the wisdom of creating states based on "ethnic and linguistic affinities". In any arrangement based on this principle, there are bound to be large numbers of small pockets of minor ethnic and linguistic groups who will necessarily find themselves grouped uncomfortably with the larger and dominant ethnic groups. Whilst in the past, such tiny tribes were undisturbed within larger units not based on tongues, they are most likely to develop genuine fears of tribal domination in any political arrangement based on the principle of language. Most of the smaller ethnic and linguistic communities have coexisted peacefully without any ill-feelings towards their bigger neighbour only because they and their neighbours belong to a larger political entity.'

'In the exercise of ascertaining the wishes of the people for the creation of States as well as the actual creation of States, no Region except the Mid-West should be left out of the operation.'

WEST: (i) *Original proposal.*

(a) First alternative: A Federation, with 'the immediate creation of more States (including a Lagos State) based on ethnic and linguistic affinities, account being taken also of territorial contiguity and economic viability'. Also 'clear-cut and less cumbersome provision for the creation of additional states in the future under conditions which should be clearly set out in the Constitution'.

(b) Second alternative: A 'Commonwealth comprising the existing Regions and such other Regions as may be subsequently created, with Lagos forming part of the present Western Nigeria'. 'Each State should have a right unilaterally to secede . . . at any time of its own choice.'

(ii) *Revised proposal*. A Federation; 'the creation of more States (including a Lagos State) based on ethnic and linguistic affinities, account being taken also of territorial contiguity and economic viability' was 'strongly recommended'. 'In the event of states not being created, Lagos shall form part of the Western Region.'

2. Head of State

EAST: The Chairman of the central executive body (see 3 below) was to act as Head of State. Annual rotation among the Regions.

MID-WEST: A President, with purely formal powers, rotating among the member States in alphabetical order. Nomination of five persons by the legislature of the State whose turn it is. Election by an electoral college consisting of all members of federal and state parliaments, etc. Also a Vice-President, drawn from the same State in the same way. Five- or six-year term of office.

NORTH: (i) No mention of any Head of State in *original proposal*

(ii) *Revised proposal* copied those of the Mid-West, with minor modifications, e.g. no Vice-President; a four-year term of office; and nominations of three not five persons.

WEST: (i) *Original proposal*

(a) First alternative: Federation. Nothing specified.

(b) Second alternative: Commonwealth. Chairman of the Council of States (see below) to act as Head of State.

(ii) *Revised proposal*. A President with purely formal powers; the office to rotate annually among the Regions.

3. Central Government

EAST: (i) *Original proposal*. An unspecified number of Secretaries of State, each responsible for a number of departments, commissions or agencies. To be paid by the Regions and subject to recall (presumably each Region appointed an equal number; this not specified). Chairman to rotate annually among the Regions.

(ii) *Revised proposal*. A Council of States. Maximum of five members per Region, appointed for a period of four years but still paid by Regions and subject to recall. As in (i) a division of responsibilities and a rotating Chairman.

MID-WEST: An Executive Council consisting of a Prime Minister and not more than 24 Secretaries of State, to be appointed on party lines but so that all Regions are equally represented (i.e. 5 per Region). In addition, not more than eighteen Parliamentary Secretaries. The Prime

Minister to hold office for the life of Parliament (four or five years; no mention of any right of dissolution).

NORTH: (i) *Original proposal.* An Executive Council, its members drawn equally from all States and its Chairman rotating annually.

(ii) *Revised proposal.* A Prime Minister and a Cabinet. The Prime Minister to be nominated every four years in rotation by the States; the State in question to designate one of its federal parliamentary representatives but the person so designated to be approved by the Federal Parliament. The Cabinet to be representative of all States equally, its members to be appointed by the Prime Minister after consultation with State Governments. They were to be *ex officio* Members of Parliament, and, like the Prime Minister, responsible to Parliament. Major issues—to be defined in advance—to be decided by unanimous decision of whole Cabinet.

N.B. The same State could not provide both the President and the Prime Minister.

WEST: (i) *Original proposal*

(a) First alternative: Federation. Nothing specified.

(b) Second alternative: Commonwealth. A Council of States comprising an equal number of delegates from each State. Rotating Chairman. To 'act on all important issues by unanimous agreement of all States'.

(ii) *Revised proposal.* A Cabinet of not more than twenty members known as Secretaries of State, each Region to nominate an equal number from among its representatives in the central legislature: to be paid by the Region and subject to recall. No Region to hold more than one of the following Ministries in any one year: Finance, Internal Affairs, External Affairs, Transport.

All major issues—defined in a schedule to the Constitution—to be decided 'by unanimous vote of the Regions represented'. One of the Secretaries of State to be nominated Prime Minister, the office to rotate annually among the Regions.

N.B. The same state could not provide both President and Prime Minister.

4. *Central Legislature*

EAST: (i) *Original proposal.* A separate legislature, consisting of Regional delegates, subject to recall. All laws to require ratification by regional governments.

(ii) *Revised proposal.* The Council of States (see 3. EAST (ii) above) to act as the legislative body.

'All laws made by the Council shall be consented to by each of the

Regional Governments before they become operative . . . where consent of all the Regions has not been obtained within three months, each Region shall be at liberty thereafter to make its own laws . . .'

MID-WEST: A unicameral Parliament, directly elected for four or five years by universal adult suffrage, each Region having an equal number of seats. 'The place of the Opposition shall be entrenched in the Constitution' (e.g. official salary for its leader; right to choose the business for discussion on certain days). To sit for not less than three-quarters of the year. In a separate memorandum detailed proposals were made for ensuring free and fair elections.

NORTH: (i) *Original proposal.* The Executive Council to legislate, in so far as such legislation was necessary.

(ii) *Revised proposal.* A Parliament consisting of an equal number of members from each State. Members of the first Parliament were to be nominated by State Governments but not subject to recall, the question of future elections being deferred for reconsideration in four years' time.

WEST: (i) *Original proposal*

(a) First alternative: Federation. A Parliament implied: mention only of 'universal adult suffrage, uniform electoral procedure, and the right of political parties to operate throughout the Federation'.

(b) Second alternative: Commonwealth. The Council of States (see 3. WEST (i) (b) above) to have powers to make law, by unanimous decision.

(ii) *Revised proposal.* Unicameral legislature; each Regional Government to nominate thirty members, for four-year term of office but subject to recall and paid by the Region. Chairman to rotate annually among the Regions. Decisions on all major issues—to be defined in the Constitution—by 'unanimous vote of the Regions'.

5. Judiciary

EAST: (i) *Original proposal.* A central Supreme Court; its original jurisdiction limited to suits against the Central Authority and between the Regions; its appellate jurisdiction limited to constitutional matters, including fundamental rights, and such cases as may be specified by regional law. Its members to be appointed 'by the Regions on the basis of equality and the Chairmanship shall rotate annually'.

(ii) *Revised proposal*: Virtually the same.

MID-WEST:

(a) 'The Judicial Service Commission should be revived'

(b) A new Federal Supreme Court, with original and appellate jurisdiction, to consist of a Nigerian President, 'and four Associate Judges . . . drawn from other Commonwealth countries'

(c) A Federal Court of Appeal 'sitting simultaneously and continuously in three-man regional panels'

(d) A code of conduct for all Judges, to be 'embodied in the constitution'.

NORTH: (i) *Original proposal.* 'Each State must have its own . . . Judiciary' with a 'central Court of Appeal'.

(ii) *Revised proposal.* Agreed with Mid-West's proposal for a Federal Court of Appeal, provided it included judges 'learned in Muslim and other customary laws to enable the court to deal with appeals in such laws'.

Disagreement with the Mid-West's proposal for a new-style Federal Supreme Court.

WEST: (i) *Original proposal*

(a) First alternative: Federation. 'Uniform judicial procedures . . . [and] uniform system of penal law throughout the Federation'

(b) Second alternative: Commonwealth. Nothing specified.

(ii) *Revised proposal.* 'There shall be an Appellate Court in each Region from which appeals will lie to the Supreme Court.'

6. Central Civil Service

PROGRESS REPORT:
No agreement.

East and Mid-West: appointments 'on the basis of equality of numbers from the Regions' and 'in making promotions to senior posts regard should, as far as possible in addition to other qualifications, be had to the Region of origin of the candidate'.

North and West: recruitment 'on population basis'.

'The East, in addition, proposes that . . . consideration should be given to the filling of the more senior posts in the Federal Service by secondment from the Regional Public Service.'

EAST: (i) *Original proposal.* 'A Central Public Service Board made up of an equal number of members from the Regions. The Chairmanship of the Board shall rotate annually.' Appointments to the Central Civil Service (and to any commissions and agencies) to be 'on an equal basis among the various Regions'.

(ii) *Revised proposal.* 'A Central Public Service Committee whose function shall be to maintain discipline and determine standards.' 'Appointments of personnel of all grades shall be made on equal basis on the recommendation of the Regions. Equal numbers of senior posts shall be allocated to the Regions, and headships of the various departments, agencies, corporations, or boards shall rotate among the Regions every two years.'

MID-WEST: 'The Public Service Commission shall consist of a Chairman, appointed in his discretion by the President, and one Member each appointed in their discretion by the Regional Governors.' 'Permanent Secretaries shall be appointed by the Public Service Commission but shall be deployed as between ministries by the Prime Minister after consultation with the PSC.'

NORTH: (i) *Original proposal.* A central Public Service Commission. Its responsibilities not specified. Personnel in the common services to 'be employed from the States in proportion to population of each State and ... as far as possible the citizens of each State shall be deployed in their respective States'.

(ii) *Revised proposal.* Recruitment 'on population basis'.

WEST: (i) *Original proposal*
    (a) First alternative: Federation. Nothing specified.
    (b) Second alternative: Commonwealth. 'Staff employed on the operation of the various Common services shall belong to the public service of the State in which they are employed and those employed in foreign legations shall be on secondment from the public service of their State of origin.'

(ii) *Revised proposal.* A federal civil service, but 'Appointments in Federal Ministries within the Federal capital and abroad shall be made on the basis of equality of numbers from the Regions.' 'Staff employed in the operation of Federal Public Service and other services such as the Railway, the Electricity Corporation, Telecommunication, Posts and Telegraphs etc. shall be drawn from the indigenes of the Regions in which the services are located.'

7. *Finance (power to raise revenue, the allocation of revenue and national debt)*
EAST: (i) *Original proposal.* 'Each Region shall keep its revenue and finance the Central Authority by equal contributions.'

(ii) *Revised proposal.* 'The Central Authority shall have no fiscal or taxing powers. All fiscal or taxing powers shall be vested in the Regions. A consultative machinery shall be created for establishing the customs tariff duties and excise duties which should be uniform throughout Nigeria. The Central Authority shall be financed by equal contributions of the Regions.'

'The existing national debt shall be the responsibility of the Regions on the basis of the location of the projects in respect of which the debt was incurred.'

MID-WEST: (i) *Original proposal.* Concurrent powers (instead of exclusively federal) for customs and excise, including export duties, and the Regions to be given exclusive responsibility (in place of the Federation) for mines and minerals, including oil, and all commodity taxes.

(ii) *Revised proposal*

(a) A Commission to be appointed to review and make recommendations on revenue allocation at regular four- to five-year intervals. S. 76 of 1963 Constitution relating to income tax and estate duty to be retained.

(b) A constitutional obligation to provide a federal grant of £2m to any newly created Region, with retrospective effect from 1 October 1960 (i.e. the Mid-West would qualify).

NORTH: (i) *Original proposal.* 'Fiscal arrangements in respect of central sources of revenue should be based on the principle of derivation.'

(ii) *Revised proposal.* (a) the Federation was to retain the exclusive right to raise revenue from mines and minerals, including oilfields, oil mining and natural gas, (b) S. 140 of the 1963 Constitution to be amended. This provides that a Region shall receive 50 per cent of any royalties and rents on minerals extracted from the Region. Minerals include oil. The reference in S. 140 to 'the continental shelf of a Region' said to be a misnomer; the continental shelf belongs to the whole country. The judgment of the US Supreme Court in US v. California 1947 quoted in support. S. 140 to 'be reviewed for a more equitable and proper application of the revenue obtained from minerals extracted from the continental shelf'.

WEST: (i) *Original proposal*

(a) First alternative: Federation. No mention of finance.

(b) Second alternative: Commonwealth. Customs and excise to be a central responsibility. 'Revenue accruing from the exercise of the responsibility of the Council of States, and the operation of the Common Services, shall be allocated to the States on the basis of derivation: but each State shall be required to make an annual subvention in equal amounts to the running of the Council of States and the Common Services.' 'The existing National Debt of the Federation should become the responsibility of the States on the basis of the location of the projects in respect of which the debt, whether internal or external, has been incurred. Any new loan obligations ... shall be met ... by the States ... in direct proportions to the degree of benefit to be derived therefrom by each State.'

(ii) *Revised proposal.* Virtual repetition of proposals under (i) (b).

8. *Defence*

Army

(i) 'There shall be a Nigerian Army which shall be organized in Regional units composed entirely in each Region of personnel indigenous to that Region.'

(ii) 'Operational control of the units in each Region will be the responsibility of the Regional Commander.'

(iii) 'Directions with respect to the maintaining and securing of public safety and public order within the Region or any part thereof may be given to the Regional Commander by the Security Committee in the Region and the Regional Commander shall comply with those directions or cause them to be complied with.'

(iv) 'The composition of the Security Committee will be as follows: the Governor of the Region; the Head of the Regional Government; the Regional Commander; the Commissioner of Police; the Minister in the Region responsible for public order.'

(v) 'Training facilities, Ordnance Depots, and other army stores shall be organized on regional basis. Recruitment shall be the responsibility of the Regional Commander acting in accordance with the policy laid down by the Security Committee.'

(vi) At the national level a Defence Council to be responsible for—

(a) 'laying down military policy which should include the strength of military personnel in each Region, types and quantities of weapons, equipment, minimum standards of recruitment, promotion, discipline, etc.'

(b) 'overall operational control of the Regional units in the event of: external aggression; inter-Regional conflict; and the Regional Security Committee requesting the Council for military assistance to cope with any security situation within the Region beyond the capability of the Regional unit.'

(c) 'the control of defence industries.'

(vii) The Defence Council to consist of: the Head of the State of Nigeria; the Head of the Central Government; the Heads of the Regional Governments; the Chief of Staff; Regional Commanders; Minister of Defence.

(viii) The office of Chief of Staff to be held in rotation by the Regional Commanders for fixed periods not exceeding twelve months.

(ix) The Defence Council to be served by a Defence Secretariat under the Chief of Staff. The personnel of the Secretariat to be drawn from Regions in equal numbers.

Navy and Air Force

Same arrangements as for the Army with the expansion of the Defence Council to include the Regional Commanders of the Navy and the Air Force.

'The *Federal Capital* shall be garrisoned in rotation for fixed periods by personnel drawn from the units of one Region at a time. (Northern Delegation reserves its position.)'

EAST: (i) *Original proposal.* 'War cannot be declared, nor peace concluded, without the consent of every Region.' 'All the armed forces . . . shall be regionalised. For the purposes of external defence, each of the Regions shall contribute part or all of its Army as occasions demand. Suitable coordination arrangements shall be worked out.'

(ii) *Revised proposal.* As in the Progress Report, with some additions and amendments:

(a) Defence Council to consist only of the Head of State, Heads of the Regional Governments and the Chief of Staff Armed Forces

(b) the Head of State and the Chief of Staff Armed Forces should not come from the same Region

(c) the Heads of Department in the Defence Secretariat should rotate annually

(d) Lagos to be garrisoned by the Region which is providing the Head of State (annual rotation)

(e) Financing of the Armed Forces to be a Regional responsibility.

MID-WEST: (i) *Original proposal.* Federal responsibility. Federal Army with Regional Units.

(ii) *Revised proposal.* As in Progress Report with additional stipulation that the Defence Council should have overall operational control of the Armed Forces in periods of emergency and in the event of any hindrance to the proper exercise of federal authority. It was proposed that Sections 70, 71, and 86 of the 1963 Constitution, which relate to such periods of emergency, should be brought together and reformulated as follows:

'. . . any period during which there is in force a resolution of Parliament, supported by the votes of not less than two-thirds of all the members of the House, declaring that:

(a) the Federation is at war;

(b) there exists a grave threat to the security of the nation;

(c) democratic institutions in Nigeria are threatened by subversion;

(d) the executive authority of a Region is being so exercised as to impede or prejudice the exercise of the executive authority of the Federation or to endanger the continuance of Federal Government in Nigeria;

(e) the continuance of Federation is endangered otherwise than by the exercise of the executive authority of a Region;

(f) law and order has broken down in any territory of the Federation'.

NORTH: (i) *Original proposal.* Each State to have its own Army and Air Force. The Navy to be 'composed of personnel in proportion to the population of each State'. Obligation to defend the country against external aggression. 'Where there is any internal trouble within a State which its forces cannot put down, the State concerned may ask the Central Executive Council to approach the other States to assist.'

'A Central Defence Commission or a similar body should be created to eliminate the danger of an arms race within the association. The Commission should have a civilian head and should not obtain external military aid without the unanimous agreement of all the States. Heads of State Forces should be included in the membership of the Commission.'

(ii) *Revised proposal.* As in Progress Report, but

(a) Defence Council to be enlarged to include the Inspector General of Police.

(b) Lagos to be garrisoned by personnel drawn from units of all States, with separate barracks for each unit.

9. *Police*

PROGRESS REPORT:

'(1) There shall be a Nigeria Police Force which shall be organised in Regional units composed entirely in each Region of personnel indigenous to that Region.

(2) The operational control of the units in each Region shall be the responsibility of the Regional Commissioner of Police.'

N.B. There was some disagreement on the right of the Regional Government to give directions to the Regional Commissioner as follows:

'Directions with respect to the maintaining and securing of public safety and public order within the Region or any part thereof may be given to the Regional Commissioner of Police by the Head of the Regional Government and the Regional Commissioner shall comply with those directions or cause them to be complied with; provided that before carrying out any such directions which may involve the use of arms the Commissioner may request that the matter should be referred to the Police Council for their directions'.

The East proposed that the words 'Police Council' should be replaced by the words 'Regional Security Committee' in order to bring it into line with the corresponding arrangement in the case of the Army.

The Mid-West reserved its position on the clause 'which may involve the use of arms'.

'(3) Training facilities, depots and stores shall be organized on a Regional basis. Recruitment shall be the responsibility of the Regional Commissioner of Police acting in accordance with the policy laid down by the Regional Government.

(4) At the national level there shall be a Police Council which shall be responsible for—

(a) Laying down general policy which should include the strength of police personnel in each Region, types and quantities of equipment, weapons, minimum standards of recruitment, promotion, discipline, etc.;

(b) overall operational control of the Regional units in the event of the Regional Governments requesting the Council for Police assistance to cope with any actual or threatened security situation within the Region beyond or likely to be beyond the capability of the Regional unit; provided that a Regional Commissioner with the consent of the Head of the Regional Government may request the Commissioner of another Region for police assistance in an urgent situation and that such a request shall not be granted or refused except with the approval of the Head of the Regional Government concerned.'

N.B. There was slight disagreement on the composition of the Police Council. There was general agreement that it should include: the Head of the Federal Government; Heads of the Regional Governments; the Inspector-General of Police; Regional Commissioners; the Minister responsible for police matters.

The North proposed in addition the Chairman of the Public Service Commission.

There was also disagreement on the terms of office of the Inspector-General of Police. 'The East and West propose that the Office of the Inspector-General of Police shall be held in rotation by the Regional Commissioners of Police for fixed periods not exceeding twelve months. The North and Lagos propose a period of three years and the Mid-West proposes that this should be held on permanent basis.'

'(5) The Police Council shall be served by a Secretariat under the Inspector-General of Police. The personnel in the Secretariat shall be drawn from the Regions in equal numbers.

(6) Five years after the new Constitution has come into effect, all local authority police forces shall cease to exist, and in the meantime there should be a progressive reduction in those local authority forces.'

EAST: (i) *Original proposal.* 'The police shall be regionalised.'

(ii) *Revised proposal.* As in Progress Report.

N.B. (a) the office of Inspector-General of Police to rotate among the Regions at least once a year

(b) the Regional Commissioner of Police to comply with *all* directions given by the Regional Government

(c) no mention made of any Minister responsible for police matters, i.e. at the centre

(d) police to be financed by the Regions.

MID-WEST: (i) *Original proposal.* Federal responsibility.

(ii) *Revised proposal.* As in Progress Report, but more precise formulation of the reservations concerning the power of a Regional Government to give binding directions to the Regional Commissioner of Police; this acceptable only 'if it is agreed in what circumstances the Premier may give such directions or what directions a Premier may lawfully give'. Additional stipulation that the Police Council have overall operational control for the purpose of S. 70, 71, and 86 of the 1963 Constitution (see above, p. 164-5).

N.B. Post of Inspector-General of Police to be a permanent appointment.

NORTH: (i) *Original proposal.* Each State to have its own Police.

(ii) *Revised proposal.* As in Progress Report.

N.B. (a) Chairman of the Public Service Commission to be included on the Police Council.

(b) Inspector-General of Police to be appointed for a period of three years.

WEST: (i) *Original proposal.* Each State to establish and control its own Police.

(ii) *Revised proposal.* As in Progress Report except:

(a) a Regional Commissioner disagreeing with any direction given him by the Head of the Regional Government could request that the matter be referred to the Regional Security Committee for its direction

(b) Police Council to be able, when necessary, to call for expert advice from the Ministry of Establishments

(c) Office of Inspector-General of Police to be held by the Regional Commissioners of Police rotating annually.

10. *External Affairs*

PROGRESS REPORT:

No unanimous agreement reached. The West, Mid-West and Lagos proposed that External Affairs should be the responsibility of the Central Authority. The East agreed subject to the following four provisos:

'(i) Appointments to foreign Missions and appointments within their establishments should be on a quota system based on equality of representation among the Regions, as has been suggested by the East, and the Mid-West Delegations in the case of item 36: "Public Service of the Federation".

(ii) All diplomatic and consular posts in the United Nations Organization, the Organization of African Unity, and in foreign and Commonwealth countries, should be held in rotation for fixed periods, as stated below, by suitable indigenes of the member Regions of Nigeria:

Head of Mission	2 years
Head of Chancery ⎫	
Counsellor ⎬	3 years
Heads of Division ⎭	
Other Staff	4 years

(iii) The following Missions, namely, London, Washington, United Nations, New York, Bonn, Paris, Brussels, Rome and Moscow, should not be headed at the same time by more than two indigenes of any one Region, and any Region that has within the preceding twelve months had one of its indigenes as Head of Mission to one of these countries should not immediately be allowed to have another representative from such a Region to head such a Mission.

(iv) The Regions shall have power to enter into treaties and agreements with foreign powers in the interest of trade and commercial development of the Region; any Region that so desires may appoint a commercial attaché or counsellor to a Nigerian Mission abroad.'

The North proposed that External Affairs should be the responsibility of the Central Authority subject to (ii) and (iii) above. The Mid-West reserved its position on (i) and the first sentence of (iv).

EAST: (i) *Original proposal*. Responsibility of the Central Authority but Regions could 'enter into treaties and agreements in the interests of' trade and economic development'. Regions also to have effective control over issue of passports and over immigration.

(ii) *Revised proposal*. Exclusive responsibility of the Central Authority subject to the four provisos as set out in the Progress Report.

MID-WEST: (i) *Original proposal*. Federal responsibility. A 'revised procedure to safeguard Regional interests' for immigration and emigration.

(ii) *Revised proposal*. Exclusive responsibility of the Federation, 'provided that appointments to Nigerian Missions abroad and appointments within their establishments should be on a quota system based on equality of representation among the Regions; and provided that any region that so desires may appoint a Commercial Attaché or Counsellor to a Nigerian Mission abroad'.

The provisions of the 1963 Constitution relating to implementation of treaties and to external and inter-regional trade and commerce to be retained. (S. 74 and S. 77).

NORTH: (i) *Original proposal.* Responsibility delegated to the Central Authority but subject to unilateral withdrawal by State Governments.

(ii) *Revised proposal.* Exclusive responsibility of the Federation, subject to all four provisos as set out in the Progress Report, except that appointments to foreign Missions should be distributed among the Regions on the basis of their population (instead of equally).

WEST: (i) *Original proposal*

(a) First alternative: Federation. Nothing specified.

(b) Second alternative: Commonwealth. Responsibility delegated to the Council of States but each State retained the right to enter into direct relations with foreign countries and international institutions, to exchange diplomatic and consular representatives and to conclude treaties; in short, concurrent responsibilities. 'A State shall be able to enter into foreign exchange commitments only to the extent of its own foreign exchange reserves.' Appointments to be shared among the States equally, and posts to be 'held in rotation for fixed periods of one or two years at a time by suitable nominees of the member States'.

(ii) *Revised proposal.* Exclusive responsibility of the Federation subject to the provisos set out in the Progress Report, with very minor modifications.

11. *Immigration and Emigration*

PROGRESS REPORT:

The Central Authority to have responsibility for: (a) 'Immigration, including visas, provided that visas and entry permits shall be issued if requested for by a State government and provided further that there shall be a branch of the Immigration Office in each Region.' (b) 'Emigration, including passports and travel certificates, provided that passports and travel certificates shall be issued to Nigerian citizens as of right to all parts of the world and provided further that there shall be a branch of the Passport Office in each Region.'

EAST: (i) *Original proposal.* The Central Authority to control immigration and issue passports and visas provided

(a) 'the Central Authority shall issue passports to Nigerian citizens only on the recommendation of the State of origin of the applicants'

(b) 'no foreigner shall be admitted into a State without the approval of that State and no foreigner permitted to enter a State shall be prevented from doing so by the Central Authority.'

(ii) *Revised proposal.* As in Progress Report but the proviso (i) (b) above maintained.

MID-WEST: (i) *Original proposal.* Exclusively a federal responsibility 'with revised procedure to safeguard Regional interests'.

(ii) *Revised proposal.* As in Progress Report.

NORTH: (i) *Original proposal.* Delegated to Central Authority.

(ii) *Revised proposal.* As in Progress Report.

WEST: (i) *Original proposal.* Nothing specified except that in the second alternative, i.e. a Commonwealth, 'each State shall be empowered to issue visas and entry permits'.

(ii) *Revised proposal.* As in Progress Report.

12. *Banking, Currency, Monetary Policy, External Loans*

PROGRESS REPORT:

All Regions, except the East, accepted the report of the Committee of Experts, which had been asked to make recommendations 'to enable each State to borrow abroad, issue its own bills of exchange and promissory notes, and to play an effective part in determining the monetary policy of the nation'. This Committee had reported as follows:

(i) *External loans* '. . . to give unfettered freedom to the Regions to borrow directly from abroad will not be consistent with maintaining a common currency, a common pool of exchange reserves and a single market for the projects for which the borrowings are to be used . . . implicit in the Federal Government's interest in loans contracted by the Regions is the need to assure foreign investors that an independent and sovereign Government with recognised international status is a party to loan agreements.

Nevertheless the Committee is of the view that some machinery should be evolved wherein Regional Governments participate fully in matters relating to the borrowing of monies. To this end we recommend the setting up of a Loans Council under the Constitution to be charged with the following functions:

(a) to receive and coordinate requests for loans submitted by the various Governments;

(b) to consider offers of loans made by foreign governments and International Financial Institutions;

(c) to determine the allocation of loans among the Governments, and to recommend accordingly, provided such recommendations shall normally be accepted by the Federal Government.

The intention is that the functions of the council shall embrace not only external loans (including Contractor-Finance and Suppliers' Credit) but also internal loans and that its recommendations shall not lightly be set aside.

We further recommend that the membership of the Loans Council shall be as follows:

(a) Governor of Central Bank (Chairman)

(b) A representative of the Central Bank, and two representatives of each Government who shall be experts in financial and economic matters.

On the question of procedure for arriving at major decisions, it was the majority view of the committee (the Eastern Regional Representatives dissenting) that such decisions shall be by two-thirds majority. It was the view of the Eastern Delegation that the Council's decisions shall be by unanimous vote.'

(ii) *Bills of exchange and promissory notes*

'Since [these] are credit instruments, we recommend that responsibility for their regulation by legislation should continue to rest with the central authority'

(iii) *Monetary policy*

'... the committee recommends that the determination of monetary policy should be entrusted to a high-powered ministerial body consisting of Finance Ministers presided over by the Federal Minister of Finance ... underpinned by a technical committee of officials and non-official experts'

(iv) *Overall economic policy*

'... monetary policy [is] closely related to other aspects of overall economic policy ... it is our hope that the possibility of setting up a high-powered body for the coordination of overall economic policy will not be overlooked. In this connection the Eastern Regional representatives disagreed with the reference to the "overall economic policy" of the country in view of the necessity for each component part to develop according to its own pace and in accordance with its own resources ... the committee considered an alternative arrangement whereby each Region is able to exercise some freedom with regard to monetary policy within its own area, such as issuing its own currency backed by its own reserves. It noted that such an arrangement would lead to different degrees of acceptability of the various currencies both internally and externally. In consequence, this would lead to restrictions of trade and payments among the Regions and also to difficulties in pursuing common policies on trade and payments with the outside world.'

N.B. The East reserved its position on the specific recommendations made in (i) and (ii).

EAST: (i) *Original proposal.* 'It is obvious that in Nigeria there exist pronounced regional differences in economic attitude, resource endowment and capacity to design and implement development plans. It is necessary therefore, to devise a monetary policy control system which, while providing a basis for monetary cooperation . . . at the same time ensures that the peculiar monetary requirements originating from regional variations in economic and financial conditions are satisfied.'

This to consist of Regional central banks; regional currencies which would be legal tender throughout Nigeria; a central Board of Governors to ensure that Regional Central Banks maintain adequate reserves and to control variations in regional rates of discount; Regions to be solely responsible for exchange control, borrowings from abroad (within a fixed limit), control of capital issues, and, in co-operation with the central authority, for bills of exchange, promissory notes, and currency.

(ii) *Revised proposal.* Highly critical of the Committee of Experts' Report. No new proposals.

MID-WEST: (i) *Original proposal.* A federal responsibility; but (a) a Region should be able to borrow up to four times its estimated revenue for the Development Plan period (b) control of capital issues to be a concurrent federal and regional power.

(ii) *Revised proposal.* Report of Committee of Experts accepted. Favoured retention of provisions of 1963 Constitution relating to Banks and Banking (S. 78).

NORTH: (i) *Original proposal.* Currency and central banking delegated to the Central Authority.

(ii) *Revised proposal.* Report of Committee of Experts accepted.

WEST: (i) *Original proposal*
   (a) first alternative: Federation. Nothing specified.
   (b) second alternative: Commonwealth. Delegation to the Council of States of responsibility for currency and central banking, 'excluding exchange control but including Bills of Exchange and Promissory Notes'.

(ii) *Revised proposal.* Agreed that the Federation should continue to have exclusive legislative responsibility for
   (a) bills of exchange and promissory notes
   (b) borrowing of moneys for the purpose of the Federation and borrowing outside Nigeria for the purpose of any Region
   (c) control of capital issues
   (d) currency, coinage and legal tender
   (e) exchange control

The recommendation of the Committee of Experts concerning the Loans Council amended slightly.

13. *Transport and Communications*

PROGRESS REPORT:

(i) Aviation, postal services, railways and meteorology: the responsibility of the central government but a Regional Government could 'establish and maintain' such services 'either by itself or through any person or authority' (this did not include the power to print postage stamps, etc.).

(ii) Highways: central government responsibility for the 'construction, alteration and maintenance of such highways as may, with the consent of all the Governments of the Regions, be declared by Parliament to be Federal Highways'.

(iii) Shipping and navigation (in tidal waters, international and interregional waterways): the responsibility of the central government as under 1963 constitution.

(iv) Ports: the central government should be responsible for 'existing ports and such new ports as may, with the agreement of the Regional Government concerned, be declared by Parliament to be Federal ports' (the East reserved its position).

(v) Wireless, broadcasting and television: the responsibility of the central government except for that 'provided by, or at the instance of, the Government of a Region'. Central responsibility for allocation of wavelengths (the East reserved its position).

EAST: (i) *Original proposal.* The Central Authority to have legislative and executive responsibility for

(a) safety of aircraft and aviation standards

(b) 'coordination' of meteorological, postal and railway services; also maintenance of existing railways

(c) navigation on the River Niger

The following were to be placed under commissions or agencies: existing ports and shipping lines; existing Nigerian airways; coordination of postal services; coordination of railways, external communications.

(ii) *Revised proposal.* The Central Authority to have responsibility for

(a) Laying down of standards for safety of aircraft, maritime shipping and for navigation on tidal waters, the Niger, etc.

(b) Coordination of railways, meteorological and postal services (including the designing of postage stamps).

MID-WEST: (i) *Original proposal.* Concurrent federal and regional powers with respect to civil aviation, meteorology, postal services, trunk roads and broadcasting. Exclusive federal responsibility for railways and the allocation of wavelengths.

(ii) *Revised proposal.* As in Progress Report.

NORTH: (i) *Original proposal.* 'Common services' for airways, civil aviation, shipping, railways, ports, waterways, postal services and telecommunications. The Niger Dam to remain under Central Authority.

(ii) *Revised proposal.* As in Progress Report, except (a) ports. 'In order to ensure that no state will be legally able to hold the rest of the country to ransom . . . the agreement of the Region . . . should not be made a condition precedent for declaring a port as a federal port.'

(b) meteorology: 'where a state intends to establish and maintain its own meteorological service, the consent of the Federal Government should first be obtained'.

WEST: (i) *Original proposal*

(a) First alternative: Federation. Nothing specified.

(b) Second alternative: Commonwealth. The Council of States to have responsibility for airways, maritime shipping, ports, harbours, railways and postal services (including savings banks). Their administration could be in the hands of Commissions: states would be represented equally; 'decisions on all major issues shall be by unanimous agreement of all States'; and 'the chairmanship shall be rotational from year to year'.

(ii) *Revised proposal.* As in Progress Report.

14. *Higher Education*

PROGRESS REPORT:

No agreement. The North, the West and Lagos, and the Mid-West proposed no change from existing arrangements, i.e. the Federal and Regional Governments have concurrent powers, but the Federal Government has exclusive responsibility for eight named institutions of higher education (all located in either the West or Lagos, except for one in the North). The East wanted higher education to be exclusively a regional responsibility.

EAST: To be a regional responsibility.

MID-WEST: Concurrent powers. Had *initially proposed* that the Federal Government should have 'responsibility for laying down uniform standards'.

NORTH: Had *initially proposed* that higher education was to be a regional responsibility. *Agreed subsequently* to maintenance of existing arrangements, with the recommendation that 'conscious effort should be made however that staff and student population in [the federal] institutions come from all the States' and that 'in view of the close proximity of the two teaching hospitals in Lagos and Ibadan . . . one of them should be transferred elsewhere'.

WEST: Not made clear in the *revised proposals* whether the Federal Government was to continue to have exclusive responsibility for the eight named institutions.

15. Concurrent Powers

PROGRESS REPORT:

The Mid-West, North, West and Lagos agreed to retain a list of powers which the central government and regional (or state) governments could exercise concurrently. Twenty-five of the twenty-nine items on the list as set out in Part II of the Schedule to the 1963 Constitution were retained. The East reserved its position 'on the ground that they should all be Regional subjects since, in its view, the concurrent list is a source of friction'.

EAST: In its *revised proposals*, after a list on matters for which a central authority was to have responsibility, it was stated

'For the avoidance of doubt, all subjects or matters not listed . . . including those on the Concurrent Legislative List or elsewhere in the 1963 Constitution . . . shall be vested in the Regions.'

WEST: In its *revised proposals*, after the list of concurrent powers, it was stated

'(a) The powers of the Central or Federal Parliament shall NOT include powers

(i) to prohibit or restrict any State or Regional Legislature from making laws with respect to the same matters . . .

(ii) to impose either directly or indirectly any charge or other obligation upon the [finances] . . . of a State or Region . . . EXCEPT with the prior consent of the Government of that State or Region

(b) No conflict or inconsistency shall be held or deemed to exist or arise as between a central or Federal law . . . and a State or Regional Law . . . unless with respect to the same specific subject matter, and to the extent that

(i) the former EXPRESSLY prohibits an act or omission which the latter EXPRESSLY permits or vice versa or (ii) it is otherwise impossible to comply with the one without disobeying or contravening the other.'

It was added that 'functions, ADDITIONAL to but not in lieu of those conferred or imposed by any central or Federal law', were not to be considered inconsistent.

16. *Planning (including the equitable distribution of capital investment)*
EAST: No specific mention.

MID-WEST: (i) *The initial memorandum* referred to the neglect of the Mid-West and listed a number of specific grievances, e.g. no army barracks, no broadcasting station, no automatic dialling telephone exchange; 'failure to develop the natural resources of the Mid-West' (in particular gas, sugar cane, gin, and rubber industries); 'federal trunk roads in the Mid-West are in worst state of disrepair in the entire Federation'.

(ii) *A subsequent memorandum* on 'Federal Agencies and Industries' drew attention to the imbalanced location of existing educational and agricultural establishments, and of industries established with federal assistance. It proposed that

(a) new Federal educational institutions and federally financed industries 'should be evenly distributed among the Regions'

(b) a Federal Industrial Development Corporation should be established 'for the purpose of stimulating industrial development at the national level, of ensuring a just and equitable distribution of federally financed industries, and of attracting private industries to less developed areas of the country in cooperation with Regional authorities'.

NORTH: The memorandum setting out the *revised proposals* refutes the argument that Lagos has been neglected. It also recommended the transfer 'elsewhere' of one of the two teaching hospitals (located in Ibadan and Lagos).

WEST: The *initial proposal* for a Federation recommended:

(a) 'A National Planning Commission which should be charged with the responsibility for planning the over-all economic development of the Nation in a manner that would ensure full employment and a fair distribution of economic projects throughout the country'

(b) 'Provision under the Constitution of machinery which will ensure the equitable distribution of resources and amenities, and the location of Federal Government sponsored industries among the States.'

APPENDIX B

A SUMMARY OF THE MORE IMPORTANT DECREES (JANUARY 1966 TO MAY 1967)

1. *The Constitution (Suspension and Modification) Decree 1966. Decree No. 1*

Dated 17 January 1966 but not published in the *Official Gazette* until 4 March 1966.

It suspended various sections of the 1963 Constitution and modified others.

It had the following effects:

(i) All parliamentary institutions, both federal and regional, were suspended

(ii) Certain executive offices, e.g. those of the Federal President, the Regional Governors, the Federal and Regional Ministers, were suspended

(iii) The Federal Military Government was given 'power to make laws for the peace, order and good government of Nigeria, or any part thereof with respect to any matter whatsoever'

(iv) The Regional Military Governors were given similar powers within their Regions but

(v) The Exclusive and Concurrent Legislative Lists were maintained and Regional Governors could not make any law with respect to any matter included in the Concurrent Legislative List without the prior consent of the Federal Military Government. The Regional Governors could however incur expenditure on any such matters without prior consent

(vi) The validity of any Decree or Edict (laws made by the Federal Military Government and by the Regional Governors) could not be challenged in any court of law

(vii) The executive authority was vested in the Head of the Federal Military Government

(viii) The executive authority in the Regions was delegated to the Regional Governors (but could be revoked at any time)

(ix) A Supreme Military Council was established consisting of
   the Head of the Federal Military Government (President)
   the Heads of the Army, of the Navy and of the Air Force
   the Chiefs of Staff of the Armed Forces and of the Army

the four Military Governors
the Federal Attorney-General
(The Attorney-General ceased to be a member except in an advisory capacity under the Constitution (Suspension and Modification) (No. 4) Decree of 1 April 1966.)

No particular functions or powers were vested in the Supreme Military Council. It acted in practice as a collective policy-making body

(x) A Federal Executive Council was established consisting of
the Head of the Federal Military Government (President)
the Heads of the Army, of the Navy, and of the Air Force
the Chiefs of Staff of the Armed Forces and of the Army
the Federal Attorney-General
the Inspector-General of the Police, and his deputy

The four Regional Governors were added by the Constitution (Suspension and Modification) (No. 4) Decree of 1 April 1966. This body acted as the Federal Government, assisted by the Permanent Secretaries of the various Ministries

(xi) An Advisory Judicial Committee was established consisting of
the Chief Justice of Nigeria (Chairman),
the Chief Justices of the four Regions and of Lagos,
the Grand Kadi of the Sharia Court of Appeal (the Muslim Court in the Northern Region),
the Federal Attorney General
This body advised on judicial appointments.

N.B. This Decree gave retrospective legal effect to arrangements worked out in practice over the preceding weeks. They are to be compared with those originally set out in the early unpublished 'Memorandum on the Organisation and Functions of the Supreme Military Council and the Federal Executive Council'. The Chiefs of Staff were not included. The Supreme Military Council was given responsibility for 'the maintenance of law and order and good government throughout the Federal Republic of Nigeria' and for 'defence and security matters'. It was served by three committees, for defence, security, and 'orientation'. The function of this last-named committee was 'to educate the public and project the image of Nigeria'. The Federal Executive Council was to 'perform the functions exercised by the former Council of Ministers', assisted and advised by a 'coordinating Committee of Officials consisting of Permanent Secretaries in key Ministries such as Finance, Economic Development, Trade, Industries etc.' Of particular interest is the reference in this memorandum to the Regions. It states that Regional Executive Councils 'will be subordinate to the Federal Executive Council' and that 'all Military-Government Budgets will be submitted by the Military Governors to the Head of the Federal Military Government and Supreme Commander of the Armed Forces for prior approval before expenditure is incurred'.

2. *The Constitution (Suspension and Modification) (No. 2) Decree 1966. Decree No. 14*

This decree gave the Federal Attorney-General power 'to institute and undertake criminal proceedings in respect of any offence created by any law in force in Nigeria or any part thereof'. Like Decree No. 1 it came into force on 17 January, although not published in the *Official Gazette* until 14 March. It is the counterpart, in the judicial field, of the centralization of administration under Decree No. 1.

3. *Public Order Decree 1966. Decree No. 33*

Dated 24 May 1966, it dissolved eighty-one political associations and twenty-six tribal and cultural associations.

The formation of any new association 'of three or more persons', having 'a political cause or objective' identical or similar to that of any of the proscribed associations, was prohibited for the next three years (penalty: not less than five years' imprisonment). No person was to take part in any meeting of such an association 'whether or not such meeting takes place in public or in private premises' (penalty: not less than two years' imprisonment). Any authorized police officer could enter and search any house, etc., where there was 'reason to believe that a meeting was being held'. The display of signs (flags, insignia, emblems) of any proscribed associations was prohibited, as was the shouting of any 'political slogan, political name or nick-name' and 'any procession of three or more persons which, in the opinion of [the police], is of a political nature . . .' (penalty: not less than three years' imprisonment).

4. *The Constitution (Suspension and Modification) (No. 5) Decree 1966. Decree No. 34* (the 'Unification Decree')

Came into force on 24 May. Under it Nigeria formally ceased to be a Federation and was renamed the 'Republic of Nigeria'. The Federal Military Government became the 'National Military Government', the Federal Executive Council became simply the 'Executive Council', and Lagos the 'capital territory'. The Regions were formally abolished, but the Provinces (the next largest administrative division below the Regions) were grouped into 'the Northern Group of Provinces', the 'Eastern Group of Provinces', etc. These Groups corresponded exactly with the previous Regions and the four Military Governors continued in office administering the same areas as before. In this respect there was no real change. Even the Regional Constitutions, as suspended and modified by Decree No. 1, remained in force. The Military Governors however lost the power to incur expenditure on their own responsibility without prior consent.

The federal and regional public services were unified into a single 'National Public Service'. Control over the most senior posts was centralized. The power to appoint and dismiss 'persons to hold or act in the office of permanent secretary to any department of government of the Republic or any other office of equivalent rank in the National Public Service' was vested in the Supreme Military Council. The National Public Service Commission was to be consulted before any such appointments were made. The power to appoint, promote, dismiss, and discipline in relation to all other administrative posts was vested in the National Public Service Commission.* This power was delegated except for the most senior posts (those carrying an initial salary of £2,292 or more) to Provincial Public Service Commissions.

The power to appoint the members of the Police Service Commission was vested in the Head of the National Military Government (under Decree No. 1 it had been vested in the Federal Executive Council).

* The National Public Service Commission had no powers over (i) police appointments which lay with the Police Service Commission; (ii) appointment of ambassadors which lay with the Government itself; (iii) Directors of Audit, other than their initial appointment; (iv) judicial appointments. The Constitution (Suspension and Modification) No. 6 Decree added the post of 'court registrar'. This decree, made on 2 June but having retrospective effect from 20 May, enabled the Government to fill a particular vacancy in the North; the rumours of this impending appointment contributed to the riots of 29 May.

5. *The Constitution (Suspension and Modification) (No. 9) Decree 1966. Decree No. 59*

Came into force 1 September 1966. It formally reinstated the Federation, which Decree No. 34 had abolished, restored the previous nomenclature (e.g. Federal Military Government), and re-established the Regions, their Public Services and their Public Service Commissions. The power to appoint members of the Police Service Commission remained however with the Head of the Federal Military Government.

Decree No. 1 was thus re-enacted, with some of the minor subsequent amendments.

6. *Eastern Region of Nigeria: Provincial Administration Edict 1966. Edict No. 33*

Dated 6 December 1966, it divided the Eastern Region into the Capital Territory of Enugu and nineteen other Provinces, and endowed each Province with organs of local self-government, namely a Provincial Council, a Provincial Executive Committee, and a Provincial Administrator.

(i) The Provincial Council
(a) is composed of an equal number of persons selected from each Division (eight Provinces consisted of two Divisions, five of three Divisions, four of four Divisions and two of five Divisions). Appointed until otherwise decided by the Governor. Members must be indigenous to the Province or of not less than three years' residence, and of Eastern Nigerian origin
(b) sits for three years, unless dissolved sooner by the Governor
(c) elects a Chairman and Vice-Chairman
(d) has power of making law for a variety of matters, e.g. chieftaincy, town and country planning, health and sanitation, primary and secondary education (excluding standards), customary marriages and succession, markets, roads, water supply, agriculture and fisheries, co-operatives, local development. A Council legislates by passing a Bill, which is submitted to the Governor for his promulgation. The Governor may return to the Council a Bill which he thinks exceeds its competence or conflicts with Constitutional or Regional law. A Bill lapses if not promulgated within 90 days
(e) may be dissolved by the Governor (on a number of grounds, e.g. 'if it performs any act in opposition to the Regional Government or acts in a manner prejudicial to the interest of Eastern Nigeria or of another Province')

(ii) The Provincial Executive Committee
(a) is composed of 'persons appointed by the Governor from all the Divisions of the Province', not members of the Provincial Council, holding office for three years, unless removed sooner by the Governor
(b) has as its function to aid and advise the Provincial Administrator 'in the exercise of his functions within the Province, except such functions as are required by law to be exercised by him at his discretion'

(iii) The Provincial Administrator
(a) is appointed by the Governor 'in rotation as between the Divisions' but the Governor 'may, if he deems it necessary, transfer a Provincial Administrator to any Province'
(b) holds office for three years, unless removed sooner by the Governor
(c) exercises the executive power of the Province 'subject to any directions given by the Governor', and is responsible to the Governor 'for the peace, order and good government of the Province, and for the proper exercise of [his] powers . . .'

(iv) Regional and Provincial Administration

(a) 'The Governor may delegate to a Provincial Administrator any function of the Regional Government due to be performed within the Province'

(b) '. . . every Province may establish and maintain such departments as may be authorised by the Governor . . .'

(c) '. . . The Governor may establish in any Province such organs, agencies, commissions or departments of the Regional Government as he may deem necessary . . .'

(d) '. . . officials of the Province shall be deemed to be persons employed in the public service of Eastern Nigeria'

(v) Finance

Expenditure is to be defrayed by

(a) 'subventions from the Regional Government'

(b) 'the revenue of the property of the Province'

(c) 'such other sources as the Governor may, from time to time, by order authorize'

The Estimates of expenditure are prepared by the Provincial Executive Committee and submitted to the Council for approval. The Estimates are then transmitted to the Governor who may disallow any item or vary any amount prescribed for any item.

7. The Constitution (Suspension and Modification) Decree 1967. Decree No. 8

Dated 17 March 1967. This Decree, which has been analysed in the text (p. 45-8), took the place of Decree No. 1.

8. Constitution (Repeal and Restoration) Decree 1967. Decree No. 13

Dated 27 May 1967. It repealed Decree No. 8, and thus restored Decree No. 1. It was motivated as follows:

Whereas executive authority in Eastern Nigeria has been so exercised as to prejudice the executive authority of the Federation in circumstances such that it is expedient and necessary to make other provisions for the continuance of federal government . . .' As such, it did not require the consent of the Military Governor of the Eastern Region but presumably had the consent of the three other Military Governors, as required by Decree No. 8. (Schedule 2. S. 70).

9. States (Creation and Transitional Provisions) Decree 1967. Decree No. 14

Dated 27 May 1967, it reconstituted Nigeria as a Federation of twelve States, with Lagos as the seat of the Federal Government. See map, p. xi.

10. *Constitutional (Financial Provisions) Decree 1967. Decree No. 15*

Dated 27 May 1967. It specified the share of the Distributable Pool Account due to each new State. This was done quite arbitrarily. Each of the six States created out of the Northern Region was to receive one-sixth of the amount previously paid to the Region. This gave them each a 7 per cent share of the Pool. The three States created out of the Eastern Region shared the amount previously paid to that Region in unequal proportions (roughly 5 : 2 : 2). This gave the Central Eastern State 17.5 per cent of the Pool. Lagos was given a 2 per cent share, at the expense of the West.

APPENDIX C

A SELECTION OF SPEECHES AND DOCUMENTS

I. BROADCAST ON RADIO KADUNA BY MAJOR NZEOGWU, 15 JANUARY 1966

In the name of the Supreme Council of the Revolution of the Nigerian Armed Forces, I declare martial law over the Northern Provinces of Nigeria.

The Constitution is suspended and the regional government and elected assemblies are hereby dissolved. All political, cultural, tribal and trade union activities, together with all demonstrations and unauthorized gatherings, excluding religious worship, are banned until further notice. The aim of the Revolutionary Council is to establish a strong united and prosperous nation, free from corruption and internal strife. Our method of achieving this is strictly military but we have no doubt that every Nigerian will give us maximum cooperation by assisting the regime and not disturbing the peace during the slight changes that are taking place. I am to assure all foreigners living and working in this part of Nigeria that their rights will continue to be respected. All treaty obligations previously entered into with any foreign nation will be respected, and we hope that such nations will respect our country's territorial integrity and will avoid taking sides with enemies of the revolution and enemies of the people.

My dear countrymen, you will hear, and probably see, a lot being done by certain bodies charged by the Supreme Council with the duties of national integration, supreme justice, general security and property recovery. As an interim measure all permanent secretaries, corporation chairmen and senior heads of departments are allowed to make decisions until the new organs are functioning, so long as such decisions are not contrary to the aims and wishes of the Supreme Council. No Minister or Parliamentary Secretary possesses administrative or other forms of control over any Ministry, even if they are not considered too dangerous to be arrested.

This is not a time for long speech-making and so let me acquaint you with ten proclamations in the Extraordinary Orders of the Day which the Supreme Council has promulgated. These will be modified as the situation improves. You are hereby warned that looting, arson, homosexuality, rape, embezzlement, bribery or corruption, obstruction of the revolution, sabotage, subversion, false alarms and assistance to foreign invaders, are all offences punishable by death sentence. Demonstrations and unauthorized assembly, non-cooperation with revolutionary troops are punishable in grave manner up to death. Refusal or neglect to perform normal duties or any task that may of necessity be ordered by local military commanders in support of the change will be punishable by a sentence imposed by the local military commander.

Spying, harmful or injurious publications, and broadcasts of troop movements or action, will be punished by any suitable sentence deemed fit by the local military commander. Shouting of slogans, loitering and rowdy behaviour will be rectified by any sentence of incarceration, or any more severe punishment deemed fit by the local military commander. Doubtful loyalty will be penalized by imprisonment or any more severe sentence. Illegal possession or carrying of firearms, smuggling or trying to escape with documents, valuables, including money or other assets vital to the running of any establishment will be punished by death sentence. Wavering or sitting on the fence and failing to declare open loyalty with the revolution will be regarded as an act of hostility punishable by any sentence deemed suitable by the local military commander. Tearing down an order of the day or proclamation or other authorized notices will be penalized by death.

This is the end of the Extraordinary Order of the Day which you will soon begin to see displayed in public. My dear countrymen, no citizen should have anything to fear, so long as that citizen is law abiding and if that citizen has religiously obeyed the native laws of the country and those set down in every heart and conscience since 1 October 1960. Our enemies are the political profiteers, the swindlers, the men in high and low places that seek bribes and demand 10 per cent; those that seek to keep the country divided permanently so that they can remain in office as ministers or VIPs at least; the tribalists, the nepotists, those that make the country look big for nothing before international circles; those that have corrupted our society and put the Nigerian political calendar back by their words and deeds. Like good soldiers we are not promising anything miraculous or spectacular. But what we do promise every law abiding citizen is—freedom from fear and all forms of oppression, freedom from general inefficiency and freedom to live and strive in every field of human endeavour, both nationally and internationally. We promise that you will no more be ashamed to say that you are Nigerian.

I leave you with a message of good wishes and ask for your support at all times, so that our land, watered by the Niger and Benue, between the sandy wastes and gulf of Guinea, washed in salt by the mighty

Atlantic, shall not detract Nigeria from gaining sway in any great aspect of international endeavour.

My dear countrymen, this is the end of this speech. I wish you all good luck and I hope you will cooperate to the fullest in this job which we have set for ourselves of establishing a prosperous nation and achieving solidarity. Thank you very much and good-bye for now.

[Source: Tape-recording. Some words indistinct]

2. BROADCAST BY GENERAL IRONSI, 16 JANUARY 1966

The Military Government of the Federal Republic of Nigeria wishes to state that it has taken over the interim administration of the Federal Republic of Nigeria following the invitation of the Council of Ministers of the last Government for the Army to do so.

For some time now there have been escalating political disturbances in parts of Nigeria with increasing loss of faith between political parties, and between political leaders themselves. This crisis of confidence reached a head during the elections in the Western Region in October last year. There were charges by the opposition parties of rigging of the elections and general abuse of power by the regional government in the conduct of the elections. Riots, arson, murder and looting became widespread in Western Nigeria since October. The situation deteriorated and certain army officers attempted to seize power.

In the early hours of the morning of 15 January 1966, these officers kidnapped the Prime Minister and the Minister of Finance and took them to an unknown destination. The revolt was widespread throughout the country and two Regional Premiers and some high-ranking army officers were killed. The whereabouts of the Prime Minister is still unknown. The vast majority of the Nigerian Army under the command of the General Officer Commanding the Nigerian Army remained completely loyal to the Federal Government and immediately took steps to control the situation.

The Council of Ministers of the Federal Government met and appraised the problems confronting the Government. They appreciated the immediate need to control the serious situation which threatened the Federation. They also saw quite clearly a possible deterioration of the situation in the light of developments on Saturday, 15 January 1966. On Sunday, 16 January, the Council of Ministers unanimously decided to hand over voluntarily the administration of the country, with immediate effect, to the Nigerian Army. This was formally done the same day by the Acting President of the Federation. The Government of the Federation of Nigeria having ceased to function, the Nigeria

Armed Forces have been invited to form an Interim Military Government for the purpose of maintaining law and order and of maintaining essential services.

The invitation has been accepted and I, GENERAL JOHNSON THOMAS UMUNAKWE AGUIYI-IRONSI, the General Officer Commanding the Nigerian Army, have been formally invested with authority as Head of the Federal Military Government and Supreme Commander of the Nigerian Armed Forces.

[Source: *The Problem of Nigerian Unity*. Appendix I. Ministry of Information. Eastern Nigeria. N.d.]

3. STATEMENT TO THE PRESS BY GENERAL IRONSI, 21 FEBRUARY 1966

I have requested this meeting in order to have the opportunity of speaking to you about matters of great importance to all of us, concerning the welfare and progress of our country. You will appreciate that since the Military Government assumed office on 17 January, it has not been an easy task either for you as moulders of public opinion, or for us as trustees of the nation. We are all faced with the problems of national reconstruction, which involves a re-examination of the principles on which our national edifice was based. In this transitional period, we seek, and we have been assured of, the cooperation of all sections of our community, including the Press, in order that we may accomplish our task with minimum friction and with maximum efficiency; we solicit the co-operation of all our people. In this connection, the Federal Military Government will in particular expect maximum co-operation from the Press in reporting the activities of Government. You are all aware of the need to create a favourable image of Nigeria both at home and overseas. This is important for our economic development, which, in a large measure, depends on foreign investments. There is a calculated attempt by some sections of the foreign press to misrepresent the circumstances which have brought the Military Government in control of the affairs of this country. Deliberate misrepresentation of the Federal Military Government cannot help Nigeria. In the foreign Press, it is deplorable; in the Nigerian Press, it is unpardonable. The Federal Military Government should be given the time to accomplish the great tasks before it. The masses of the people have welcomed the new regime. It will be the duty of the Press to prevent its publications being used as a medium to revive unwelcome associations of the past order.

This meeting is, therefore, summoned to appeal to you once again to exercise a sense of loyalty, responsibility and restraint in the performance of your duties. You should avoid reports in your newspapers which are likely to incite one section of our people against another. You should also avoid the dangerous practice of rumour mongering which is so much in evidence in our country today. On this point, it might be necessary to sound a note of warning. While it is not the intention of the Military Government to muzzle constructive Press comments on matters of public interest, it should be realized that it is the duty of any responsible Government to ensure that confidential matters of State are not being made the subject of sensational Press speculation, especially where such matters have not been officially cleared for release to the public. Whenever in doubt about anything, you should always check up your facts from the Ministry of Information, who will either furnish you with the correct answers, or make enquiries from the proper quarters on your behalf. It is not part of the policy of Government to curb the freedom of the Press but, at the same time, you will agree that it is the duty of the Government to prevent any section of the community taking advantage of liberties which will not be conducive to the well-being of the country, its citizens and Government. Our country is reputed to have the freest Press in all Africa, and is among one of the freest in the world. It is the intention of my Government to keep it so. But we must not forget that the exercise of freedom also carries with it correlative responsibility. This is what is demanded of responsible journalism.

I would therefore wish to take this opportunity to emphasize the need for your co-operation in tackling our gigantic and urgent problems of economic and social development within the framework of national unity in the concept of 'one Nigeria'. The public would like to know the kind of administrative reforms we intend to undertake and the organs we propose to establish in order to attain our objectives. As a first step, administrative reforms are essential in order to lay a solid foundation not only for the present but for the future as well. Here the Press should reflect the thinking of the people and provide a forum for public discussion and constructive suggestions. The country needs a sort of nerve centre which will give the necessary direction and control in all major areas of national activities, so that we will be in a position to plot a uniform pattern of development for the whole country. Matters which were formerly within the legislative competence of the regions will need to be reviewed, so that issues of national importance could be centrally controlled and directed towards overall and uniform development in the economic and social fields; effective liaison and co-ordination should be established between the Federal authority and its provincial counterparts, if we are to avoid the pitfalls of the recent past and make a more significant impact both internally as well as externally. The works programme of the Supreme Military Council and the Federal Military Government will necessarily include the establishment of certain essential organs which are indispensable for accelerated development in some major and sensitive areas where proper planning has been neglected, haphazard or unco-ordinated. We are undertaking a review of commercial and industrial development, details of which will be announced shortly. Other equally important problems requiring early attention are: the formulation of an educational policy related to the needs of a developing country such as Nigeria, manpower training tailored to meet the demands of the country, unemployment and its attendant social evils. The solution to these problems, you will admit, cannot be effected overnight. The new regime should be given time to tackle the heavy programme of work it has been called upon to shoulder. We need maximum co-operation from all sections of the country and resources to the utmost in order to lay a proper foundation for the present as well as for the future.

On the question of the political future of the country, the experiences and mistakes of the previous governments in the Federation have clearly indicated that far-reaching constitutional reforms are badly needed for peaceful and orderly progress towards the realization of our objectives. I have already touched on some of the major issues involved in my recent broadcast to the nation. It has become apparent to all Nigerians that rigid adherence to 'regionalism', was the bane of the last regime and one of the main factors which contributed to its downfall. No doubt, the country would welcome a clean break with the deficiencies of the system of government to which the country has been subjected in the recent past. A solution suitable to our national needs must be found. The existing boundaries of governmental control will need to be re-adjusted to make for less cumbersome administration. We are determined that constitutional changes, which are prerequisite to the re-establishment of parliamentary system of government, will be undertaken with the consensus of various representatives of public opinion. Proposals for constitutional changes will involve careful and detailed analysis, so that the nation will eventually have a system of parliamentary government best suited to the demands of a developing country in modern times. We expect that when the system of government acceptable to the people of Nigeria has been formulated, all elections to parliament will be by universal adult suffrage. It will be necessary to review also the method of selection for future ministerial appointments, in order that the destiny of the country will be placed in the hands of the men capable of shouldering the heavy responsibilities of modern government; capable of commanding the respect and admiration of their fellow citizens and capable of reflecting a proud image of Nigeria outside her borders. In the new order of things, there should be no place for regionalism and tribal consciousness, subjugation of personal service to personal aggrandizement, nepotism and corruption.

The Military Government has no political affiliation or ambition, nor did it come into power with the fiat of any political party. It has no desire to prolong its interim administration of government longer than is necessary for the orderly transition of the country to the type of government desired by the people. Study groups are being set up, details of which will be announced shortly, to study and submit working papers on constitutional, administrative and institutional problems in the context of national unity. A constituent assembly will in due course examine constitutional proposals followed by a referendum before the new constitution comes into being.

In this transitional period, all citizens have a useful part to play in shaping the destiny of our country, and the Press which serves as one of the important media of public opinion also has a responsible and constructive role to play. The measure of confidence which the Military Government reposes on the Press will in turn depend upon the confidence inspired in the Government by the Press.

[Source: *New Nigerian*, 23 February 1966]

4. BROADCAST BY LT-COL GOWON, 30 NOVEMBER 1966

Fellow Countrymen,

I wish to speak to you this evening about the measures which the Federal Military Government will implement to save the country from disintegrating. You are all aware that the Ad Hoc Committee has been adjourned indefinitely. They had run into difficulties which made it impossible for them to meet. In those circumstances there was little hope of the Committee evolving reasonable solutions to our present crisis. I shall deal later with the conditions under which the Committee could continue the work it started so well.

Our problems demand urgent solutions. The Federal Military Government has therefore worked out a clear and objective programme for saving Nigeria. Our non-partisan programme will not favour any particular group or groups.

The foremost preoccupation of the Federal Military Government is to lessen tension and maintain peace in the country. On the Military front, I am in constant touch with all the Military Governors and we are all confident that the Nigerian Army in conjunction with other Armed Forces and Police can still save this country. I do appreciate that the recent tragic events have shaken the basis of mutual confidence in the Army but my colleagues and I will gradually rebuild it. We can succeed with the help of honest Nigerians.

My long-term aim is the preservation of one Nigerian Army and one country. For a start, however, and because of the general distrust and suspicion in the country, the bulk of the army in each Region must be drawn from the indigenous people of that Region. In furtherance of this aim, steps are being taken to recruit more Westerners into the Nigerian Army. I have already given instructions for recruitment to commence next week. Those who advocate the withdrawal of Northern soldiers from the Western Region admit that any immediate wholesale withdrawal of Northern soldiers from the Western Region is not practicable. Law and order and the entire national security arrangements in the Western Region will break down if the troops were withdrawn at once.

The seat of the Federal Government is in Lagos. The Head of the Federal Government must therefore make special security arrangements for Lagos. This is not in dispute in all responsible quarters.

We are all aware, however, that Nigeria's troubles started from bitter political strife and inordinate ambition for personal power. We must therefore try to avoid such bitterness and selfish manœuvres in our approach to national problems. Political activities will therefore remain banned. We must also discourage any attempt to revive tribal consciousness and worsen Regional animosities. I have received some co-operation from Nigerian leaders in this respect but there must be greater restraint in all quarters if we are to succeed in reducing tensions everywhere. The press, the radio and other mass communication media must exercise a greater sense of responsibility in what they publish in these difficult times.

I now come to the immediate political programme of the Federal Military Government. As soldiers, my colleagues and I are ready to go back to the barracks any day. But the work of national reconstruction must be completed; public confidence in our institutions restored; and civilian leaders demonstrate to the nation that they are ready to take over and project a better image of the country than it had just before January 1966.

There are five main issues which the Federal Military Government will deal with in the course of national reconstruction. The first is the reorganization and long-term reintegration of the Nigerian Army. The second is the implementation of a nationally co-ordinated resettlement and rehabilitation programme for displaced persons. The third is the preparation of the Second National Development Plan. The fourth is to continue the fight against corruption in public life and the fifth is the preparation of a new Constitution for the country.

I have already spoken about my long-term aims for the Nigerian Army. For security reasons, I do not intend to discuss in public the internal affairs of the Armed Forces.

The Federal Military Government recognizes the need for a nationally co-ordinated resettlement and rehabilitation programme for displaced persons. I appreciate the valuable work done by the Regional Governments and voluntary organizations in providing emergency relief for displaced persons. Nevertheless, the Federal Military Government must do all it can to provide national leadership for tackling the problems of resettling these unfortunate persons as part of its efforts to restore normalcy in the country. The Federal Military Government will provide a fair proportion of the funds required for implementing the national programme to be worked out in consultation with the Regional Military Governments. This is a matter to which I attach the greatest urgency.

One of the major tasks of the Federal Military Government is to guarantee the safety of investment, foreign and Nigerian. Genuine investors therefore have nothing to fear from our current difficulties.

Every effort will be made to ensure that the Nigerian economy will continue to grow without serious interruptions. To this end, the Government will press on with the preparation of the Second National Development Plan. It is quite clear that in the next stage of our industrial development we shall enter such fields as iron and steel, petrochemicals, fertilizers and industries based on agriculture where the entire Nigerian market is almost too small. This is one reason why we should preserve Nigeria as one economic unit on terms acceptable to ordinary Nigerians in every part of the Federation.

Regarding the eradication of corruption from our public life, the Federal Military Government will take appropriate action on the Reports of the Enquiries recently held into the Nigerian Railway Corporation, the Electricity Corporation of Nigeria and the Lagos City Council. Similar enquiries will be held into the other Federal Corporations. The Decree on the declaration of assets will be implemented and the investigations into the assets and liabilities of those who held public offices from 1960 to 1966 will be continued. Those involved will include former Ministers, Chairmen of Statutory Corporations, Board Members, Permanent Secretaries and other Senior Civil Servants, General Managers and the top Executives of the Public Corporations. The Government has been handling these investigations in a quiet way because it does not want to give the impression of witch-hunting. Those found guilty of ill-gotten gains will be appropriately dealt with. There will also be a special administrative tribunal to enquire into the allocation of Federal State lands in Lagos and elsewhere.

Coming now to the Constitutional issue I reiterate my previous statements that it is not the intention of the Federal Military Government to impose a Constitution on the country. It is obvious to the Government, however, that the general sentiment among most Nigerians is that the country must be preserved as one entity. I should emphasize that the idea of a temporary confederation is unworkable. In a confederation there will be no effective central authority. Each Region as a virtually sovereign state can contract out or refuse to join any common service. For example, the Mid-West may not like to contribute to the Nigerian railways, the East may not want to use electricity from Kainji Dam, the North may not want to use coal or refined petroleum products from the East and the West may prefer to pull out of the Nigerian Airways and so the process of disintegration will be complete in a very short time. Once we adopt the so-called temporary confederation because of the current difficulties it will be hard to come together again. This is not the future to which our children are entitled and we have no moral right to commit future generations of Nigerians to this disastrous course.

I am confident that Nigerians can agree on a Constitution which will preserve the integrity of the country and satisfy the aspirations of the vast majority of our people. It is important that all shades of opinion should be given full expression. I therefore propose to summon a fully representative Constituent Assembly to draw up a new Constitution which will reflect the genuine wishes of all Nigerians as distinct from regional blocs, tribal groups and vested political interests. The Federal Military Government will announce the detailed machinery for selecting delegates to the Constituent Assembly. The assembly will consist of at least one person from each of the existing administrative divisions in the country and the representatives of special interests such as Trade Unions, Professional Associations, Chambers of Commerce and Industry, and Women's Organizations.

To facilitate the work of the Constituent Assembly, I am appointing a drafting committee to prepare the outline of the draft Constitution to be submitted to the Constituent Assembly. The drafting instructions to the committee will be based on the decisions of the Supreme Military Council which will soon meet to consider the findings of the various Constitutional groups including the agreed recommendations of the Ad Hoc Committee submitted to me in their Progress Report of 30 September. If all delegates to the Ad Hoc Committee can meet within Nigeria and agree to carry on from where they left off in early October, their further conclusions would assist the drafting committee in its task.

The draft Constitution will reflect the generally expressed desire for a stable Federation. It is quite clear that our common need in Nigeria is that no one Region or tribal group should be in a position to dominate the others. The new Federal Constitution must therefore contain adequate safeguards to make such domination impossible. In the stable Federation, no Region should be large enough to be able to threaten secession or hold the rest of the Federation to ransom in times of national crisis. This brings me to the major question of the creation of new States.

I wish to make it clear to the nation that honestly I personally have no vested interest in the creation of any particular state. But there is no doubt that without a definite commitment on the states question, normalcy and freedom from fear of domination by one Region or the other cannot be achieved.

The principles for the creation of new States will be:

(i) no one State should be in a position to dominate or control the Central Government;

(ii) each State should form one compact geographical area;

(iii) administrative convenience, the facts of history, and the wishes of the people concerned must be taken into account;

(iv) each State should be in a position to discharge effectively the functions allocated to Regional Governments;

(v) it is also essential that the new States should be created simultaneously.

All these criteria have to be applied together. No one principle should be applied to the exclusion of the others. To give an illustration of what I have in mind: given the present size and distribution of the Nigerian population and resources, the country could be divided into not less than eight and not more than fourteen States. The exact number of States will be determined through the detailed application of these criteria and will be fully debated in the Constituent Assembly.

Meanwhile, I am still taking steps to associate some civilians with the Federal Executive Council in carrying out the programme I have just outlined. They will be persons known to believe strongly in the continued existence of Nigeria as an effective Federation and they are to help me in projecting the national image. They will not be persons who were actively involved in the partisan politics which divided us so bitterly. They will be men of undoubted integrity and of independent character. I shall select men who have no intention to seek elective political office on the completion of this programme and who will not compete with professional politicians for office in the next civilian government.

Dear countrymen, I have outlined a programme which I trust will further reduce tension and enable us to proceed with the preparation of a new Constitution in a calm atmosphere. As I have promised on several occasions, I shall do everything in my power and use the resources of the Federal Government to guarantee the continued existence of Nigeria as one political and economic unit.

As part of our deliberate policy to reduce tension, I have preferred to ignore certain unfounded allegations and provocative statements against me and the Federal Military Government. My studied silence should not be taken as a mark of weakness. My belief is the less we talk and the more we act honestly in the interest of the whole nation, the better for everyone. It is easy enough for me to mobilize enough forces to deal with any dissident or disloyal group. But I have always preferred peaceful solutions to our current crisis. We have had enough bloodshed in this country. But if circumstances compel me to preserve the integrity of Nigeria by force, I shall do my duty to my country.

I am aware that some Nigerians and their foreign collaborators have been engaging in illegal arms trafficking. I need not spell out the grave consequences of such actions. I warn such misguided Nigerians to desist from these criminal acts.

I want to take this opportunity to appeal to the people of Nigeria to remain law abiding citizens and help us to maintain peace. My main concern is with the personal safety of you all and you must not allow yourselves to be misled by ill-motivated persons. I appeal to all soldiers, sailors and airmen to remember that this is a Military Government and any unlawful act on your part is a discredit to your Government. Your discipline and loyalty must not be shaken. My appreciation goes to all of you and members of the Nigeria Police for maintaining the necessary calm which is so essential for the restoration of trust and confidence so vital at this time. I appeal to all Nigerian leaders from all walks of life to come forward and help us in saving this country from falling apart. If we fail, we will deny future generations the opportunity to do better than we have done. If we fail, the whole of Africa and the black race will not forgive us. So help us God.

With the genuine co-operation of you all, I am confident that we shall carry out this programme successfully. We shall give the country a workable Constitution and the basis for a return to normal political life and rapid economic progress.

Long live the Federal Republic of Nigeria.

Thank you and good night.

[Source: *New Nigerian*, 1 December 1966]

5. ADDRESS BY LT-COL HASSAN KATSINA, MILITARY GOVERNOR IN THE NORTH, TO A MEETING OF EMIRS AND CHIEFS IN LUGARD HALL, KADUNA, 19 APRIL 1967

Since the Military Regime came into being a number of reforms have been introduced by the Military Government. Among the most important of such reforms in Northern Nigeria are:

(1) that in future Native Authority personnel shall not be allowed to take part in politics whilst at the same time remaining in Native Authority employment; and

(2) that as from 1 April 1968 all Native Courts shall be taken over by Government to be administered as part of the Judiciary under the Chief Justice, while Emirs' and Chiefs' Courts of Grades 'A' and 'A' Limited shall cease to function as from 1 April this year.

Reports coming from all the Provinces, as expressed in both oral and written comments by the general public, indicate the overwhelming support these measures have received.

However security and intelligence reports have shown that there are certain disgruntled and mischievous elements who have been trying to create dissatisfaction in the minds of people especially of the Emirs and Chiefs against these reforms particularly those on the Native Courts.

These shortsighted persons who have no respect for the liberty and well-being of the common man and whose memory is so short that they cannot even reflect on our present situation and the forces which brought it about, have been going round talking to people with a view to inciting them to contempt against the Government.

Some of these mischievous elements have even gone to the extent of writing and sending seditious letters to you Emirs and Chiefs condemning these reforms and trying to incite you against me and my advisers. Some of you have in fact handed in these letters to your Provincial Secretaries which was the very proper thing to do. Needless to say that measures are being taken to trace out and deal severely with these enemies of our society.

These mischievous elements are trying to create dissatisfaction in your minds by falsely telling you that the Court reforms are intended to reduce your powers and minimize your prestige and integrity. The circumstances leading to these court reforms have already been fully explained to you in a circular dated 13 February 1967, addressed to all Provincial Secretaries with copies to Native Authorities. Subsequent to that circular some of you—one from each Province—were present at a meeting of my Executive Committee when further explanation was given on the reforms. So I trust that being in fact fully aware of the background and reasons for these reforms you will not be misled by these mischievous elements.

It is the declared policy of the Military Government to maintain the Chieftaincy Institution and to uphold the dignity, prestige and integrity of Chiefs and at the same time to safeguard the interests of the common man. In pursuance of this policy it is my duty to try and remove all causes of dissatisfaction and friction, and those obstacles to the smooth running of Government both at Regional and Native Authority level. That the present Native Courts system has been such an obstacle and a source of dissatisfaction and friction has been recognized as far back as 1958. It was in that year that the Civilian Government appointed a Panel of eminent jurists to examine our Court system and make recommendations to the Government.

One of the main features of the Panel's recommendations was a closer control of the native courts by the Government. The taking-over of the native courts by the Government was in fact accepted in principle by the civilian Government and judging from some of the legislation it had passed since 1958 there is no doubt that it was working towards that goal.

You will therefore see that the idea of the Government taking over of native courts was not hatched out when the Military Government came into power and when I assumed my present office as Military Governor of the Region. The issue was an old story. However, since the Military Government came into power in January last year people seem to have taken advantage of the change of Government to be freely expressing their feelings on issues. The utterances both written and oral together with the intelligence and security reports on the native courts system, led me to the inevitable conclusion that the time had come for some reform in the system.

My decisions on these reforms were only taken after long and careful consideration. The decisions were based on recommendations of learned men who are as much interested in the welfare of this country as you and I. Their recommendations were in turn made after a close study of our Court system and a careful consideration of that system in relation to our present state of social and political advancement

When you look back into the history of our court system, before the advent of the British and after, you will clearly see that the system has been a developing one, and at every stage the change has been dictated by the social and political demands of the time.

We have now reached a stage when these reforms must be made if you as the rulers are to continue to enjoy the respect and the confidence of your subjects. If we were to shut our eyes and close our ears to the need for these reforms, it is quite certain that sooner or later we would be faced with a popular uprising. It is my duty to you and to the people, having foreseen the possibility of such a situation to take steps to avert it. In any case, just as it is important to separate the executive from the legislature, if Governments are to fulfil their sacred function of governing justly in the interest and welfare of their people, it is no less important to separate the executive from the judiciary.

In this regard, I intend, as soon as my other engagements permit, to convene another meeting of leaders of thought to stress to them that good government can only be nurtured and the liberty of the individual guaranteed upon this separation of functions. I repeat, it is vital that the Executive, the Judiciary and the Legislature must each operate within their own sphere. It is the duty of the Military Regime to lay this foundation firmly before handing over the reign of Government to civilians.

But there is still much work ahead which must be faced resolutely despite the current situation in Nigeria. The intransigence of Eastern Nigeria must be checked to avoid ruining our country and bringing untold misery to the common man. The ills of the past are being corrected as everybody knows. Inquiries have been concluded into the affairs of Public Corporations and their recommendations are being followed up and implemented. Personal assets of individuals involved in the findings of the inquiries are also being investigated with despatch.

The question of probes into the personal assets of both past and present office holders in accordance with Decree No. 51 is also under active consideration for execution.

I would also like you to look at these reforms within the context of international relations. Today, we are living in a world that is getting smaller and smaller. With the modern developments on all fronts our social and economic contacts are growing. We can no longer sit back and feel indifferent to what other peoples think of us. Our court system is one of the things that we must shape in such a way that we may favourably be regarded by outsiders. The following aspects of our native court system would obviously be obstacles to our gaining international respect.

(1) We were the only country in the world in which there existed authorities on whom were vested the powers of legislation, adjudication and execution all at the same time.

(2) We were the only country in the world in which appointments to certain executive posts would automatically place the appointee as president of a court of law of unlimited jurisdiction.

(3) We were the only country in the world in which courts of law of unlimited jurisdiction might be presided over by persons who were not learned or trained in the law.

With these reforms such unfavourable aspects of our native courts system have been removed.

By giving up judicial functions the Chiefs are giving up responsibilities that carry with them their own unseen and unsuspected weakness and which therefore may be more dangerous than useful. There have been a number of cases decided by appeal courts in which decisions of the lower courts were quashed on the ground that a person cannot be a judge in a cause wherein he is interested either personally or in his official capacity.

Because of the dual capacity in which Chiefs were acting their court decision would always be in danger of being challenged on this principle, and this danger was more real as people became more enlightened and sophisticated.

The mischievous elements try to mislead you to think that by stopping you from performing judicial functions the Government wishes to reduce your powers. I am not sure if judicial functions can be aptly described as powers when related to Emirs and Chiefs or to anyone for that matter. By this aspect of the reforms I hope that Emirs and Chiefs will now have more time to concentrate on their other functions for the benefit of their people and be more readily available in assisting me in the administration of the Region.

Without judicial functions the responsibilities of the Emirs and Chiefs are still many and varied. One only needs to read through the Native Authority Law to realize this. To mention one of the responsibilities, I want particularly to remind you of your duty to maintain law and order. You will also not forget that you are the guardians of your people, who will never stop coming to you with their complaints and petitions. You should patiently listen to them. If a dispute is on a matter which you can settle administratively, do settle it; if it is a matter for the Court then direct that the complainant be taken to the appropriate Court. Your subjects will still look to you for guidance and solace.

Residents and District Officers had extensive judicial functions including jurisdiction in capital cases under the Provincial Courts Ordinance. They lost these functions completely in 1935 when the Ordinance was repealed and the Provincial Courts of the time were replaced by the High Court and Magistrates' Courts of the Protectorate. I have every reason to believe that many of them felt this keenly, and thought that it was a dangerous derogation from their authority that they could ill afford to suffer.

But of course they accepted the change loyally as they were bound to do, and I doubt whether anybody can be found to say that their authority as a result was really diminished in the slightest; their powers and influence over the administration of their Provinces were as great as they had ever been. Indeed, the Administrative section of the Regional Government does function satisfactorily without any judicial duties. I think there is much to be learnt from these examples.

In conclusion I would like to emphasize two points. Firstly, you can rest assured that it is the declared policy of the Military Government to maintain and uphold the dignity and prestige of Emirs and Chiefs.

Secondly, the recent reforms have been introduced in the interest of the Region as a whole and having regard to the social and political developments in the country they are timely. Progress, the result of social and economic developments, is not bestowed on a country as a gift but is achieved by the people themselves through hard work, decent living and the willingness to look constantly into the nation's social orders to see what modifications changing conditions demand in them, while at the same time maintaining and enriching the nation's basic tradition and culture.

These forces are constantly at play in the life of any nation and it would be catastrophic if anyone were to interfere with them, since in the last resort the sovereign powers of any nation rest on the ordinary man whose interest and welfare must remain supreme and not be subordinated to that of any class or group, and where this is reversed the position will not endure before the ordinary man reasserts himself.

Finally, I wish you a successful deliberation on any matter you may wish to discuss and a safe return home.

[Source: *New Nigerian*, 25 April 1967]

6. REPORT OF THE SPEECH BY CHIEF AWOLOWO TO THE
   MEETING OF WESTERN REGION 'LEADERS OF THOUGHT' AT
   IBADAN, I MAY 1967

'I consider it my duty to Yoruba people in particular and to Nigerians in general to place four imperatives, two of them categorical, and two conditional.

1. Only a peaceful solution must be found to arrest the present worsening stalemate and restore normalcy.

2. The Eastern Region must be encouraged to remain part of the Federation.

3. If the Eastern Region is allowed by acts of omission or commission to secede from or opt out of Nigeria, then Western Nigeria and Lagos must also stay out of the Federation.

4. The people of Western Nigeria or Lagos would participate in the Ad Hoc Constitutional Committee or any similar body only on the basis of absolute equality with other Regions of the Federation.'

Speaking to the first point he said:

'If the East attacked the North it would be for the purpose of revenge pure and simple. Any claim to the contrary would be untenable. If it is claimed that such a war is being waged for the purpose of recovering the real and personal properties left behind in the North by Easterners two insuperable points are obvious. Firstly, the personal effects left behind by Easterners have been wholly locked up or destroyed, and could no longer be physically recovered; secondly, since the real property is immovable in any case, recovery of it can only be by means of forcible military occupation of these parts of the North on which this property is situated.

'On the other hand, if the North attacked the East, it could only be for the purpose of further strengthening and entrenching its position of dominance in the country. If the North claimed that an attack on the East was going to be launched by the Federal Government and not by the North, as such, and that it was designed to ensure the unity and integrity of the Federation, two other insuperable points also became obvious.

'First, if a war against the East becomes a necessity, it must be agreed unanimously by the remaining units of the Federation', he declared.

He added that in this connection the West, Mid-West and Lagos have declared their implacable opposition to the use of force in solving the present problem.

'In the face of such a declaration by the three out of the four territories of Nigeria a war against the East could only be a war favoured by the North alone. Secondly, if the true purpose of such a war is to preserve the unity and integrity of the Federation, then these ends can be achieved by the very simple device of implementing the recommendation of the committee which met on 9 August 1966, as reaffirmed by a decision of the Military Leaders at Aburi on 5 January 1967, as well as by accepting such of the demands of the East, West, Mid-West and Lagos as are manifestly reasonable and essential for assuring harmonious relationships and peaceful co-existence between them and their brothers and sisters in the North.'

Chief Awolowo condemned the idea of an attack on the East, which he said was being advocated by some persons who compared such an attack to that of the war President Lincoln of America waged against the Southern States of America.

He pointed out that the Lincoln war was for the abolition of slavery.

He said that a war against the East in which Northern soldiers would be predominant 'will only unite the Easterners or the Ibos against their attackers, strengthen them in their belief that they are not wanted by the majority of their fellow Nigerians and finally push them out of the Federation'.

Chief Awolowo went on 'We have been told that an act of secession on the part of the East would be a signal in the first instance for the creation of the COR state by decree which would be backed if need be, by use of force.

'With great respect, I have some dissenting observations to make on this declaration. There are eleven national or linguistic groups in the COR area, with a total population of over five millions. These national groups are as distinct from one another as the Ibos are distinct from them or from the Yorubas or Hausas. Of the eleven, the Efik, Ibibio, Annang national groups are 3.2 million strong as against the Ijaws, who are only about 700,000 strong.

'Ostensibly, the remaining nine national groups number 1.4 millions. But when you have subtracted the Ibo inhabitants from among them, what is left ranges from the Ngennis, who number only 8,000 to the Ogonis, who are 220,000 strong.

'A decree creating a COR state without a plebiscite to ascertain the wishes of the peoples in the area, would only amount to subordinating the minority national groups in the state to the dominance of the Efik-Ibibio-Annang national group. It would be perfectly in order to create a Calabar state or a Rivers state by decree and without a plebiscite: each is a homogeneous national unit, but before you lump distinct and diverse national units together in one state, the consent of each of them is indispensable, otherwise, the seed of social disequilibrium in the new state would have been sown. On the other hand, if the COR state is created by decree after the Eastern Region shall have made its severance from Nigeria effective, we should then be waging an unjust war against a foreign state. It would be an unjust war, because the purpose of it would be to remove ten minorities in the East from the dominance of the Ibos only to subordinate them to the dominance of the Efik-Ibibio-Annang national groups.

'I think I have said enough to demonstrate that any war against the East, or vice versa, on any count whatsoever, would be an unholy crusade for which it would be most unjustifiable to shed a drop of Nigerian blood. Therefore, only a peaceful solution must be found, and quickly too to arrest the present rapidly deteriorating stalemate and restore normalcy.'

Chief Awolowo went on to refer to what he regarded as the second categorical imperative. 'It is my considered view,' he said, 'that whilst some of the demands of the East are excessive within the context of a Nigerian union, most of such demands are not only well-founded, but are designed for smooth and healthy association amongst the various national units of Nigeria. For instance, the East has demanded the creation of separate regional monetary authorities, the demolition of the appellate jurisdiction of the Federal Supreme Court, and the dependence of the Federal Government on financial contributions from the regions. These and other suchlike demands, I do not support. Demands such as these, if accepted, will lead surely to the complete disintegration of the Federation, which is not in the interest of our people. But I wholeheartedly support the following demands among others, which we consider reasonable and most of which are already embodied in our memoranda to the Ad Hoc Committee:

'That mines and minerals should be residual subjects: that revenue should be allocated strictly on the basis of derivation; that is to say, after the Federal Government has deducted its own share for its own services, the rest should be allocated to the regions to which they are attributable; that the existing public debt of the Federation should become the responsibility of the regions on the basis of the location of the projects in respect of each debt, whether internal or external; that each region should have and control its own militia and police force; that, with immediate effect, all military personnel should be posted to their regions of origin.

'I can advance cogent reasons in support of these demands, but as the time for such an exercise is not available today, I will confine myself to bringing to your notice certain facts relating to our public debt, as a sample of the cogency and reasonableness of the above demands. Under the current six-year plan which ends next year on 31 March the summary of the location and external debt element of the projects is as follows:

Lagos: Total value of projects £36.79 million; external debt element £12.8 million. In addition, expenditure on aircraft and warships £10.93 million, with external debt element on that £2.8 million.

West: Total value of projects £5.88 million; external debt element £3.75 million.

East: Total value of projects £18.8 million (including the Niger bridge); external debt element £7.86 million.

North: Total value of projects £127.21 million (including Kainji Dam); external debt element £60.1 million.

Mid-West: £6.95 million (excluding Niger bridge); external debt element—nil.

'If we are to live in harmony with one another as Nigerians it is imperative that these demands and others, which are not here related, should be met without further delay by those who have hitherto resisted them. To those who may argue that the acceptance of these demands will amount to transforming Nigeria into a Federation with a weak central government, my comment is that any link, however tenuous, which keeps the East in the Nigerian union, is better, in my view, than no link at all.

'Before the Western delegates went to Lagos to attend the meetings of the Ad Hoc Committee, they were given a clear mandate that if any Region should opt out of the Federation of Nigeria, then the Federation should be considered to be at an end, and that the Western Region and Lagos should also opt out of it. It would then be open to Western Nigeria and Lagos, as an independent sovereign state to enter into association with any of the Nigerian units of its own choosing and on terms mutually acceptable to them.

'I see no reason for departing from this mandate', he went on, 'if any Region in Nigeria considers itself strong enough to compel us to enter into association with it on its own terms. I would only wish such a Region luck. Luck, I must warn, will, in the long run, be no better than that which has attended the doings of all colonial powers down the ages!

'This much I must say in addition, on this point. We have neither the military might, nor the overwhelming advantage of numbers here in Western Nigeria and Lagos. But we have the justice of a noble and imperishable cause on our side, namely: the right of a people to unfettered self-determination. If this is so, then God is on our side and God be with us—then we have nothing whatsoever in this world to fear.

'The fourth imperative, and the second conditional one, has been fully dealt with in my recent letter to His Excellency, the Military Governor of Western Nigeria and in the representation which your deputation made last year to the Head of the Federal Military Government. As a matter of fact as far back as November last year, a smaller meeting of leaders of thought in this region decided that unless certain things were done, we would no longer participate in the meeting of the Ad Hoc Committee. But since then, not even one of our legitimate requests has been granted. I will, therefore, take no more of your time in making further comments on a point with which you are well familiar.

'As soon as our humble and earnest requests are met, I shall be ready to take my place on the Ad Hoc Committee, but certainly not before.' Finally he offered what he called 'this piece of advice' in order to resolve this crisis amicably and in the best interests of all Nigerians.

'Certain attributes are required on the part of Nigerian leaders— military as well as non-military leaders alike—namely: vision, realism, and unselfishness.

'But above all, what will keep Nigerian leaders in the North and East unwaveringly in the path of wisdom, realism and moderation is courage and steadfastness on the part of Yoruba people in the course of what they sincerely believe to be right, equitable and just.

'In the past five years, we in the West and Lagos have shown that we possess these qualities in a large measure. If we demonstrate them again, as we did in the past, calmly and stoically, we will save Nigeria from further bloodshed and imminent wreck and, at the same time, preserve our freedom and self-respect into the bargain.'

[Source: *Daily Times*, 2 May 1967]

7. BROADCAST BY COLONEL ADEBAYO, 3 MAY 1967

My fellow countrymen.

I have decided to speak to you about the general situation in the country and the position of Western Nigeria in it all. As you are well aware, it is my avowed policy to keep the generality of our people informed about the momentous events which shaped their destiny. The need to do so has never been greater than now and I trust that this broadcast will help all of you, whatever your station in life may be, to pause and reflect soberly about circumstances in which we find ourselves.

I will speak first about the political situation because it is that which causes all of us the greatest anxiety. We feel anxious because we see the economic prosperity of our country with its hopes, dwindling before our very eyes whilst our present circumstances make it difficult to arrest the deterioration. We feel anxious because we find ourselves slowly but inexorably moving towards a conflagration which, if allowed to happen, may engulf all of us and produce disastrous consequences for us and for future generations. We are anxious also because we feel that this country, for which many patriots laboured intensely and even gave their lives to raise up to the height it attained before and after independence, is in real danger of disintegration.

I have no doubt that the political problem is at the centre of the long-drawn national crisis. The question it poses is 'how can we live and work together as one country given the events before and after January 1966?' We tried at Aburi to find the basis for a solution but there was not enough confidence to build upon that basis. As a result, follow up action was slow and argument developed which further impaired confidence. When at last decree No. 8 was passed by the Supreme Military Council, we could not carry the Eastern Region with us.

An aspect of the question as to how we can live and work together as one country is the alternative between the use of force for settling the Nigerian crisis and the use of peaceful methods. My personal conviction and by my assessment of the wishes of the overwhelming majority of the people of the region, the choice is for a settlement by peaceful methods. I consider wise and patriotic the solemn pledge signed by the military leaders at Aburi and re-affirmed at the recent meeting of the Supreme Military Council to the effect that force will not be used. I need not tell you what horror, what devastation and what extreme human suffering will attend the use of force. When it is all over and the smoke and dust have lifted, and the dead are buried we shall find as other people have found, that it has all been futile, entirely futile, in solving the problem we set out to solve. It is therefore with deep satisfaction that I note the voice of our people from all parts denouncing the use of force and commending the wisdom of the choice already made by the Supreme Military Council. And I am grateful to the representatives of the people of this region who in their deliberation two days ago, left me in no doubt about their own choice.

In essence the programme of action recently published as part of a communiqué at the end of the last meeting of the Supreme Military Council has this aim in view. I believe firmly in that purpose and I have worked strenuously and ceaselessly to achieve it. It was to that end you will recall that I arranged to meet my colleague, the Military Governor of the East at Onitsha on Easter Monday. At that meeting he and I exchanged frank views on the problems which unfortunately continue to plague us until now, including the problem of displaced persons of Western Nigeria origin who were ordered to leave the East. The most important problem was, of course, how to arrange a full meeting of the Supreme Military Council which I considered, and I still consider, to be of primary importance to the solution of the Nigerian crisis.

I must emphasize that in all the efforts I have made as an individual what has been uppermost in my mind is the preservation of the unity of Nigeria. I am glad to say that the collective view of the members of the Supreme Military Council in drawing up the latest programme of action was the same. Every right-thinking man whatever may be his region of origin ought to see that it is not in the best interest of this country that any of its component parts should cease to be part of it. An atmosphere must therefore be created to keep all the regions together in a way that the people may feel a sense of belonging.

During the nine months that I have been Military Governor I have seen my duty in three parts, namely: as a member of the Supreme Military Council with responsibility for the government of the nation as a whole; as a Military Governor with responsibility for the welfare and progress of the people of Western Nigeria, and as a senior member of the Nigerian Army. I have never considered these responsibilities irreconcilable. The object of my efforts in all three directions is the welfare of the people.

It is right and proper that we in Western Nigeria should be concerned about the state of affairs in our country. But we also have the equally important obligation of putting our own house in order. We can hardly expect to have an effective voice in attending to national issues in the absence of a secured and well-organized home base. It is for this reason that despite my exertions in other directions I have endeavoured to find time to address my mind to problems on the home front. It may be useful for me to recall some of these things briefly in this broadcast. The old provincial system of administration having fallen into disuse particularly from the point of view of day to day administration of public affairs, the region has now been regrouped into 28 administrative divisions. Henceforth the focal point of administration will be around these units. It is the primary objective of this reform to bring the machinery of government closer to the people and to provide the necessary impetus for social and economic developments from below. For reasons which I have already mentioned the old provincial grouping in the region has now been formally abandoned. For the purpose of effective supervision the 28 administrative divisions have been grouped into four zones at headquarters. I must emphasize that this zonal arrangement carried no political implications of any kind.

I have in my budget speech drawn attention to the precarious state of our finances and the need to raise additional revenue. The Ministry of Finance as well as the new divisional offices in the field will be devoting a good deal of their time during this year to ways and means of raising additional revenue so as to make it possible for us to continue to meet existing commitments and future requirements. I count on the willing cooperation of all of you in the task. I am sure you will be glad to know that the appeal court for the region, promised in my budget speech will be inaugurated on 1 June 1967.

The training depot for the Army, promised in April has now been commissioned and the monthly intake of Yorubas into the Nigerian Army has now been raised to 200 with the likelihood of further increase in the monthly intake of trainees. I know that this will go some way towards meeting the genuine fears of the people of this region as it will afford us the facility for improving the strength of Yoruba personnel within the Nigerian Army and make for more harmonious relationship between us and our fellow Nigerians in other regions. The No. 2 area command of the Nigerian Army has now been established at Ibadan on the basis of equality of status with similar formations in other parts of the country. Plans are in hand to fill the yawning gap in the personnel of the Nigeria Police contingent within Western Nigeria. To this end efforts will be made to provide additional physical facilities.

In response to the demand and the wishes of the people, I have appointed a commission to investigate the assets of public officers who have held office in this region since 1960 and those connected with them. The commission held its public sitting on 17 April. As you will have seen from the recent communiqué issued by the Supreme Military Council, it is the firm resolution of us in the army that the country should be assisted to get back on its feet by purging it of corrupt elements so as to pave the way for the establishment of an honest civilian government in due course.

I and senior Army officers of Western Nigeria origin have spent the last 24 hours in consultation with the Head of the Federal Military Government. Let us face it there is no region now without its acute problems brought about by recent events; there is nowhere the people do not have their fears. Ours in Western Nigeria have been spelt out again and it has been my duty every time to bring them to the notice of the Head of the Federal Military Government and my other colleagues in the Supreme Military Council. I have just returned from performing such a duty with respect to the resolutions which the leaders of thought passed three days ago. These resolutions indicate that the people of this region are frustrated and are impatient on account of the protracted crisis. This I have made clear to the head of the Federal Military Government. I am glad about his reactions and about the understanding of the need for speedy action to remove the causes of frustration and inhibition felt by our people.

I have left him in no doubt about the desire of the people of Western Nigeria that Nigeria should continue as one country and that an honourable place should be guaranteed for all parts of the country within it. Unhappily, the use of various political labels has, during the past few months, acquired over-tones and emotive meanings which have contributed in no small way to our problems. Among a section of the nation the word 'confederation' is almost a dirty one. I should like to take this opportunity to restate what is perhaps obvious. It is clear to all honest men that it is well nigh impossible, in the present circumstances of the country, to produce an ideal federal constitution with a strong centre or anything like we had prior to the events of 1966. But I sincerely believe that there is an opportunity for working out a constitution which will keep the country together while removing the fears of those who are genuinely concerned about preserving the unity of the country. It is neither in the interest of the people of this region nor of the country for anyone to contemplate doing anything that might disrupt the economy or interfere with the vital communication links between the various parts of the country. I say this with reference to the position of the West and other parts of the country particularly the North. The trade links and communication lines between us have been established for generations and they serve as channels of commercial and cultural intercourse between us. I should like to repeat solemnly that it has not occurred to responsible opinion here in Western Nigeria that these vital links should be interfered with in any way. In this connection, I would wish to appeal to our foreign friends to assist us, by discouraging the circulation of wild and irresponsible rumours.

As I have said earlier in this broadcast, all our energies should be directed towards creating the right atmosphere for representatives of all sections of the country to meet and discuss our common problems with sincerity and on the basis of complete equality. To those members of the public who have expressed anxiety about the nature of the responsibilities of military governors I will say this: we have found from bitter experience in the past that the only valid and enduring basis of government of any kind is to be found in the consent of those who are to be governed. It follows therefore that a true leader, military or civil, must be in close and constant consultation with all shades of opinion, and must seek to reflect and represent the people honestly. Otherwise government will become utterly impossible. I made this point earlier in this broadcast, but I think it can bear repetition. I would remind listeners that even during the early days of the military regime, in April and June 1966, the military leaders discovered very quickly that the advice and views of civil elements are indispensable to good administration. This is the only way that any kind of government can be run and it is my intention to continue to consult representative opinion in the region in all matters involving our future.

In my recent consultation with the Head of the Federal Military Government, I have found it necessary to restate that Western Nigeria is not in collusion with the Eastern region or with any other section of the country. Our primary concern is to ensure the solidarity of the nation and to find an honourable place for all of us within it. I am glad to say that my colleagues on the Supreme Military Council understand our purpose perfectly.

It is my earnest hope that the good people of Nigeria will continue to support the Supreme Military Council in finding a peaceful solution to the problems of the nation. I must ask you during these trying times to exercise a little of the habit of self-discipline. We need to cut down on ostentatious and extravagant entertainment. This is the time for hard work and sober reflection. We should desist from loose talk and rumour mongering such as are likely to frustrate all attempts at rebuilding our country. We require more than before to demonstrate a united purpose and to be charitable towards one another. I have an abiding faith in the

ability of the people of this region and I know also that in spite of
appearances and occasional outbursts, we nevertheless are a united
people dedicated to the noble course of doing honour to the Yoruba
race, and our country, Nigeria. As a gesture of my abiding faith I have
today ordered that all persons in detention should be released in the hope
that the people concerned will do everything possible to justify my
confidence.

You may well agree that our record in the West during this period
has not been unimpressive, but you will also have sensed that we are
being denied the pride and comfort of achievement as a result of the
overall situation in the country. How then do we get out of this rut?
This is obviously a task beyond the scope of any single individual among
us. I have no doubt that a resolution of our problems is within our
reach and competence, if the nation as a whole will agree to work
towards a common purpose. This we can do by continuing in our
efforts to allay the fears of all those who are genuinely concerned about
the protection of their legitimate interests within the country.

We in Western Nigeria are firmly convinced that the grave problems confronting the nation do not admit of the use of force. We
believe, very strongly, that we in the country have a common destiny
and that Nigeria, as we know it today, will not survive if any part
of it were to be severed from the rest. It is as well to bear in mind that
the only way of bringing about a settlement is to work resolutely
and peacefully for a fair and just solution which will meet with the
active support and approval of all those who are genuinely concerned.

[Source: *Daily Times*, 5 May 1967]

8. ADDRESS BY LT-COL OJUKWU TO THE JOINT MEETING OF
THE ADVISORY COMMITTEE OF CHIEFS AND ELDERS AND
THE CONSULTATIVE ASSEMBLY, 26 MAY 1967

Highly respected Chiefs and Elders, Loyal Patriots of Eastern Nigeria,
Distinguished Fellow Countrymen,

Once again it is my privilege to welcome you to this Assembly.
I do this with all humility and a sense of duty. Although we have not met
in this body for some time, I have continuously and daily met people
from all walks of life, visited various places and discussed with the people.

In tackling the day-to-day problems which have confronted us, my
task has been made much lighter than it would otherwise have been by
your absolute support and understanding in all we have tried to do.
On all the occasions I have had the privilege of addressing you, either
personally as I am now doing, or through other media of communication, I have made it clear that my paramount aim as the Military

Governor of this Region has always been to preserve the integrity of this Region, to provide adequate security for its citizens, to assure peace and progress amongst us and to prevent any recurrence of ill-treatment and atrocity against this Region and its people; and also, in consultation with my military colleagues, to establish a framework within which all the component units of this country could work together in the future on a basis of absolute equality. These have been the joint objectives of everyone of us and our paths towards them have always been made very clear and unmistakable.

Your meeting today is very crucial. The East is at the cross-roads. Since our last meeting everything possible has been done by enemies of the East to escalate the crisis in an attempt to bring about the collapse of this Region. They have failed and will continue to fail. Nevertheless, I find it necessary to put all the facts before you, indicating the issues, the difficulties and the dangers, so that you can examine them fully and advise me on the path we are to follow from now on. As usual, I call upon you to be free, frank and objective.

For a better understanding and a proper appreciation of the problems facing the country today, and in particular of the attitude of Eastern Nigeria to them, we need to go back to the historic statements on Nigerian unity made by leaders of Northern Nigeria.

We all know that before the amalgamation in 1914 of Southern and Northern Nigeria, the North was administered as an entity quite distinct from the South. The amalgamation was, however, not intended to, and did not in fact, result in a fusion of either the peoples of both areas or of their institutions. When, for example, a Legislative Council was established in 1922, it could not, and did not, legislate for the North; rather the Governor-General in Lagos legislated for the North by means of Proclamations. This was so because the amalgamation was forced on Northerners who made no secret of their dislike for it. The late Sir Ahmadu Bello, in his book, *My Life*, at page 135, said:

The Colonial master who ruled Nigeria introduced a system of unitary government not for the present or future unity or well-being of all the indigenes of the country but for his own administrative convenience. Lord Lugard and his amalgamation were far from popular amongst us at that time.

In 1953, the late Sir Abubakar Tafawa Balewa in a speech in the Legislative Council, said:

Since the amalgamation of the Southern and Northern Provinces in 1914, Nigeria has existed as one country only on paper. It is still far from being united. The country is inhabited by peoples and tribes who speak different languages, who have different religions, different customs, and traditions and entirely different historical backgrounds in their way of life, and who have also attained different stages of development. . . . We do not want our southern neighbours to interfere in our development. . . . But I should like to make it clear to you that if the British quitted Nigeria now at this stage the Northern people would continue their interrupted conquest to the sea.

'Interrupted conquest'! That has always been the Northern intention. Thank God that the East has now awakened to its responsibilities, and with that awakening, that ambitious dream will never be fulfilled in this country.

The Self-Government motion in the Central Legislature in March 1953 evoked the following reply from the late Sir Ahmadu Bello:

It is true that we politicians delight in talking loosely about unity of Nigeria. . . . What is now called Nigeria consisted of large and small communities all of which were different in their outlooks and beliefs. The advent of the British and of Western education has not materially altered the situation and these many and varied communities have not knit themselves into composite unit. . . . In 1914, the North and South were amalgamated though the administration of the two sections are distinctly different. Since then, no serious attempt has been made by the British or by the people themselves to come together *and each section has looked upon the other with suspicion and misgiving.*

In supporting him, Isa Kaita said:

'The mistake of 1914 has come to light and I should like to go no further.'

During this period, secession was the talk of every Northern leader, and Sir Ahmadu again said during one of the Legislative Council Debates:

. . . There were agitations in favour of secession; we should set up on our own; we should cease to have anything more to do with the Southern people; we should take our own way.

. . . I must say it looked very tempting. We are certainly 'viable', to use the current phrase; we could run our own show; the Centre would have to hand over to us our share of Nigeria's accumulated sterling assets. We had the men and production and minerals and the will to act.

The Northern House of Assembly debated the issue of self-government for Nigeria later that year, and in the course of this, her leaders adopted the now famous 8-point proposal, the purport of which is that the political arrangement best suited to Nigeria was complete regional autonomy with common services maintained by a central agency which would have neither legislative nor executive powers.

This attitude of the North delayed Nigerian Independence for two years. History will record that leaders from Southern Nigeria, and from Eastern Nigeria in particular, preached and worked for twenty years to achieve the unity of this country. History will also bear witness to the fact that the North had for so long resisted the idea of unity, and had, on four occasions in the recent past, expressed this resentment through brutal killings.

In 1964, when the most farcical election in Nigeria took place, a Northerner, Mallam Bala Garuba, published the following statement in the 30 December issue of the *West African Pilot*:

The conquest to the sea is now in sight. When our godsent Ahmadu Bello said some years ago that our conquest will reach the sea shores of Nigeria, some idiots in the South were doubting its possibilities.

Today have we not reached the sea? Lagos is reached. It remains Port Harcourt. It must be conquered and taken after December 30, 1964.

I remember when the N.C.N.C. and the A.G. were boasting about their day-dreams of snatching power from us. Today, their great brains are in our bag. Imagine such personalities as Akintola, Benson, Davies, Akinjide, Olowofoyeku . . .

I still hope that it will not be long when Okpara, Adegbenro and Aminu Kano will come to beg. Osadebay and other Mid-West leaders are half way to us. As for Awo, he will spend the last day of his term of imprisonment there for his inordinate ambition. Some Southern fools must understand that to suggest secession after their defeat is suicide for them. Let them think about all these things and understand the implications in secession.

(a) Where is the Nigerian Military Academy? (b) Where is the Nigerian Air Force base built? All these are up here in our region.

After the election, we will call upon our leaders to make a Northerner the leader of the Nigerian Army. Those who propose Ironsi are day-dreaming.

'After the next five years those southern so-called educated fools must realize where they are. *Once we will be able to connect the Bornu Railway with those of our brothers in the neighbouring country and from there to Egypt, we can allow secession to take place.*

Our exports could be sent out through that way. Thanks to Allah that the Kainji Dam will soon be completed. It is up to Tarka to come back now or face what will follow when we achieve our aim.

We must do anything possible to win the coming jihad. But we must keep our weather eyes open on those from the West as they could do anything at any time. Immediately we win, we can lose some members from the West at any time. We must not take things for granted.

With our 167 seats in the North we can go it alone. There is no need sharing the post of Prime Ministership and Presidentship with anyone. I have a genuine fear that we keep the posts and then concede some important ministries to some Yoruba members.

The time has come. *We are going to show these intellectual fools that we are only in the morning of our leadership of this country.*

We try N.N.D.P. in the next five years and see whether they will be too forward and ambitious as the ungrateful N.C.N.C. and A.G. If some still doubt that we haven't conquered our way to the sea, let them go through these facts.

(a) Who is the Prime Minister of the country?

(b) Who is the Minister of Lagos Affairs? Is Lagos not our capital?
Our only obstacle are the Ibos. They have played their card. They will sink.

This statement summarizes the stand of the North in relation to the rest of the country. In August 1966, just after the murder of Major-General Aguiyi-Ironsi, Gowon stated publicly *that there was no basis for Nigerian unity*.

I have quoted these and other statements in order to remind us of the consistency of the North in their feeling of separateness except where they are in relation to other peoples of Nigeria as Master is to servant.

In May 1966, the ill-fated Decree No. 34 was promulgated after it had been discussed and approved by General Aguiyi-Ironsi's Supreme Military Council which was composed as follows:

North (Two members)	Lt-Col Hassan.
	Lt-Col Gowon.
East (Two members)	Lt-Col C. Odumegwu Ojukwu.
	Lt-Col G. T. Kurubo.
West and Lagos (Three members)	Lt-Col F. A. Fajuyi.
	Commodore J. Wey.
	Brigadier B. O. Ogundipe.
Mid-West (One member)	Lt-Col D. Ejoor.

At the same time, his Federal Executive Council consisted of:

North (Three members)	Lt-Col Hassan.
	Lt-Col Gowon.
	Alhaji Kam Selem—Deputy Inspector-General of Police.
East (Three members)	Lt-Col C. Odumegwu Ojukwu.
	Mr L. E. Edet, Inspector-General of Police.
	Lt-Col G. T. Kurubo.
West and Lagos (Three members)	Lt-Col F. A. Fajuyi.
	Commodore J. Wey.
	Major M. Johnson.
Mid-West (One member)	Lt-Col D Ejoor.

The Heads of the Federal Civil Service were distributed as follows:

North	8
East	3
West and Lagos	5
Mid-West	7

The Heads of Federal Corporations and institutions then were distributed thus:

North	6
East	3
West	12
Mid-West	1

I have given you these facts because after the promulgation of Decree No. 34, evil-minded persons in the North and elsewhere propagated the mischievous lie that Easterners were dominating the affairs of the country. At no time since independence did Easterners dominate the politics of the Federation.

The reaction of the North to Decree No. 34 was to massacre Easterners in the North and to loot their property in May 1966.

Thereafter, the Supreme Military Council decided that a tribunal should be set up to enquire into the causes of that disturbance. Northern Emirs rejected it and demanded the secession of the North from the Federation. Nonetheless, the tribunal was scheduled to begin its sittings on 2 August 1966. On 29 July, and for several days thereafter, Northern soldiers in conspiracy with Northern civilians unleashed against defenceless Easterners the bloodiest acts of brutality. Major-General Aguiyi-Ironsi was murdered. His host, Lt-Col Fajuyi, was also murdered. Dead they are but their memories will live from age to age as a shining example of heroism, courage and loyalty.

In the heat of these outrageous acts, Gowon, a fairly junior Colonel in the Army, and himself one of the rebels, hoisted himself on the seat of the Supreme Commander; his first act was to demand secession for the North as a condition for stopping the massacre. I was left with no other alternative than to agree. However, on the advice of certain foreign nationals, he abandoned the idea, telling his people of the North that Allah had once more put the Government of Nigeria into the hands of 'another Northerner'.

On 8 and 9 August 1966, representatives of all the Military Governors met in Lagos and recommended, among other measures, that—

(a) Troops should be sent back to barracks in their region of origin.

(b) All decrees which centralized affairs in Lagos should be abrogated.

(c) Lagos should be garrisoned in a manner to be determined by the Military Governors.*

(d) A Constitutional Conference should be constituted to work out a constitution for Nigeria.

These recommendations were ignored by Gowon, and to this day

* According to the official minutes of that meeting: 'the Supreme Commander in consultation with the Military Governors'. Ed.

Northern troops have been stationed in Lagos and Western Nigeria. The proposed Constitutional Conference began its sitting on 12 September 1966. Gowon charged it to discover a form of association suitable for Nigeria no matter the name by which it may be called. Memoranda were exchanged by the Delegates, and vital features of some of them are as follows . . .

[Here Lt-Col Ojukwu cited the North's *original* proposal and the West's *alternative* proposal. See Appendix A. Ed.]

You can see that the position of the West then was very similar to the Northern proposal which suggested the loosest type of association for Nigeria. In the words of the late Sir Ahmadu Bello, this association would be:

A looser structure for Nigeria while preserving its general pattern—a structure which would give the Regions the greatest possible freedom of movement and action: a structure which would reduce the powers of the Centre to the absolute minimum.

The Gowon junta now preaches unity not because it believes in unity but because the dominating position of the North is threatened.

The *Ad Hoc* Constitutional Conference sat for about three weeks, and when it looked as if it was going to achieve a form of association unsuitable to Northerners, the pogrom of September and October was unleashed. The story of this pogrom is now being recorded by the Atrocities Commission in the interest of posterity.

The events of that period have made fundamental changes in the structure and pattern of Nigeria society and government. Some two million Eastern Nigerians have returned to the East. All the Northerners in the East have gone home. Relationship between peoples of the two Regions have come to an end, and if ever revived, will be on an entirely different basis.

I refused to recognize Gowon for reasons which I gave at Aburi. To recognize him would mean to accept the authority of a rebel in the Army, and that would be bad for discipline. The stalemate which followed culminated in the Aburi Meeting.

The main decisions reached at Aburi were . . .

[Here Lt-Col Ojukwu gave a summary. See Appendix D. Ed.]

It is to be noted that the meeting of 4 and 5 January at Aburi was held largely on my own initiative. Although I had strong forebodings about the outcome of the meeting, I went to it with a genuine desire to make it succeed. I decided that as soon as I set foot on the Ghana soil, I should be nothing but a Nigerian. It was my aim that the Military Leaders must come to an arrangement whereby the right climate could be created for all of us to carry out the duties and responsibilities to which we had dedicated ourselves. I wanted an atmosphere created for a return of normalcy, peace and confidence in country, an atmosphere in which all sources of fear and suspicion would be removed.

My genuine desire for all these was borne out by the fact that, before the start of the meeting, I pressed for a resolution eschewing the use of force in the settlement of our problems. I did so because of the widespread fear and suspicion in other parts of the country that the East was planning an attack. Nobody with knowledge or discernment could doubt our ability, even at that time, to take effective actions of revenge against the North, or even Lagos, if we had wanted. But our aim was and has remained that we should avoid further bloodshed, even though it has been the innocent blood of Easterners that has been most wantonly shed. Subsequent events seem to indicate that our opponents mistook my action in pressing for that resolution on the use of force as a sign of weakness.

On the question of political and administrative control of the country as a whole, executive and legislative powers were vested in the Supreme Military Council. In other words, all what used to be the legislative powers of the Nigerian Parliament, and what used to be the executive and policy-making powers of the Council of Ministers, under the civilian regime, were vested in the Supreme Military Council as a collective organ. To make sure that the Regions had effective voice in all decisions affecting the whole country, all such decisions must receive the concurrence of all Military Governors; and where any Military Governor was unable to attend a meeting of the Supreme Military Council, any decision reached in his absence must be referred to him for comments and concurrence.

This principle of concurrence by Military Governors was prompted by an appreciation of the special responsibilities which each Military Governor had over his area of authority. Having regard to the general welfare of the people under his charge, he should be in a position to delay any decision affecting the country as a whole until a consensus was reached.

As far as the Regions were concerned, it was decided that all the powers vested by the Nigerian Constitution in the Regions and which they exercised prior to 15 January 1966, should be restored to the Regions. To this end, the Supreme Military Council decided that all decrees passed since the Military take-over, and which tended to detract from the previous powers of the Regions, should be repealed by 21 January, after the Law Officers should have met on 14 January to list out all such decrees.

None of these agreements has been carried out. The meeting of

Military Officers was abandoned because Gowon withdrew the Federal representatives. The Law Officers met on 14 January as agreed and listed out the relevant decrees which had detracted from the previous powers and positions of the Regions, to enable the Supreme Military Council to promulgate the necessary decree by 21 January as decided at Aburi. The Officers of the Ministry of Finance never met within the time stipulated at Aburi because the Permanent Secretary of the Federal Ministry of Finance did not consider that such a meeting would serve any useful purpose.

I have said that what the decisions at Aburi amounted to in terms of political and military control of the country was that the country should be governed as a Confederation. As soon as we came back from Aburi, I considered it my duty to explain to the Eastern Nigeria public, through the press, the decisions taken at Aburi, and, as far as my sense of responsibility allowed me, the implications. In Lagos, the Permanent Secretaries there studied the recommendations and, to their credit, brought out clearly and unmistakenly their meanings and implications. Having seen these, however, they unfortunately went beyond their rights and duty as civil servants to advise against the implementation of the Aburi agreements. From here our difficulties started and have taken us to our present stalemate.

This leads me to the publication by Lagos of the controversial Decree No. 8. That is the Decree by which Gowon and his group claim to have implemented the Aburi agreements. I have mentioned that aspect of the Aburi decisions which stipulated that a Decree restoring the Regions to their position before the military take-over should be passed by 21 January 1967. The Law Officers met, as required, on 14 January but no signs of action appeared forthcoming from Lagos after that meeting. On or about 19 January, I despatched a telegram calling for the necessary draft decree to be circulated for concurrence.

Gowon's reply was the negative one of giving untenable reasons for his failure to carry out that aspect of the Aburi decisions. He, however, assured me that the decree was being drafted and asked for an urgent meeting of the Supreme Military Council. I promptly replied to his telegram as follows:

Glad learn Decree being drafted to repeal all decrees or aspects of decrees which detracted from position and powers of regional governments as they existed before 15 January 1966. Imperative that repealing decree be published immediately in order to confirm confidence and clear way of meeting Supreme Military Council. I agree that matters affecting constitution for which there were questions or reservations should be referred to Supreme Military Council which should follow soon after publication of decree repealing over-centralizing decrees or aspects of decrees. Surprised that my press statement embarrassed anyone. I know people with vested interests have tried through representations to you and others to capitalize viciously on that press conference. Honest acquaintance with and appreciation of feelings in East would show that it was in the interest of all that the conference was given. Silence would be misinterpreted here and difficulties created for smooth return to normalcy and of confidence. Every word spoken at Press Conference completely in accord with transcript of Aburi meeting.

You will see in that telegram my willingness to attend the Meeting of the Supreme Military Council provided the repealing Decree acceptable to all was published without delay. Such an action on the part of Gowon would have proved his sincerity to keep faith and honour agreements in the interest of public confidence. I should add here that the West Military Governor took the same stand with us on the need for an immediate publication of the repealing Decree.

Eventually a draft decree came forward from Lagos; but it was a document which was a complete departure from, indeed the very opposite of, what was intended at Aburi. It was even at variance with the agreements reached by the Solicitors-General at their Benin meeting of 14 January. Both the West and ourselves rejected the draft outright. Then followed a period of public controversy, confusion and uncertainty, until it was agreed that officials of the different Governments, led by their respective Secretaries to the Military Governments, should meet at Benin to advise on how best the Aburi agreements should be implemented.

The officials of the five Governments of the Federation held meetings on 17 and 18 February and at the end made recommendations which have since been published and which I believe you all have seen.* Another draft decree was prepared by Lagos. Although it must be admitted that this draft (which, incidentally, was, I am told, the 5th attempt!) was an improvement on the first one, yet it contained extraneous features which, at best, went contrary to the agreements of the officials and, at worst, were directed against the East. We promptly raised our objections to those features, but without any further comments from the Federal Government a meeting of the Supreme Military Council was arranged to be held in Benin on 10 March.

They expected me to attend that meeting even though they knew perfectly well that I could not do so for three obvious reasons. First, Northern troops were still present in the West and Lagos, and, secondly, all the confidence and marks of good faith generated at Aburi had been systematically undermined by Lagos. Thirdly, the passing of the right decree had been my pre-condition for attending such a meeting.

* See Appendix E. Ed.

However, they met on 10 March and, that very day, approved their Decree No. 8.

As if to underline their action of perfidy and double-dealing, a message was sent through, even after they had taken a final decision on the Decree, for Law Officers of the Regions to meet in Lagos to finalize a draft Decree. As a mark of my genuine desire for a peaceful settlement and return to normalcy, I sent my Law Officers to the meeting in Benin, where they were simply told that as the Decree had been passed by the Supreme Military Council, there was really nothing for them to do! All the same, our men reduced into writing and handed to their colleagues, this Region's objections. A few days later, on Friday, 19 March*, the Decree was formally published.

The Decree gave Gowon a veto power over the concurrence of all the Military Governors in matters affecting the exercise of legislative and executive powers of the Federation; it gave the Supreme Military Council power to declare a state of emergency in a Region against the wishes of the Governor. It is important that you should know that two days after the promulgation of the Decree, Gowon requested the other members of the Supreme Military Council to approve his proposal for a declaration of a state of emergency in the East. But for the wisdom of some members of the Council who refused to be so used, the story of the past two months would have been different.

For the foregoing reasons, I found Decree No. 8 unacceptable and rejected it. It was a Northern instrument for political power over the South. An important fact to bear in mind is that at Aburi it was agreed that all the members of the Supreme Military Council should meet to appoint the Commander-in-Chief and Head of the Federal Military Government. Up till now that decision has not been implemented.

I think I should here tell you my personal efforts since July to ensure a quick, realistic and peaceful settlement of our problems. Soon after the 29 July rebellion and the usurpation of office by Gowon, I told him that even though I was not prepared to accept him either as the Supreme Commander or the Head of the Federal Government, I would be prepared to co-operate with him in the task of keeping the country together, stopping further bloodshed and ensuring a quick return to normalcy.

It was for that reason that I sent representatives of this Region to Lagos on 8 August although I knew perfectly well the type of risks to which they were at that time exposed. It was for that reason that I did everything to make it possible for the meeting of the *Ad Hoc* Constitutional Conference to be held in Lagos with our representatives attending. All along Gowon and I were keeping in daily contact with

* Correct date is 17 March. Ed.

each other on the telephone. Even after the pogrom which started on 29 September and which has, more than anything else, changed our previous conception of Nigeria as one country, I continued the daily dialogue with Gowon.

There was a meeting of Secretaries to the Military Governments immediately followed by that of Advisers to the Military Governors. The outcome of these efforts was the famous Aburi meeting of 4 and 5 January.

Although the attitude of Lagos to the Aburi agreements was nothing but a catalogue of bad faith, I still felt that all chances of a peaceful settlement, which would lead to the maintenance of this country as a unit, had not all been lost. Meanwhile the Federal Government was owing us heavy amounts of money due to us as our right under the Constitution. I pressed that this debt should be paid promptly in view of our pressing needs for funds to meet our refugee problems. Nothing was done; the drift continued; the stalemate persisted, and the clouds thickened.

On 16 February, I sent a lengthy letter to Gowon with copies to Commodore Wey and other Military leaders. Because of its interest a copy of that letter has been printed as an appendix to this speech for you to see. I shall, therefore, not recount the details of that letter, but in it I brought out as forcefully as possible the dangers inherent in the continued stalemate. I pointed out to Gowon that, in spite of all his public protestations to that effect, he was not serious about saving the country. I repeated this Region's absolute stand on the Aburi decisions. I then gave him a catalogue of his acts of bad faith and perfidy following the Aburi meeting. Finally I gave the warning that if by 31 March the Aburi agreements were not implemented, I would have no alternative but to feel free to take whatever measure was possible to implement the decisions unilaterally. I ended my letter with these words:

I say this with the deepest sense of regret and fully conscious of the consequences of such unilateral action. But, I shall be able to tell the world when the time comes what part I have played at different stages and in different circumstances since the emergency which started in May last year, to avoid the situation. The responsibility will not be mine.

I still hope that good sense will prevail and that God will save us from such a bleak future. Let us at once implement the Aburi agreements, and preserve the country as one.

There was no reaction from Gowon to that letter. We continued to drift. On 10 March, a meeting of the Supreme Military Council was held in Benin, and on Friday, 19 March, the so-called Decree No. 8 was promulgated. The financial year was coming to an end, as was fast approaching my date-line of 31 March.

My aim was still to avoid a point of no return. Thus, on Easter Sunday, 26 March, I paid a visit to Ghana for discussions with General Ankrah and his colleagues on the National Liberation Council. I explained to them the position of this Region and the dangerous consequences of Gowon's continued indifference. I undertook not to take unilateral action provided Lagos paid its debt to us before 31 March. General Ankrah and his colleagues for their part undertook to bring together in Ghana all the officials of the Nigerian Governments to discuss the settlement of Federal debts to this Region.

On Monday the 27th, I held a meeting at Onitsha with Colonel Adebayo, Military Governor of Western Nigeria, accompanied by Commodore Wey, Head of the Navy, and Mr Omo-Bare, Deputy Inspector-General of Police. We held a lengthy, detailed and frank talk, in which I made the position of the East absolutely clear. The meeting ended on a high note of optimism. The delegation undertook to get Gowon to do two-things: first, to make sure that the debt owed to the East was paid by 31 March; secondly, either to suspend Decree No. 8 or to repeal those sections which were obnoxious to the East. They also suggested that the North should express public apology to the East for their atrocities.

I should also have mentioned that I had previously paid a visit to my colleague and friend, Lt-Col David Ejoor with whom I held intimate discussions. I had made quite clear to him the course open to the East unless there was a change of attitude in Lagos.

True to their word, the Ghanaian authorities were able to bring together in Ghana representatives of the Governments of the Federation, comprising economists, financial experts and legal experts for a meeting which was held on Wednesday, 29 March. The painful result of that meeting was the knowledge that the Federal Government had no intention of paying to this Region debts owed to it.

Here, I must place on record my unqualified gratitude and tribute to General Ankrah and his colleagues for the untiring efforts in trying to help this country solve its problems. The sincerity in all their approaches has always been transparent. Apart from telephone contacts and letter correspondence, the Ghanaian Government has sent representatives to Nigeria on several occasions to hold personal discussions, all aimed at helping us resolve our difficulties. Even if it turns out that Nigeria cannot remain as one, the efforts of Ghana in trying to avoid that situation will never be forgotten. If in the end some other solution is achieved, Nigeria will have yet greater reason to be grateful to the Government and people of that sister country of Africa.

Eventually, the date-line of 31 March arrived, and I considered it my duty to take appropriate actions effected through Edicts. Not surprisingly the Federal Government and its associates immediately read everything vicious into my action. I think I should here explain again the reasons behind the various edicts passed since 31 March:

Revenue Collection Edict

The purpose of this edict was to make sure that the Federal Government is no longer in a position to owe this Region its statutory revenues. It is legitimate that we take what belongs to us; it did not attempt to change the formula for revenue allocation as provided in the Nigerian Constitution, nor to take away what rightly belonged to the Federal Government. The truth of this statement is borne out in our estimates for this year where the revenues expected from Federal sources have been shown strictly on the existing formula.

Legal Education Edict

Following the disturbances of 1966, our students in the Lagos Law School were compelled to return to this Region. As a result of the stalemate, it became clear that they would never return to Lagos for their studies. We asked Lagos to open a law school at our expense but they refused even though under the Act it was possible. These students had a right to continue with their legal studies and also to practise their chosen profession. This Government would have failed in its duty to them if it did not take appropriate action to safeguard their interests. Our action was guided by the same principle that led us to establish a Medical School and a Teaching Hospital.

Statutory Bodies Council Edict

As part of its acts of retaliation and repression the Federal Government stopped the payment of salaries and wages to the employees of the various Federal statutory bodies operating in this Region, stopped the supply of necessary equipment, material and spare parts for them, and suspended the services of some of them, while making every effort to stifle others. The aim of the edict was to enable this Region take over the control and administration of these bodies to ensure coordination and efficient management. I do not need to mention that the Federal Government had failed to honour the Aburi agreement to pay employees of Governments and Statutory Corporations up to 31 March. The result is that this Government had to take over responsibility for the payment not only of the salaries and wages of refugees, but even of other employees of those Corporations operating in this Region. As at the end of April, this Government had spent £600,000 on this account.

Court of Appeal Edict

This edict was enacted to ensure that our people have opportunities of prompt justice and redress. The Federal Supreme Court last held sessions in the East in February 1965. As a result of the events which started in July 1966, our people, as lawyers or clients, could not pursue their appeals in Lagos. As the Federal Chief Justice was unwilling to arrange sittings of the Court in the East, the representative of Eastern Nigeria on the Supreme Court has since returned to the East, and the Bar Association of Eastern Nigeria has taken a resolute stand against its members going tò Lagos for cases, we saw no alternative than to enact an edict establishing our own final Court of Appeal.

Registration of Companies Edict

This edict requires companies to be registered in Eastern Nigeria; it does not deal with incorporation. It will enable us to collect and collate statistics of businesses operating in this Region for the purposes of planning.

No sooner had the Revenue Edict been passed than Lagos stopped all flights of Nigeria Airways, of which this Region is a joint-owner, to the East. Business and official travel has been disrupted and movement of mails has been disturbed. Talking of mails, I can illustrate the situation by mentioning that a letter signed in the Cabinet Office in Lagos on 28 April and addressed to my office was not received until 19 May.

In addition to this Lagos ordered that Federal employees serving in this Region, whether in Government or Corporations, should not be paid their salaries and abandoned all financial responsibility for Federal projects established in this Region.

As if all these were not enough, Gowon convened a meeting of his Military colleagues and presented to them a memorandum seeking authority for diplomatic, military and further economic sanctions against the East. You know the details of that iniquitous memorandum, which I promptly published as soon as it came into my hands.

You have heard about the withdrawal of diplomatic passports from citizens of this Region, the stoppage of postal order transactions between this Region and the rest of the country. There is, of course, the blockage of foreign exchange not only against this Government as such, but also against Statutory Corporations and institutions and even private industrial concerns in which this Government has a financial interest.

Importers from this Region have been denied import licences, and our industries the right to import essential raw materials for their operations. Further, Lagos has sent emissaries abroad to interfere with this Region's sale of its produce. Lagos has done everything within its power to strangle this Region economically.

I think that here I must mention the radio announcement by Gowon that his sanctions against the East have been lifted with effect from Tuesday the 23rd of this month. The unfortunate thing is that Gowon should tag on to his announcement the suggestion that the East should reciprocate by repealing the different Edicts which I have already mentioned and even the release of Railway rolling stock. If Gowon's action is to be taken as a sign of a change of heart, belated though it may be, let him go further and support it by paying to the East all moneys owed by Lagos, pay all Federal Corporation staff, reconstitute the Federal Supreme Court in a manner acceptable to all. No, we have had and known enough of Lagos not to be so foolish as to take Gowon's words on their face value. There must be concrete proof of genuine intentions and good faith.

Let me give you the background to Gowon's announcement about the lifting of his sanctions against this Region. I had repeatedly stated categorically that neither I nor my representatives would attend any further meeting to discuss the problems of Nigeria while the economic strangulation continued. I said it to the last delegation from Ghana; I said so to Mr Justice Arthur Prest who came here as a representative of a body called the Nigerian Peace Committee; I said so to Chief Awolowo and others who came as the representatives of the so-called National Conciliation Committee.

Indeed I should say a little more on the visit of Chief Awolowo and his group. They had come, in the name of the so-called National Conciliation Committee, to plead with us to send delegates to attend a meeting of that Committee. We could not understand the basis on which the Committee was constituted; it contained two self-exiled Eastern Nigerians resident in Lagos, in whom we have no confidence. The Committee has, however, invited two prominent men in this Region to serve as members, Sir Francis Ibiam, my Adviser, and Sir Louis Mbanefo, my respected Chief Justice. I informed the delegation that, as my Adviser, Sir Francis could not be expected to serve on a Committee to mediate between me and other military leaders; I told them that in this Region we regard the Judiciary as sacrosanct and would not want it involved in political matters of this nature.

However, we offered concrete proposals which were reduced into writing as follows:

1. The East is willing, and indeed prepared, to participate in discussions designed to resolve the present Nigerian crisis.

2. With regard to the request made by the delegates of the Conciliation Committee that the Eastern Government should appoint

representatives to the Committee, it would appear anomalous that whilst the other members of the Committee have been personally invited by the sponsors/conveners, the Eastern delegates should be appointed by their own Government.

3. Other members of the Committee, therefore, ought also to be appointed by their respective Governments. A Committee constituted in this way would be in a better position to achieve effective results.

4. Such a Committee should be set up in such a way that it is made up of people who have the authority and mandate of their Governments, with the Regions having equal representation and equality of status.

5. Necessary preparations should be made to ensure that there are:

(a) agreed agenda, with emphasis on the terms of association between the Regions;

(b) an acceptable venue, with due regard to conditions of safety and free discussion; and

(c) a time limit set for the completion of the work of the Committee so that the discussions do not become unduly protracted.

6. If the delegates are to participate in the discussions in an atmosphere of freedom and equality, then—

(a) the economic strangulation of the East should be discontinued;

(b) the occupation of West and Lagos by Northern troops should end.

We have heard that the Committee subsequently met, and submitted recommendations to Gowon, who has accepted them. Gowon is, of course, always prepared to accept recommendations from any body or any organization provided the Eastern viewpoint is not represented.

Last week, Gowon sent me a telegram informing me that he had arranged with the British Government to supply two companies of British troops to neutralize Benin or nearby so that the Military leaders might meet and that as an alternative to the supply of troops the British Government had agreed to make available an aircraft carrier or frigate on which we could hold a meeting. I, of course, promptly rejected the proposals in a telegram which read as follows:

'Reference British invasion Mid-West. Proposal not acceptable for following reasons—

(1) Meeting of Military Leaders without proper preparation and agreed agenda cannot achieve good results;

(2) Request for British troops without prior consultation with East makes whole business suspicious in the extreme;

(3) British agreement not in consonance with their policy of non-intervention nor your declared policy of non-internationalization of crisis;

(4) Presence of British troops in Benin will be regarded inimical to East.

In view of British attitude in present crisis other alternative not acceptable. East will resist British or Northern incursion into Mid-West with force.

If, however, you are now prepared to approach matter with realism and sincerity meeting of Military Leaders should be preceded by meeting of Government representatives on an agenda mutually agreed. Representatives would be fully briefed by respective Military Leaders so that they can reach agreement for ratification by Military Leaders or place proposals for them to decide upon. In any case, the East will not repeat not attend any meeting whilst subject to economic strangulation. *See* my letter of 16 May.

Two days before, I had addressed what I regarded as a final letter to him part of which read as follows:

The purpose of this letter is to tell you that in the face of all these unfriendly and destructive acts, deliberate and well calculated against this Region, we have no alternative but to make plans for a separate existence in the interest of self-preservation. Contrary to what you have chosen to believe, and have taken great pains to get the world to believe, it has always been my genuine desire to keep this country in existence. But for this desire I could have taken all the measures now taken or proposed to be taken, six months ago, and there would have been no power to stop us. I believed that this country should exist as one in a realistic form of association. Since this wish cannot be fulfilled the responsibility is yours and history will know where to lay the blame.

Before I go on, I should like here to stress that while Gowon is only too anxious to ask Britain for troops, his attitude towards the efforts of African Heads of State and the OAU to mediate has been one of stout and consistent rebuff bordering on contempt.

Having said that, there are certain facts which we must bear in mind. In the context of Nigeria, the history of this Region has been one of retarded progress because we are too prone to compromise and sacrifice in the interest of national unity.

The year 1966 has been for us a year of great lessons, opening our eyes to realities and dispelling our illusions. We came to this position months ago, but unfortunately we were alone. We had seen the need that if this country was to be saved, its component parts were to move apart. For this we were misunderstood and even abused. But because we believed our stand to be right we stuck to it.

One thing that has come out of the evils of 1966 is that they have clearly identified for us areas of conflict and friction as well as what powers can be used or abused by one authority to the detriment of others.

I am happy that at last our brothers in the South have come to realize the wisdom and sanity of what we have been advocating these last months. A great deal has, however, happened that our people are now demanding sovereignty.

Another good sign of the recent weeks is the acknowledgement by the people of the South that the stand of the East against the North has not been a mere struggle for itself; but a struggle against all forms of injustice, and for the natural rights of every citizen to have and enjoy life and property in an atmosphere and under environments free from fear and molestation. It has been a struggle of progress against reaction. If then, by hitherto standing alone, we have been able to convince others that we have been championing their cause as well as ours, we have every reason to feel proud of our stand, without regret for whatever sacrifices we have so far sustained.

Those of you who have been following the utterances in the North and Lagos during the past months would have heard threats of force against this Region. May I take this opportunity to assure you all that there is no power in this country, or in Black Africa, to subdue us by force. I make this statement not to intimidate anyone but to reassure you all, as well as to warn those who might be misguided.

As I pointed out in my letter of 16 May to Gowon, he seems to believe that time is on his side and against us. We know that the Federal Government has been importing arms, and preparing troops for purposes best known to them. We shall not launch an attack on anybody. But should anybody want to use force against this Region, he will find us neither unprepared nor inadequate. I think a word to the wise should be sufficient.

No Easterner would want to pass through the events of the past ten months again. Only a loose association, call it confederation or what you may, can ensure this. But Gowon and the North have categorically rejected confederation. The position of the East, and indeed the West and Mid-West on the one hand, and that of the North on the other, are at once irreconcilable. It is for you as the representatives of the 14 million people of Eastern Nigeria to choose from (a) accepting the terms of the North and Gowon and thereby submit to domination by the North, or (b) continuing the present stalemate and drift, or (c) ensuring the survival of our people by asserting our autonomy. If we have no alternative to the third choice, we shall leave the door open for association with any of the other Regions of the country that accepts the principle of association of autonomous units.

In such a situation the present units of the country would emerge as sovereign units each capable of maintaining its integrity at home and abroad but at the same time co-operating in the operation of common services in such fields as transport and communications, particularly shipping, harbours and ports, railways and airways. This form of association would envisage the movement of goods and services across the borders without customs restrictions. Appropriate machinery could be devised for co-ordination in currency management and monetary policy.

While I cannot here go into the details of this arrangement, the association could provide for dual citizenship so that nationals of the associating units need not carry passports from one territory to another.

It is my belief that such arrangements are the only practicable and realistic ones in the present circumstance and hold greater promise for the future than complete disintegration. Given good faith on all sides we cannot rule out the possibility of closer ties in the near future.

I consider it my duty to warn that if we are compelled to take that decision we must be prepared for a period of real sacrifice, hardship, and inconvenience. To start with, we may be without friends for a period. We may have to face the hostilities of the North acting in desperation. For a time there would be financial and economic difficulties. There will be the problems of external communications, of immigration, including passports.

All these would prove uncomfortable but only for a while. But we are bound to pull through it all. We have already made contingency plans to mitigate as much of those difficulties as possible. I shall not pursue the point, except to warn that time is running out. The people of this Region are totally tired of the present stalemate and state of uncertainty. We do not have much longer to wait. If Lagos and the North are now prepared that we settle the matter peacefully, they must act quickly.

We have a way of life and proud heritage to defend and preserve. We want to preserve our democratic and free institutions as a progressive society unhampered in its progress and development by feudalistic and reactionary forces with which it has been our misfortune to contend all these years.

As I said at the beginning of this address, I shall need your advice and guidance on the path we are to follow from now on. If, as is now customary, the Lagos and Kaduna authorities continue to spurn our genuine proposals for a form of association of sovereign units, merely because they wish to dominate the entire country, through a strong central government, I would expect the people of this Region to resist to the last man their aggressive designs on this Region. I am encouraged by the massive demonstrations throughout the Region supporting the Government's stand in this crisis. There have also been persistent requests and appeals to me for a formal break with some parts of the country. I now look to this august assembly for clear guidance on what to do should all our peaceful and constructive overtures fail.

Before concluding, I should like to refer to a few matters which are of particular interest to everyone in this Region at this moment. It has come to my notice that a number of expatriates have been worried about their future and personal safety. I want to assure them that Eastern Nigeria is safe for all friends; we need their services and their assistance and friendship. We guarantee them the safety and security not only of their persons but also of their property and business. I regret that in the past week or so circumstances have arisen where the people of this Region have had to react unfavourably towards a long-established expatriate business in this Region. I personally regret the incident and do sincerely hope that the type of circumstances borne [sic] out of the present crisis will not occur again.

This speech has been fairly long, and I must bring it to an end. Quite a number of you here might be wondering what this Government has been doing to give effect to the new Provincial Administration system. I want to assure you that everything is being done in this direction. There has been a lot of administrative and technical details to be completed before the system can come into full operation. What could be done has been done, such as the posting of administrative officers to the new Divisions and Provinces. What remains to be done will be done as expeditiously as possible.

I also appreciate the inconvenience which the absence of Customary Courts has caused to every man and woman of this Region as well as to the Local Government authorities, which have been handicapped in the collection of rates and in the maintenance of law and order. Here again things have been moving as fast as practicable and I hope, within a short time, to announce the constitution and members of the different Customary Courts.

Finally, it remains for me to thank you all for coming to this meeting. I do not need to extol the value of your understanding and co-operation which you have all along extended to me in the present crisis. The struggle has been the people's struggle not the struggle of one individual. With God on our side we shall emerge from the dark clouds now overshadowing us into a glorious and happy future.

APPENDIX I

Ref: EMG/S.62   16 FEBRUARY 1967
LT-COL YAKUBU GOWON,
SUPREME HEADQUARTERS,
DODAN BARRACKS,
LAGOS.

It is increasingly and ominously clear to me that we are not really serious to save the country in spite of our public protestations to that effect. For so long our country has been in continuous stalemate and it is now time to put an end to this state of affairs.

2. After the Aburi meeting, everybody rejoiced that it had been a

success. From our mood in Ghana, I was convinced that this was the feeling of us all. Personally, I returned to Enugu satisfied that we had faced our problems in earnest and realism. I therefore lost no time in re-assuring the people of the East, who had good reasons to doubt the usefulness of our meeting, that they had been wrong in their doubts and misgivings. It is a shame that subsequent developments tend, in fact, to prove them right and me wrong.

3. At Aburi, certain decisions were taken by the Supreme Military Council—the highest authority of the land under the present Regime. For my part, I became dedicated to those decisions, only to discover soon that you and your Civil Service advisers, along with selfish and disgruntled politicians in Lagos, and perhaps elsewhere as well, did not feel the same. As a result you have seen to it that the decisions taken at Aburi are systematically vitiated or stalled.

4. Soon after our return from Aburi meeting you on your own voli-tion got in touch with me to discuss the Federal publication 'Nigeria 66'. You wondered if it would be advisable in the light of the spirit of Aburi to go ahead publishing the document. We discussed and agreed that since the publication had not already been put out to the public it might be wise to withhold it at least for some time. On 15 January the publication came out. I got in touch with you and you assured me that it was not a deliberate act but a leakage. This informa-tion turned out to be a deceit because evidence soon came through that the publication was, in fact, formally launched in Washington, London, Cotonou and other foreign capitals. What is more, its intro-duction shows that the draft was completed after the Aburi meeting, most likely even after our discussion.

5. Your Press conference to the world on the Aburi meeting virtually amounted to a denunciation of the agreements reached at Aburi. At that Press conference you even brought in issues which were never discussed at Aburi, no doubt in order to embarrass me and cause dis-satisfaction in the East. My reaction to that Press conference was clearly shown in my letter EMG/S.62 of 30 January, addressed to Military Governors and copied to you.

6. Contrary to the decisions at Aburi, recruitment into the Army has continued with publicity in different parts of the country except the East; contrary to those agreements, you have proceeded to appoint Ambassadors without reference to the Supreme Military Council; contrary to the agreements, purchase and importation of arms have continued. The meeting of Military Officers to discuss the reorganiza-tion of the Army as agreed at Aburi has been unilaterally postponed by you. The Meeting of Finance Officials, with particular reference to the problem of rehabilitation, has not even been held because your

Finance Permanent Secretary in Lagos does not think it will serve any useful purpose.

7. You failed to publish the Decree on 21 January repealing all Decrees or aspects of Decrees which detracted from the previous powers and positions of the Regional Governments. After strong pressure from me and the Military Governor of the West, you have got a comprehensive Decree drafted which, for all intents and purposes, aims at strengthening the powers of the Federal Government at the expense of the Regions. You have denounced the decision (which incidentally was taken on your own personal initiative and proposal at Aburi) to pay employees who had been compelled to flee their places of work in other parts of the country until 31 March.

8. In support of these defaults on your part, you and your Federal advisers have looked for one reason or another. You have described the Press statement I gave soon after my return, as causing 'serious embarrassment to all', when, in fact, my honest motive was to assure the people of the East of the sincerity and determination of the Military Regime to face realities and save the country from ruin.

9. You have on another occasion accused me of distorting the decisions of Aburi, when in fact, I was very careful in my choice of words to conform with the actual ones we used. Another reason to support your efforts to abandon the Aburi agreements is the ridiculous one that I went to the meeting prepared while others were not. This is an information which has repeatedly filtered through to me and it surprises me that mature people should expose themselves to such ridicule. It was our first meeting since 29 July and it certainly could not be a picnic but business. The agenda was prepared beforehand in consultation with all concerned. If anybody went to that meeting unprepared, then one can only infer that he was not seriously concerned with the sad problems which had set the country, let alone with how to solve those problems.

10. Following your denunciation of the agreement to pay fleeing employees up to the end of March, your officials have given the fact that railway wagons are now in the East as excuse. When the decision was taken at Aburi, everybody knew that those wagons were here. One should have thought that the implementation of the Aburi agreement would be a pre-condition for the release of these wagons and not the other way round. Your Government has further complicated matters by denying the Coal Corporation the right to collect their just debts from the Nigerian Railway Corporation, and have refused to send the necessary funds for the payment of salaries for railway workers. These acts are nothing but a deliberate attempt to cause trouble and disaffection among the people of Eastern Nigeria,

because you and your Federal officials know the large number of persons involved and the seriousness of their dissatisfaction following non-payment of their salaries at the beginning of a new year when they have to meet commitments for their children's school fees and other personal matters.

11. The authorities in Lagos have not stopped there. They are using all their power to impede the smooth operation of private industries in this Region. Not only are they doing everything to obstruct investors and industrialists coming to do business here, they are doing everything to kill even those industries which are operating in this Region.

12. On the political front, I have evidence that the Federal Government is encouraging acts of subversion and sabotage within this Region, all of which are unfriendly and unbecoming of a people who regard themselves as belonging to one corporate country.

13. I have in this letter tried to catalogue some of the actions of the Federal authorities which are nothing but breaches of faith and exhibition of hostility towards this Region. I do not want to go over what I have often repeated and of which you are well aware, of similar acts prior to the Aburi meeting and beginning from 29 July.

14. Since your assumption of office you have constantly told me one thing and done another. You have never honoured any of our mutual agreements, let alone those reached by accredited representatives of our Governments at conferences. I had thought that the meeting would put an end to all these acts of hostility and deception.

15. As far as I am concerned, I have now on my hands one million, eight hundred thousand refugees who must be catered for. In addition to these people thousands of people have left Secondary Schools and other training institutions, and have entered the labour market looking for employment in the East. I accept with disfavour the attempts on the part of the Federal authorities to increase this problem by refusing to pay the railway employees up till 31 March as agreed, following your own personal suggestion at Aburi, and of doing everything to see that the Coal Corporation folds up. I have separately addressed you on the subject of the Federal Government's refusal to pay this Region its statutory share of revenue.

16. Now that I have been driven right to the wall, I have no alternative but to consider certain actions of which I have always hated to think. But I have responsibilities and as a soldier of honour, I will not run away from them. The people of this Region have a right to decent life, peace and harmony. As a people who once claimed the honour of being looked upon as the most matured in Africa, the leaders of this country must show that maturity by honouring agreements. Organized

society, confidence, good faith and progress cannot exist if people who call themselves civilized cannot honour agreements voluntarily and maturely taken. The survival of this country, its normalcy and peace, hinge on the implementation of the Aburi agreements. I would be the last to say that those agreements were perfect. I have already on several occasions said that I took them as no more than interim arrangements for the smooth running of the Military Regime. Having admitted that they could not be perfect, I believe that they may have to be modified in the light of experience in their operation.

17. We are coming to the end of our fiscal year when estimates must be finalized and plans made for the coming year. These are not possible under the present stalemate and unsettlement. If, therefore, the Aburi agreements are not implemented by 31 March, I shall have no alternative but to feel free to take whatever measure is unilaterally possible to carry out the spirit of the Aburi agreements. I say this with the deepest sense of regret and fully conscious of the consequences of such unilateral action. But, I shall be able to tell the world when the time comes what part I have played at different stages and in different circumstances since the emergency which started in May last year, to avoid the situation. The responsibility will not be mine.

18. I still hope that good sense will prevail and that God will save us from such a bleak future. Let us at once implement the Aburi agreements, and preserve the country as one.

[Source: The Government Printer, Enugu, n.d.]

9. BROADCAST BY LT-COL GOWON, 27 MAY 1967

Dear countrymen: As you are all aware Nigeria has been immersed in an extremely grave crisis for almost 18 months. We have now reached a most critical phase where what is at stake is the very survival of Nigeria as one political and economic unity. We must rise to the challenge and what we do in the next few days will be decisive.

The whole world is witness to the continued defiance of Federal authority by the Government of the Eastern Region, the disruption of the Railways, the Coal Corporation, the normal operations of the Nigerian Ports Authority, the interference with the flight schedules of the Nigeria Airways and other illegal acts by the Eastern Region Government culminating in the edicts promulgated last month by that Government purporting to seize all Federal Statutory Corporations and Federal revenues collected in the East.

The consequence of these illegal acts has been the increasing deterioration of the Nigerian economy. It has also produced uncertainty and insecurity generally and pushed the country with increasing tempo towards total disintegration and possible civil war and bloodshed on massive scale.

It has also led to increasing loss of foreign confidence in the ability of Nigerians to resolve the present problems. This has been reflected in the stoppage of the inflow of much badly needed additional foreign investment, it has put a brake on economic development so essential to the well-being of the common man and the ordinary citizen whose only desire is for peace and stability to carry on his daily work.

In the face of all these, I have shown great restraint hoping that through peaceful negotiations a solution acceptable to all sections of the country can be found. Unfortunately, the hopes of myself and my other colleagues on the Supreme Military Council have been disappointed by the ever increasing campaign of hate by the Governor of the Eastern Region.

Lt-Col Ojukwu has continuously increased his demands as soon as some are met in order to perpetuate the crisis and lead the Eastern Region out of Nigeria. We know very well the tragic consequences of such a misguided step. Not only will the regions themselves disintegrate further but before then, pushed by foreign powers and mercenaries who will interfere, the dear country will be turned into a bloody stage for chaotic and wasteful civil war. When the tragic events of 15 January 1966 occurred, the country acquiesced in the installation of a military regime only because it desired that order and discipline should be restored in the conduct of the affairs of this country, that swift reforms will be introduced to produce just and honest government, to usher in stability and ensure fair treatment of all citizens in every part of the country. The citizens of this country have not given the military regime any mandate to divide up the country into sovereign states and to plunge them into bloody disaster.

As I have warned before, my duty is clear—faced with this final choice between action to save Nigeria and acquiescence in secession and disintegration. I am therefore proclaiming a state of emergency throughout Nigeria with immediate effect. I have assumed full powers as Commander-in-Chief of the Armed Forces and Head of the Federal Military Government for the short period necessary to carry through the measures which are now urgently required.

In this period of emergency, no political statements in the Press, on the Radio and Television and all publicity media or any other political activity will be tolerated. The Military and Police are empowered to deal summarily with any offenders. Newspaper editors are particularly urged to co-operate with the authorities to ensure the success of these measures.

I have referred earlier to some illegal acts of the Eastern Region

Government. You all know that about one-third of the entire rolling stock of the Nigerian Railways, including 115 oil tankers, have been detained and that the services on the Eastern District of the Nigerian Railway have been completely disrupted for many months.

You are also aware of the fact that they have disrupted the direct movement of oil products from the refinery near Port Harcourt to the Northern Region. They have hindered the transit of goods to neighbouring countries and have even seized goods belonging to foreign countries.

These acts have flagrantly violated normal international practice and disturbed friendly relations with our neighbours. That refinery is owned jointly by the Federal Government and Regional Governments.

Illegally, since last year the authorities at Enugu have interfered with the flight routes of the Nigeria Airways. Only recently they committed the barbaric crime of hi-jacking a plane bound for Lagos from Benin.

They have placed a ban on the residence of non-Easterners in the Eastern Region—an action which is against the Constitution and the fundamental provisions of our laws.

They have continuously on the Press and radio incited the people of the Eastern Region to hatred of other Nigerian peoples and they have indulged in the crudest abuse of members of the Supreme Military Council especially myself.

Despite all these, I have spared no effort to conciliate the East in recognition of their understandable grievances and fears since the tragic incidents of 1966. To this end I agreed with my other colleagues on the Supreme Military Council to the promulgation of Decree No. 8 which completely decentralized the government of this country and even went further than the Republican Constitution as it existed before 15 January 1966. But what has been the response of the Eastern Region Government? Complete rejection of Decree No. 8 and insistence on its separate existence as a sovereign unit.

Only recently, a group of distinguished citizens formed themselves into the National Conciliation Committee. They submitted recommendations aimed at reducing tension. These included the reciprocal abrogation of economic measures taken by the Federal Military Government and the seizure of Federal Statutory Corporations and Federal revenues by the Eastern Government. These reciprocal actions were to be taken within one week, that is by 25 May 1967. It is on record that I accepted the recommendations and issued instructions effective from Tuesday, 23 May. Indeed, I now understand that certain vehicles of the Posts and Telegraphs Department which went to the East in resumption of services have been illegally detained in that Region. The response of the East has been completely negative and they have continued their propaganda and stage-managed demonstrations for 'independence'.

Fellow citizens, I recognize, however, that the problems of Nigeria extend beyond the present misguided actions of the East Regional Government to that of all sections of the country with equality. The main obstacle to future stability in this country is the present structural imbalance in the Nigerian Federation. Even Decree No. 8 or Confederation or 'loose association' will never survive if any one section of the country is in a position to hold the others to ransom.

This is why the first item in the political and administrative programme adopted by the Supreme Military Council last month is the creation of states for stability.

This must be done first so as to remove the fear of domination. Representatives drawn from the new states will be more able to work out the future constitution for this country which can contain provisions to protect the powers of the states to the fullest extent desired by the Nigerian people.

As soon as these are established, a new revenue allocation commission consisting of international experts will be appointed to recommend an equitable formula for revenue allocation taking into account the desires of the states.

I propose to act faithfully within the political and administrative programme adopted by the Supreme Military Council and published last month.

The world will recognize in these proposals our desire for justice and fair play for all sections of this country and to accommodate all genuine aspirations of the diverse people of this great country.

I have ordered the re-imposition of the economic measures designed to safeguard Federal interests until such time as the Eastern Military Governor abrogates his illegal edicts on revenue collection and the administration of the Federal Statutory corporations based in the East.

The country has a long history of well articulated demands for States. The fears of minorities were explained in great detail and set out in the report of the Willink Commission appointed by the British in 1958. More recently, there have been extensive discussions in Regional Consultative Committees and leaders-of-thought conferences. Resolutions have been adopted demanding the creation of states in the North and in Lagos.

Petitions from minority areas in the East which have been subjected to violent intimidation by the Eastern Military Government have been widely publicized.

While the present circumstances regrettably do not allow for consultations through plebiscites, I am satisfied that the creation of new states as the only possible basis for stability and equality is the over-whelming desire of the vast majority of Nigerians.

To ensure justice, these states are being created simultaneously.

To this end, therefore, I am promulgating a decree which will divide the Federal Republic into 12 states.

The 12 states will be six in the present Northern Region, three in the present Eastern Region, the Mid-West will remain as it is, the Colony Province of the Western Region and Lagos will form a new Lagos State and the Western Region will otherwise remain as it is.

I must emphasize at once that the decree will provide for a state Delimitation Commission which will ensure that any divisions or towns not satisfied with the states in which they are initially grouped will obtain redress. But in this moment of serious national emergency, the co-operation of all concerned is absolutely essential in order to avoid any unpleasant consequences.

I wish also to emphasize that an Administrative Council will be estab-lished at the capitals of the existing Regions which will be available to the new states to ensure the smoothest possible administrative transition in the establishment of the new states.

The states will be free to adopt any particular names they choose in the future. The immediate administrative arrangements for the new states have been planned and the names of the Military Governors already announced.

The allocation of federally collected revenue to the new states on an interim basis for the first few months has also been planned. The suc-cessor states in each former region will share the revenue of that region in the equitable basis of their populations until a more per-manent formula is recommended by the new Revenue Allocation Commission. Suitable arrangements have been made to minimize any disruption in the normal functioning of services in the areas of the new states.

It is my fervent hope that the existing Regional authorities will co-operate fully to ensure the smoothest possible establishment of the new states. It is also my hope that the need to use force to support any new states will not arise. I am, however, ready to protect any citizens of this country who are subject to intimidation or violence in the course of establishment of these new states.

My dear countrymen, the struggle ahead is for the well-being of the present and future generations of Nigerians. If it were possible for us to avoid chaos and civil war merely by drifting apart as some people claim that easy choice may have been taken. But we know that to take such a course will quickly lead to the disintegration of the existing regions in condition of chaos and to disastrous foreign interference.

We now have to adopt the courageous course of facing the fundamental problem that has plagued this country since the early fifties.
There should be no recrimination. We must all resolve to work
together. It is my hope that those who disagreed in the past with the
Federal Government through genuine misunderstanding and mistrust
will now be convinced of our purpose and be willing to come back and
let us plan and work together for the realization of the political and
administrative programme of the Supreme Military Council and for
the early restoration of full civilian rule in circumstances which would
enhance just and honest and patriotic government.

I appeal to the general public to continue to give their co-operation
to the Federal Military Government; to go about their normal business
peacefully; to maintain harmony with all communities wherever they
live; to respect all the directives of the Government, including directives
restricting the movements of people while the emergency remains.
Such directives are for their own protection and in their own interest.

Let us therefore march manfully together to alter the course of this
nation once and for all and to place it on the path of progress. Let us
so act that future generations of Nigerians will praise us for our
resolution and courage in this critical stage of our country's history.
Long live the Federal Republic of Nigeria.

[Source: *New Nigerian*, 29 May 1967]

APPENDIX D

The Supreme Military Council held its meeting in Ghana on 4-5 January. Those present were:

> Lt-Col Yakubu Gowon
> Colonel Robert Adebayo
> Lt-Col Odumegwu Ojukwu
> Lt-Col David Ejoor
> Lt-Col Hassan Katsina
> Commodore J. E. A. Wey
> Major Mobolaji Johnson
> Alhaji Kam Selem
> Mr J. Omo-Bare

Secretaries

Mr S. I. A. Akenzua	Permanent Under-Secretary, Federal Cabinet Office.
Mr P. T. Odumosu	Secretary to the Military Government, West.
Mr N. U. Akpan	Secretary to the Military Government, East.
Mr D. P. Lawani	Under-Secretary, Military Governor's Office, Mid-West.
Alhaji Ali Akilu	Secretary to the Military Government, North.

Opening

The Chairman of the Ghana National Liberation Council, Lt-General J. A. Ankrah, declaring the meeting open, welcomed the visitors to Ghana and expressed delight that Ghana had been agreed upon by the Nigerian Military Leaders as the venue for this crucial meeting. He considered the whole matter to be the domestic affair of Nigeria, and as such, he refrained from dwelling on any specific points. The General, however, expressed the belief that the Nigerian problems were not such that cannot be easily resolved through patience, understanding and mutual respect. Throughout history, he said, there has been no failure of military statesmen and the eyes of the whole world were on the Nigerian Army. He advised that soldiers are purely statesmen and not politicians and the Nigerian Military Leaders owe it as a responsibility to the fifty-six million people of Nigeria to successfully carry through their task of nation-building. Concluding, the General urged the Nigerian Leaders to bury their differences, forget the past and discuss their matter frankly but patiently.

2. Lt-Col Gowon invited the Nigerian Leaders to say a 'joint thank you' to their host, and all said thank you in unison in response to Lt-General Ankrah's address.

3. At this point the General vacated the Conference table.

Importation of Arms and Resolution Renouncing the Use of Force

4. Lt-Col Ojukwu spoke next. He said that the Agenda was acceptable to him subject to the comments he had made on some of the items. (A copy of the Agenda with Lt-Col Ojukwu's comments is attached to these minutes as Annexure A.) Lt-Col Ojukwu said that no useful purpose would be served by using the meeting as a cover for arms build-up and accused the Federal Military Government of having engaged in large-scale arms deals by sending Major Apolo to negotiate for arms abroad. He alleged that the Federal Military Government recently paid £1 million for some arms bought from Italy and now stored up in Kaduna. Lt-Col Ojukwu was reminded by the Military Governor, North, and other members that the East was indulging in an arms build-up and that the plane carrying arms which recently crashed on the Cameroons border was destined for Enugu. Lt-Col Ojukwu denied both allegations. Concluding his remarks on arms build-up Lt-Col Ojukwu proposed that if the meeting was to make any progress, all the members must at the outset adopt a resolution to renounce the use of force in the settlement of Nigerian dispute.

5. Lt-Col Gowon explained that as a former Chief of Staff, Army, he was aware of the deficiency in the country's arms and ammunition which needed replacement. Since the Defence Industries Corporation could not produce these, the only choice was the order from overseas and order was accordingly placed to the tune of £¾ million. He said to the best of his knowledge the actual amount that had been paid out was only £80,000 for which he signed a cheque on behalf of the General Officer Commanding. The £80 million about which so much noise has been made was nothing but a typographical error in the Customs in recording the payment of £80,000. As to why these arms were sent up to the North, Lt-Col Gowon referred to lack of storage facilities in Lagos and reminded his Military Colleagues of the number of times arms and ammunition had been dumped in the sea. This was why, he said, it became necessary to use the better storage facilities in Kaduna. The arms and ammunition had not been distributed because they arrived

only two weeks previously and have not yet been taken on charge. After exhaustive discussion to which all members contributed and during which Lt-Col Ejoor pointed out that it would be necessary to determine what arms and ammunition had arrived and what each unit of the Army had before any further distribution would take place, *the Supreme Military Council unanimously adopted a Declaration proposed by Lt-Col Ojukwu, that all members:*

(a) *renounce the use of force as a means of settling the Nigerian crisis;*

(b) *reaffirm their faith in discussions and negotiation as the only peaceful way of resolving the Nigerian crisis; and*

(c) *agree to exchange information on the quantity of arms and ammunition available in each unit of the Army in each Region and in the unallocated stores, and to share out such arms equitably to the various Commands;*

(d) *agree that there should be no more importation of arms and ammunition until normalcy was restored.*

The full text of the Declaration which was signed by all members is attached as Annexure B to these minutes.

Reorganization of the Army

6. The Supreme Military Council, having acknowledged the fact that the series of disturbances since 15 January 1966 have caused disunity in the Army resulting in lack of discipline and loss of public confidence, turned their attention to the question of how best the Army should be reorganized in order to restore that discipline and confidence. There was a lengthy discussion of the subject and when the arguments became involved members retired into secret session. On their return *they announced that agreement had been reached by them on the reorganization, administration and control of the army on the following lines:*

(a) *Army to be governed by the Supreme Military Council under a chairman to be known as Commander-in-Chief of the Armed Forces and Head of the Federal Military Government.*

(b) *Establishment of a Military Headquarters comprising equal representation from the Regions and headed by a Chief of Staff.*

(c) *Creation of Area Commands corresponding to existing Regions and under the charge of Area Commanders.*

(d) *Matters of policy, including appointments and promotion to top executive posts in the Armed Forces and the Police to be dealt with by the Supreme Military Council.*

(e) *During the period of the Military Government, Military Governors will have control over Area Commands for internal security.*

(f) *Creation of a Lagos Garrison including Ikeja Barracks.*

7. In connection with the re-organization of the Army, the Council discussed the distribution of Military personnel with particular reference

to the present recruitment drive. The view was held that general recruitment throughout the country in the present situation would cause great imbalance in the distribution of soldiers. After a lengthy discussion of the subject, *the Council agreed to set up a Military Committee, on which each Region will be represented, to prepare statistics which will show:*

   (a) *Present strength of Nigerian Army;*
   (b) *Deficiency in each sector of each unit;*
   (c) *The size appropriate for the country and each Area Command;*
   (d) *Additional requirement for the country and each Area Command.*

The Committee is to meet and report to Council within two weeks from the date of receipt of instructions.

   (8) *The Council agreed that pending completion of the exercise in paragraph 7 further recruitment of soldiers should cease.*

   (9) In respect of item 3 (b) of the Agenda, implementation of the agreement reached on 9 August 1966, it was agreed, after *a lengthy discussion, that it was necessary for the agreement reached on 9 August by the delegates of the Regional Governments to be fully implemented.* In particular, it was accepted in principle that army personnel of Northern origin should return to the North from the West. It was therefore felt that a crash programme of recruitment and training, the details of which would be further examined after the Committee to look into the strength and distribution of army personnel had reported, would be necessary to constitute indigenous army personnel in the West to a majority there quickly.

Non-recognition by the East of Lt-Col Gowon as Supreme Commander

   10. The question of the non-recognition by the East of Lt-Col Gowon as Supreme Commander and Head of the Federal Military Government was also exhaustively discussed. Lt-Col Ojukwu based his objection on the fact, *inter alia,* that no one can properly assume the position of Supreme Commander until the whereabout of the former Supreme Commander, Major-General Aguiyi-Ironsi, was known. He therefore asked that the country be informed of the whereabout of the Major-General and added that in his view, it was impossible, in the present circumstances, for any one person to assume any effective central command of the Nigerian Army. Lt-Col Ejoor enunciated four principles to guide the meeting in formulating an answer to the question of who should be Supreme Commander. These were the:

   (a) Problem of effective leadership;
   (b) Crisis of confidence in the Army;
   (c) Disruption in the present chain of Command;
   (d) Inability of any soldier to serve effectively in any unit anywhere in the country.

Lt-Col Gowon replied that he was quite prepared to make an announcement on the matter and regretted that a formal announcement had been delayed for so long but the delay was originally intended to allow time for tempers to cool down. He reminded his colleagues that they already had the information in confidence. After further discussion and following the insistence by Lt-Col Ojukwu that Lt-Col Gowon should inform members of what happened to the former Supreme Commander, members retired into secret session and subsequently returned to continue with the meeting after having reached an agreement among themselves.

11. At this point, the meeting adjourned until Thursday, 5 January. The Communique issued at the end of the first day's sitting is attached as Annex D.

The Powers of the Federal Military Government, vis-à-vis *the Regional Governments*

12. When the meeting resumed on 5 January, it proceeded to consider the form of Government best suited to Nigeria in view of what the country has experienced in the past year (1966). *Members agreed that the legislative and executive authority of the Federal Military Government should remain in the Supreme Military Council to which any decision affecting the whole country shall be referred for determination provided that where it is not possible for a meeting to be held the matter requiring determination must be referred to Military Governors for their comment and concurrence. Specifically, the Council agreed that appointments to senior ranks in the Police, Diplomatic and Consular Services as well as appointments to super-scale posts in the Federal Civil Service and the equivalent posts in Statutory Corporations must be approved by the Supreme Military Council.* The Regional members felt that all the Decrees or provisions of Decrees passed since 15 January 1966, and which detracted from the previous powers and positions of Regional Governments should be repealed if mutual confidence is to be restored. After this issue had been discussed at some length the Council took the following decisions:

The Council decided that:

(i) *on the reorganization of the Army:*

(a) *Army to be governed by the Supreme Military Council under a Chairman to be known as Commander-in-Chief of the Armed Forces and Head of the Federal Military Government.*

(b) *Establishment of a Military Headquarters comprising equal representation from the Regions and headed by a Chief of Staff.*

(c) *Creation of Area Commands corresponding to existing Regions and under the charge of Area Commanders.*

(d) *Matters of policy, including appointments and promotion to top executive posts in the Armed Forces and the Police to be dealt with by the Supreme Military Council.*

(e) *During the period of the Military Government, Military Governors will have control over Area Commands for internal security.*

(f) *Creation of a Lagos Garrison including Ikeja Barracks.*

(ii) *on appointment to certain posts:*
The following appointments must be approved by Supreme Military Council:

(a) *Diplomatic and Consular posts.*

(b) *Senior posts in the Armed Forces and the Police.*

(c) *Super-scale Federal Civil Service and Federal Corporation posts;*

(iii) *on the functioning of the Supreme Military Council—*
Any decision affecting the whole country must be determined by the Supreme Military Council. Where a meeting is not possible such a matter must be referred to Military Governors for comment and concurrence;

(iv) *that all the Law Officers of the Federation should meet in Benin on 14 January and list out all the Decrees and provisions of Decrees concerned so that they may be repealed not later than 21 January if possible;*

(v) *that for at least the next six months, there should be purely a Military Government, having nothing to do whatever with politicians.*

A statement on the Supreme Military Council is attached as Annex C.

Soldiers involved in Disturbances on 15 January 1966 and thereafter

13. Members expressed views about the future of those who have been detained in connection with all the disturbances since 15 January 1966, and *agreed that the fate of soldiers in detention should be determined not later than end of January 1967.*

Ad Hoc Constitutional Conference

14. The Council next considered the question of the resumption of the *Ad Hoc* Constitutional Committee and the acceptance of that Committee's recommendations of September 1966. After some exchange of views, *it was agreed that the Ad Hoc Committee should resume sitting as soon as practicable to begin from where they left off, and that the question of accepting the unanimous recommendations of September 1966 be considered at a later meeting of the Supreme Military Council.*

The Problems of Displaced Persons

15. The Council considered exhaustively the problems of displaced persons, with particular reference to their rehabilitation, employment and property. The view was expressed and generally accepted that the Federal Government ought to take the lead in establishing a National Body which will be responsible for raising and making appeal for funds.

Lt-Col Ojukwu made the point, which was accepted by Lt-Col Katsina, that in the present situation, the intermingling of Easterners and Northerners was not feasible. After each Military Governor had discussed these problems as they affected his area, *the Council agreed:*

(a) *on rehabilitation, that Finance Permanent Secretaries should resume their meeting within two weeks and submit recommendations and that each Region should send three representatives to the meeting;*

(b) *on employment and recovery of property, that civil servants and Corporation staff (including daily-paid employees) who have not been absorbed should continue to be paid their full salaries until 31 March 1967 provided they have not got alternative employment, and that the Military Governors of the East, West and Mid-West should send representatives (Police Commissioners) to meet and discuss the problem of recovery of property left behind by displaced persons. Lt-Col Ejoor disclosed that the employment situation in his Region was so acute that he had no alternative but to ask non-Mid-Westerners working in the private sector in his Region to quit and make room for Mid-Westerners repatriated from elsewhere. Lt-Col Ojukwu stated that he fully appreciated the problem faced by both the Military Governor, West and the Military Governor, Mid-West, in this matter and that if in the last resort, either of them had to send the Easterners concerned back to the East, he would understand, much as the action would further complicate the resettlement problem in the East. He assured the Council that his order that non-Easterners should leave the Eastern Region would be kept under constant review with a view to its being lifted as soon as practicable.*

16. On the question of future meetings of the Supreme Military Council, *members agreed that future meetings will be held in Nigeria at a venue to be mutually agreed.*

17. On the question of Government information media, *the Council agreed that all Government information media should be restrained from making inflammatory statements and causing embarrassment to various Governments in the Federation.*

18. There were other matters not on the Agenda which were also considered among which were the form of Government for Nigeria (reported in paragraph 12 above) and the disruption of the country's economy by the lack of movement of rail and road transport which the Regional Governors agreed to look into.

19. The meeting began and ended in a most cordial atmosphere and members unanimously issued a second and final communique a copy of which is attached to these minutes as Annex E.

20. In his closing remarks the Chairman of the Ghana National Liberation Council expressed his pleasure at the successful outcome of the meeting and commended the decisions taken to the Nigerian leaders for their implementation. Lt-Col Gowon on behalf of his

colleagues thanked the Ghanaian leader for the excellent part he had played in helping to resolve the issues. The successful outcome of the meeting was then toasted with champagne and the Nigerians took leave of the Ghanaians.

21. The proceedings of the meeting were reported verbatim for each Regional Government and the Federal Government by their respective official reporters and tape-recorded versions were distributed to each Government.

AGENDA FOR PROPOSED MEETING OF HEADS OF GOVERNMENTS TO BE HELD ON 4 JANUARY 1967

COMMENTS BY MILITARY GOVERNOR, EASTERN NIGERIA

Agenda	Comments
1. Opening address by the Head of State of Host Country.	Better be deleted. If host wishes to make opening address this should entirely be his decision.
*2. Response by Head of the Federal Republic of Nigeria and Supreme Commander of the Nigerian Armed Forces.	Not acceptable.
3. Review of the Current Situation in Nigeria, with particular reference to: (a) Organization of the Nigerian Army; (b) Implementation of the agreement reached on 9 August 1966 in regard to the disposition of Army personnel.	
4. Resumption of talks by the *Ad Hoc* Constitutional Committee. Acceptance of unanimous recommendations in September 1966.	Should read 'Acceptance and implementation of unanimous recommendations of *Ad Hoc* Constitutional Committee in September'. This along with 3 (b) of draft agenda would inspire confidence and reassure public of good intentions.
5. Problems of displaced persons, with particular reference to: (a) Rehabilitation; (b) Employment; (c) Property.	
6. Arrangements for future meetings of the Supreme Military Council and the Federal Executive Council.	Should read 'Arrangements for future meetings'.
7. Communique (to become item 8).	New item 7 should be—'Government information media'.

*N.B. Alternatively, this item to read 'Response' only.

DECLARATION ON USE OF FORCE

We, the members of the Supreme Military Council of Nigeria meeting at Accra on 4th day of January, 1967, hereby solemnly and unequivocally;

(i) DECLARE that we renounce the use of force as a means of settling the present crisis in Nigeria, and hold ourselves in honour bound by this declaration.

(ii) REAFFIRM our faith in discussions and negotiation as the only peaceful way of resolving the Nigerian crisis.

(iii) AGREE to exchange information on the quantity of arms and ammunition in each unit of the Army in each Region, and also on the quantity of new arms and ammunition in stock.

ANNEX C

STATEMENT ON THE SUPREME MILITARY COUNCIL

The Supreme Military Council now meeting in Ghana has agreed on the following reorganization of the Army:

(a) The Army is to be governed by the Supreme Military Council the chairman of which will be known as Commander-in-Chief and Head of the Federal Military Government.

(b) There will be a Military Headquarters on which the Regions will be equally represented and which will be headed by a Chief of Staff.

(c) In each Region there shall be an Area Command under the charge of an Area Commander and corresponding with the existing Regions.

(d) All matters of policy including appointments and promotions of persons in executive posts in the Armed Forces and Police shall be dealt with by the Supreme Military Council.

(e) During the period of the Military Government, Military Governors will have control over their Area Commands in matters of internal security.

2. The following appointments must be approved by the Supreme Military Council:

(a) Diplomatic and Consular posts.

(b) Senior posts in the Armed Forces and the Police.

(c) Super-scale Federal Civil Service and Federal Corporation posts.

3. Any decision affecting the whole country must be determined by the Supreme Military Council. Where a meeting is not possible such a matter must be referred to Military Governors for comment and concurrence.

MEETING OF THE SUPREME MILITARY COUNCIL OF NIGERIA
HELD IN GHANA ON 4 JANUARY 1967

Communique

A meeting of the Supreme Military Council of Nigeria was held in Ghana on 4 January 1967. Present were:

> Lt-Col Yakubu Gowon
> Colonel Robert Adebayo
> Lt-Col Odumegwu Ojukwu
> Lt-Col David Ejoor
> Lt-Col Hassan Katsina
> Commodore J. E. Wey
> Major Mobolaji Johnson
> Alhaji Kam Selem
> Mr J. Omo-Bare

The meeting which was held in a most cordial atmosphere was opened with an address by the Chairman of the National Liberation Council of Ghana, Lt-General J. A. Ankrah.

The meeting discussed a number of issues and took decisions. These included a declaration renouncing the use of force as a means of settling the present crisis in Nigeria and holding themselves in honour bound by the declaration. They also reaffirmed their faith in discussions and negotiation as the only peaceful way of resolving the Nigerian crisis.

The meeting has adjourned to resume in the same venue tomorrow, 5 January 1967.

MEETING OF THE SUPREME MILITARY COUNCIL OF NIGERIA
HELD IN GHANA 5 JANUARY 1967

Second and Final Communique

The Supreme Military Council of Nigeria resumed its meeting in Ghana on 5 January and continued and concluded discussion of the remaining subjects on the Agenda. The Council reached agreement on all the items.

On the powers and functions of the Federal Military Government the Council reaffirmed its belief in the workability of the existing institutions subject to necessary safeguards.

Other matters on which agreements were reached included the following:

(i) Reorganization, administration and control of the Army.

(ii) Appointments and promotions to the senior ranks in the Armed Forces, the Police, Diplomatic and Consular Services as well as appointments to super-scale posts in the Federal Civil Service and the equivalent posts in the Federal Statutory Corporations.

On the question of displaced persons the Supreme Military Council agreed to set up a committee to look into the problems of rehabilitation and recovery of property. In this connection the Military Governor of the East assured the Council that the order that non-Easterners should leave the Eastern Region would be reviewed with a view to its being lifted as soon as practicable. Agreement was also reached that the staff and employees of Governments and Statutory Corporations who have had to leave their posts as a result of recent disturbances in the country should continue to be paid their full salaries up to the end of 31 March 1967, provided they have not found alternative employment.

The Council agreed that the *Ad Hoc* Committee on the constitutional future of the country should be resumed as soon as practicable and that the unanimous recommendations of the committee in September 1966 will be considered by the Supreme Military Council at a later meeting.

The Council unanimously agreed that future meetings of the Council should be held in Nigeria at a venue to be announced later.

The entire members of the Supreme Military Council express profound regret for the bloodshed which has engulfed the country in the past year and avow to do all in their power to ensure there is no recurrence of the unhappy situation.

The Members of the Supreme Military Council place on record their profound appreciation and gratitude for the constructive initiative and assistance rendered by the Chairman of the National Liberation Council, the Government and people of Ghana.

[Source: Published by the Federal Ministry of Information: *Meeting of the Nigerian Military Leaders*; and by the Eastern Nigeria Military Government: *The Meeting of the Supreme Military Council, Aburi*]

APPENDIX E

EXTRACTS FROM MINUTES OF THE MEETING OF
SECRETARIES TO THE MILITARY GOVERNMENTS
AND OTHER OFFICIALS OF THE FEDERAL REPUBLIC
OF NIGERIA HELD IN THE MILITARY GOVERNOR'S
OFFICE, BENIN CITY, MID-WESTERN NIGERIA,
ON 17 AND 18 FEBRUARY 1967

The Minutes complement those reproduced in Appendix D. They make clear the difficulties standing in the way of an agreed interpretation of the decisions taken at Aburi. This extract reproduces

(i) the paragraphs relating to the crucial question of regional consent to federal action (Paragraphs 15–42) and

(ii) the Summary of Conclusions.

Draft Constitution (Suspension and Modification) Decree, 1967

15. After these preliminary statements by the leaders of the respective delegations, it was agreed that the crucial issue on which the meeting should focus attention was the draft Constitution (Suspension and Modification) Decree, 1967. It was suggested that the decree should be examined in the light of the relevant decisions of the Supreme Military Council. On the procedure to be adopted in this regard, Alhaji Akilu (Secretary to the Military Government, Northern Nigeria. Ed.) suggested that the law officers should be constituted into a committee to examine, for the consideration of the meeting, a draft decree aimed at ensuring consistency with the Aburi decisions.

16. The Chairman (Mr H. A. Ejueyitchie, Acting Secretary to the Federal Military Government. Ed.) held a contrary view, believing that the whole issue hinged upon the location of the legislative and executive authority of the Federation. In this connection, he pointed out that the Aburi decision was that powers in this regard should be vested in the Supreme Military Council. He contended, however, that the decision was apparently based upon the misconception that, in the past, these powers were vested in that body. The position, as he understood it, was that this had never in fact been so. For, under the terms of Decree No. 1 of 1966, two separate bodies were set up, *viz.*,

(i) the Supreme Military Council; and

(ii) the Federal Executive Council.

When it was found that this dichotomy was undesirable, an amending decree enlarging the Federal Executive Council had to be promulgated. The Mid-Western and the Western Nigeria delegations did not agree with this analysis as they both felt that the correct position was that both the Supreme Military Council and the Federal Executive Council had executive and legislative jurisdictions within certain limits. (See Appendix B. Decree No. 1. Ed.)

17. There was divergence of opinion on the procedure to be adopted in determining the extent to which the draft decree had conformed with the Aburi decisions. (A reference to a draft decree prepared by the Federal Military Government and circulated to Military Governors. Ed.) While some members held the view that the draft decree should form the basis for considering the matter, others thought that the starting point should be the minutes of the relevant meeting of the Supreme Military Council. In the end it was decided that the essential import of the Supreme Military Council's decisions should be determined as a basis for examining the decree. At this juncture attention was drawn to the decision recorded as follows in paragraph 12 of the relevant minutes:

Members agreed that the legislative and executive authority of the Federal Military Government should remain in the Supreme Military Council to which any decision affecting the whole country should be referred for determination provided that where it is not possible for a meeting to be held requiring determination must be referred to the Military Governors for their comment and concurrence.

There was general agreement that it was the intention of the meeting of the military leaders that the legislative and executive authority of the Federation should vest in the Supreme Military Council. As it stood, however, the draft decree did not reflect this intention. Members were unanimous in the view that the appropriate decree, in order to give effect to the decisions of the military leaders, should faithfully reflect this intention.

18. After the question of the location of the legislative and executive authority of the Federation had been settled, the meeting then proceeded to consider the manner in which it was intended that this authority should be exercised. On this issue Mr Giwa-Amu, Solicitor-General for Mid-Western Nigeria, pointed out that the intention of the military leaders was, to some extent, explained in paragraph 12 of the minutes of their meeting at Aburi.

The essential point to note, he said, was the agreement that 'any decision (of the Supreme Military Council) affecting the whole country should be referred for determination provided that where it is not possible for a meeting to be held the matter requiring determination must be referred to the Military Governors for their comments and concurrence". Continuing, Mr Giwa-Amu pointed out that no clear-cut drafting instructions were given to the law officers with respect to the manner of exercising the Supreme Military Council's legislative and executive authority within the context of the Aburi decisions and that it was with a view to clarifying the decisions that the questions posed on page 11 of the minutes of the meeting of the law officers on 14th and 15 January, 1967, were referred to the Supreme Military Council for determination. (See below, pp. 257–8. Ed.) As far as he was aware, these issues had not been determined and, despite this fact, the Federal Government had proceeded to draft a decree.

19. A prolonged discussion on the subjects in respect of which the concurrence of Military Governors was considered necessary ensued. The Federal delegation, as represented by the views expressed by Mr Atta (Permanent Secretary, Federal Ministry of Finance. Ed.) felt that, in dealing with the issue of the extent to which the right of con-currence should be conceded, care should be taken that it did not extend, for instance, to the approval of estimates as it was foreseen that any deadlock arising from the approval of estimates would have the effect of bringing the processes of the Federal Government to a complete stand-still. Mr Atta warned that the greatest possible caution should be exercised in determining the extent of concurrence by Regional Governors in the decisions of the Supreme Military Council in the exercise of its legislative and executive authority since most aspects of the activities of the Federal Military Government could have far-reach-ing implications on the international plane. He considered that if the powers of concurrence granted to Regional Governors were too ex-tensive, the overall national interests would be jeopardized and the nation would become a laughing stock in the estimation of the outside world.

20. The Eastern delegation, on the other hand, stressed that account should be taken of the fact that the existing constitutional situation was entirely different from what it was under the civilian regime. With the suspension of Parliament and the Federal Council of Ministers, the Supreme Military Council combined all the powers previously exercised by the two bodies. In such circumstances, it was essential that due regard was given to the feelings of the Regions in arriving at decisions affecting the whole country. Emphasizing the same point, Mr Giwa-Amu endorsed the view that the existing situation in the country was entirely different from what it was under the civilian regime. Under the latter, he pointed out, there was a well organized military force which could ensure that the laws enacted by Parliament were enforced. At present, however, it could not be said that there was a unified army as it was a well-known fact that the army was, to all

intents and purposes, organized in regional units with each unit owing allegiance, so to speak, to the respective Regional Governments. He stressed that it would be over-optimistic to expect that, under the prevailing circumstances, it would be possible to enforce Federal enactments in the same way as they were enforced under the old regime. For this reason, he felt that a sufficiently wide scope ought to be given to Regional Governors for expressing concurrence in or disagreement with the decisions of the Supreme Military Council. Accordingly, he suggested that in demarcating the areas of concurrence in the decisions of the Supreme Military Council by Regional Military Governors, attention should be focused on the following issues:

(i) amendment of the entrenched provisions of the Republican Constitution;

(ii) legislation affecting the territorial integrity of a Region;

(iii) legislation affecting the economy of a Region;

(iv) legislation affecting the effective administration of a Region.

The Western and Northern delegations thought that these matters were far too wide to be conceded to Military Governors.

21. Another approach to which the Western and Eastern Nigeria delegations lent support was that the entrenched provisions as contained in section 4 of the Republican Constitution, 1963, should be the subject of concurrence by the Regional Military Governors. In addition, it was felt that the exclusive legislative list should be examined serially in order to determine which matters at present contained in the list should be made the subject of concurrence by Military Governors within the context of the Aburi decisions. Chief Dina's suggestion that, in addition to statutory safeguards, the old national consultative organs (e.g., the National Economic Council, the Joint Planning Committee, the National Council on Establishments, etc.) should be revived in order to give the ultimate decisions of the Supreme Military Council a national character and so inspire confidence in them, received general acceptance.

22. The Secretary to the Midwestern Nigeria Military Government thought that the areas of dispute were likely to be enlarged if any attempt was made to extend the scope of concurrence by the Regional Military Governors to matters on the exclusive list. Accordingly, he suggested that the right of concurrence should be limited in the meantime to the entrenched provisions as contained in section 4 of the Republican Constitution, 1963. At the same time the need to re-convene the Ad Hoc Committee, which had already done some good work on a future re-distribution of powers, so that it could complete its assignment leading to more permanent solutions to the country's problems, was stressed.

23. While the Northern delegation agreed with this view on the ground that the meeting would be going beyond the normal contemplation of the Aburi decision if the exclusive list were to be invaded, the Eastern and Western delegations felt strongly that unless this was done the decision of the Aburi meeting could not be said to have been faithfully implemented.

24. The Mid-Western and Northern Nigeria delegations suggested that, considering the divergence of opinion which occurred over the interpretation of the relevant decision of the Supreme Military Council, a further approach should be made to the Council with the request that the precise intention of the council with regard to the scope of concurrence by Regional Military Governors should be defined. The Northern delegation, in particular, felt that it would be beyond the competence of civil servants to dabble too much into the intricate political issues connected with the determination of the manner in which concurrence should be exercised by the Military Governors including, perhaps, for the Federal Territory, the Military Administrator of Lagos. The Eastern Nigeria delegation countered this suggestion by making it clear that the Military Governor of Eastern Nigeria had made no secret of the fact that he would be unable to attend any meeting of the Supreme Military Council until the decree on the suspension and modification of the Constitution was issued as agreed at Aburi.

25. The meeting was unable to reach agreement on the scope of concurrence to be allowed to Military Governors (including, maybe, the Military Administrator of Lagos) in the decisions of the Supreme Military Council before it rose for a luncheon break at 1.45 p.m.

26. When the meeting re-assembled at 3.15 p.m., it was still impossible to arrive at a decision on the issue, despite an appeal for objectivity and detachment by the Chairman. For this reason it was decided to defer consideration of the subject until the next day.

27. Other matters raised thereafter include:

(i) powers of Regional Governments with regard to the amendments of their respective constitutions;

(ii) provisions of the draft decree considered inconsistent with the Aburi decisions.

With regard to the first issue no decision was reached on the first day of the meeting. As for the second, it was observed by the Western Nigeria delegation that although it was agreed among the military leaders at Aburi that appointments to diplomatic and consular posts, senior posts in the armed forces and super-scale Federal civil service and corporation posts should be subject to approval by the Supreme Military Council, this decision was not reflected in the draft decree.

It was suggested that the draft decree should reflect the decision with the proviso that in respect of appointments to super-scale posts in the Federal civil service (*i.e.*, posts graded in Group 9 and above), the Federal Public Service Commission should act in an advisory capacity. The Secretary to the Mid-Western Nigeria Military Government supported this proposal in principle but felt that it would be too much to expect the Supreme Military Council to be saddled with the responsibility of approving appointments, with all its implications, to posts as low in status as Group 9. He therefore suggested that the powers of the Supreme Military Council in this regard should be confined to Staff Grade and equivalent posts. The Eastern Nigeria delegation had no objection to this amendment. On its part, however, the Northern Nigeria delegation thought that it would be unrealistic to attempt to determine at what point the powers of the Supreme Military Council with regard to appointments should end until an accurate assessment of the volume of responsibility involved was made. As for the definition of 'senior posts' in the armed forces and the police, it was thought that the expression used was far too vague and that a clearer definition should be obtained from the Supreme Military Council. In this connection, the meeting saw nothing wrong in attempting a definition for consideration by the Council.

28. On these issues, no precise decision was reached before the day's meeting was brought to an end at 5.10 p.m. The next day's meeting was fixed for 9.30 a.m.

29. The next day's session commenced at 9.50 a.m. with all members present and with Mr Ejueyitchie, Secretary to the Federal Military Government, still presiding. Before introducing discussion on the day's business, the chairman appealed once again to members to be conscious of their responsibilities as civil servants.

Questions referred by the law officers to the Supreme Military Council for determination

30. The Chairman suggested, and it was agreed, that before proceeding to consider the items deferred at the previous day's sitting, the meeting should look into the questions posed on page 11 of the minutes of the law officers' meeting of 14th and 15th January, 1967, for the Supreme Military Council's determination, in an effort to see what practical proposals it might be able to present to the Supreme Military Council on the issues raised. The questions are reproduced below for ease of reference:

(a) Whether it is the intention of the Accra agreement that a meeting of the Supreme Military Council would not be properly constituted and so cannot properly be held unless all the Military Governors are present.

(b) Whether where all the Military Governors are present at a meeting of the Supreme Military Council, decisions of the Council can properly be taken only with the concurrence or unanimity of all the Military Governors present, or by a majority of the Military Governors present, *or else* by a majority of all the members present.

(c) Whether where one or more Military Governors are not present at the meeting of the Supreme Military Council, their concurrence in decisions taken at such a meeting will still be necessary before the decisions can be implemented.

(d) Whether all decrees (whether affecting the whole country or not) are to be formally approved by the Supreme Military Council before they are signed by the Head of the Federal Military Government.

(e) In what manner should the concurrence of the Military Governors in the making of decrees (in their capacity as members of the Supreme Military Council) be signified that is, for instance, whether it will be enough for this to be signified orally in the course of a meeting of the Supreme Military Council or by writing under their respective hands or whether there should be a column in the decree for the appending of their signatures.

31. With regard to question (a), it was the concensus of opinion that the Aburi decision with regard to the exercise of the Supreme Military Council's legislative and executive authority could not be construed as implying that a meeting of the Council could not be held or be properly constituted unless all the Military Governors were present. With regard to question (b), however, a number of divergent views were expressed. The Attorney-General for Northern Nigeria, Alhaji Buba Ardo, contended that decisions taken at meetings of the Supreme Military Council should require the support or consent of a majority of the Military Governors present, with this reservation that, on issues of vital importance or national significance, the comments of Military Governors who are absent at such meetings should be obtained. As for routine matters it was his view that a simple majority of the Council would be enough to render a decision of the Supreme Military Council valid.

32. Mr Akpan, Secretary to the Eastern Nigeria Military Government, considered that the suggestion that decisions of the Supreme Military Council should require the consent of a majority of Military Governors or members of the council present, as the case might be, was contrary to the normal cabinet procedure whereby questions are determined not by vote but by collective decision. On this point, Alhaji Ali Akilu, Secretary to the Northern Nigeria Military Government, was in complete agreement with Mr Akpan. It was, however, his view that the question under consideration did not in any way arise in view of the fact that the intention of the Supreme Military Council was quite obvious from the decision recorded in paragraph 12 of the minutes of the Aburi meeting. According to him, it was clear that,

where a meeting was held even in the absence of some members, the usual cabinet procedure should apply. Continuing, he pointed out that the Aburi decision, to which reference had been made dealt specifically with the procedure to be adopted where it was not possible for a meeting of the Supreme Military Council to be held and not the other way round. The Chairman concurred and added that these observations seemed incontestable on a fair and proper construction of the relevant portion of the minutes of the Aburi meeting.

33. Mr Tokunboh (Permanent Secretary, Federal Ministry of Establishments. Ed.) felt that it would be futile to place too literal an interpretation on the Aburi decision which, he confessed, had, unfortunately, not been expressed in very precise terms. It was understandable that most members, having not had the opportunity of knowing how the particular decision was arrived at, were in difficulty in understanding its precise intention. For this reason, he suggested that the right approach to adopt was to find out to what extent the decision, as recorded, was practicable. Where the decision would be difficult to implement, it was the duty of the meeting to find out how the inherent difficulty could be surmounted. Mr Tokunboh's views received the support of Mr Imoukhuede, Secretary to the Mid-Western Nigeria Military Government.

34. Contributing to the discussion, Dr Ajayi, Solicitor-General for Western Nigeria, recalled that the crux of the matter had been discussed extensively at the previous day's meeting. In his view, the whole issue centred around the interpretation of the Supreme Military Council's decision concerning issues affecting the whole nation in respect of which the concurrence of the Military Governors must be obtained before any decision could be valid. For this reason, he contended that the limits within which Military Governors' right of concurrence to decisions of the Supreme Military Council must be exercised had to be determined first before a proper answer could be found to question (b) (see paragraph 30 above). He therefore suggested that the categories of matters requiring Military Governors' concurrence, as proposed by Mr Giwa-Amu on the previous day, be carefully re-examined. This suggestion was accepted and on the basis of a paper presented by him, it was agreed to recommend to the Supreme Military Council that the following matters should be subject to the concurrence of Military Governors in the exercise of the Council's legislative and executive jurisdiction:

(i) power to make decrees affecting the territorial integrity of a region or altering any of the entrenched provisions listed in the proviso to section 4 (1) of the Constitution of the Federation, 1963, to be revived with necessary modifications;

(ii) power to make laws or to administer existing laws of economic character affecting the whole country, for instance, laws with respect to trade, commerce, industry, transport and communications, labour, public service and public finance (other than the approval of the Federal estimates, but including the approval of new capital projects in such estimates);

(iii) power to make new laws or to administer existing laws of international or security character affecting the whole country, for instance, laws with respect to external affairs, defence, naval, military and air forces, the Nigeria Police, arms and ammunition, administration of the affairs of a region, maintenance and securing of public order, public safety and essential supplies and services;

(iv) power to make new laws or to administer existing laws of a higher educational or professional character, for instance, laws with respect to higher education generally, existing higher educational institutions and the professions;

(v) power to exercise executive authority affecting the country with respect to any of the matters mentioned in (i)-(iv) above.

35. Another aspect of the exercise of the Supreme Military Council's legislative and executive authority within the context of the Aburi decision, to which the meeting directed its attention, was the necessity for making provision in the proposed decree enabling the Supreme Military Council to delegate some of the legislative and executive powers now being vested in it at the Federal level on a wider scale than was provided for in the previous decrees. It was, for instance, observed that both in Decree No. 1 of 1966 and in the draft decree circulated to the meeting, the power of the Supreme Military Council to delegate its authority was limited to the power to delegate *only* to its own members. It was considered that in the interest of efficiency and for the convenience of day-to-day administration, it would be necessary for the Council to be able to delegate its executive powers as well as many of its powers under existing statutes to any other person or authority as it might deem fit. It was unanimously agreed that the proposed decree should contain a provision enabling the Supreme Military Council to delegate its powers not only to its members, as at present, but also to any other person or authority, provided that:

(i) the Supreme Military Council should not delegate any of its powers to make decrees;

(ii) where the Council considered it necessary to delegate the exercise of its executive authority with respect to any of the matters mentioned in items (i) to (iv) listed in the preceding paragraph, such delegation should be effected only with the concurrence of all the Military Governors.

Exercise of the Executive Authority of Regional Governments

36. The meeting then proceeded to consider whether the suspended section 86 of the Constitution of the Federation (which dealt with the executive authority of the Regions) should be restored. The Eastern Nigeria delegation felt strongly that it was entirely unnecessary to revive section 86 of the Constitution as care was taken in all previous decrees to suspend this provision of the Constitution. In any case, they thought that the revival of the section was purely academic in the present circumstances of Nigeria. They did not consider that what was necessary to keep the Federation together was the revival of this provision of the Constitution. On the contrary, they suggested that the best way of keeping the country together and of avoiding the possibility of secession by any component part of the Federation was to take effective steps to normalize relations between all parts of the Federation. They urged that, in approaching the issue account should be taken of the fact that the prevailing circumstances in the country could in no way be compared with what they were during the first republic. Before the inception of the Military Government, there was a disciplined armed force which could be relied upon in guaranteeing the safety of the whole Federation. At present, however, the position had changed completely and it was impossible to speak of a properly organized armed force which could guarantee the safety of all Nigerians irrespective of their Regions of origin. In recognition of these altered circumstances, they considered that it would be entirely undesirable to attempt to limit the powers of the Regions in the manner implicit in the revival of section 86 of the Constitution.

37. The Chairman argued that it was necessary to suspend section 86 of the Constitution under Decree No. 1 of 1966 because at that time extensive powers were concentrated at the centre and there could be no question of the Regions, which were indeed in the process of being unified, exercising their powers in a manner prejudicial to the existence of the country. He observed that circumstances had since changed and that the obvious tendency was towards the restoration of the powers previously exercised by the Regional Governments. Under such circumstances, it was necessary to guard against the possibility of Regional Governments exercising their authority in a manner likely to endanger the very existence of the Federation.

38. On its part, the Northern Nigeria delegation emphasized that the essential issue to be borne in mind was that the fundamental intention of the Aburi decisions was to restore to the Regional Governments the powers vested in them prior to the inception of military rule. That intention implied that the constitutional safeguards operative

during the old regime should be equally revived. Unless this was
done, it would be well-nigh impossible to preserve the Federation.
Indeed it was the view of the Northern delegation that the exclusion
of provisions identical to those contained in section 86 of the Constitution would leave the regions free to secede from the Federation if
they so desired.

39. Mr Imoukhuede (Secretary of the Mid-West Government. Ed.)
thought that it would be invidious to discuss this issue in isolation as
he considered that it was inextricably bound up with the question
concerning the extent to which Military Governors would be allowed
to exercise the right of concurrence in decisions by the Supreme
Military Council on which agreement had been reached as recorded in
paragraph 34 above.

40. Side by side with the desirability of reviving section 86 of the
constitution, the question whether the declaration of emergency in a
Region under sections 70 and 71 of the Republican Constitution should
be grouped among matters in respect of which the Supreme Military
Council should not arrive at a decision without the concurrence of the
Military Governors was considered. The Eastern Nigeria delegation
was strongly opposed to the idea of including this subject in the list of
matters calling for the concurrence of Military Governors. At the same
time, it was opposed to the resuscitation of sections 70, 71 and 86 of the
Republican Constitution which, if restored, would have the combined
effect of strengthening the control of the Federal Government over the
Regions. With particular reference to the provisions of the Republican
Constitution with regard to the declaration of emergency, it was the
view of the Western Nigeria delegation that, as most of the law officers
appreciated at their meeting, the current situation in the country had
all the features of an emergency and that it would be illogical to talk
of an emergency within an emergency. For this reason, the Western
delegation felt that the emergency provisions of the Republican Constitution should not be revived nor should section 86 be restored. Both
the Federal and Northern Nigeria delegations held strongly to the view
that unless these sections of the Republican Constitution were restored,
the Federal Government would be left completely impotent. In such a
situation, it would be impossible to guarantee the safety of the Federation.

41. Mr Giwa-Amu, Solicitor-General for Mid-Western Nigeria,
felt that in the national interest, it was necessary to revive the sections
of the Republican Constitution under consideration. He was of the
opinion that the expression 'emergency' should be viewed from a perspective wider than that contemplated by the East and the West. He
thought that the Federal Government should be in a position to take

effective steps to quell any riot or any plot calculated to undermine the authority of any Regional Government within its area of jurisdiction.

42. The meeting was unable to reach agreement on these issues and it was decided that they should be referred to the Supreme Military Council for determination. In addition, it was agreed that a separate paper setting out the divergence of views expressed on the issues should be submitted to the Supreme Military Council, along with other papers connected with the proposed decree.

SUMMARY OF CONCLUSIONS

The Conclusions reached on the various subjects considered at the meeting may be summarized as follows:

1. *Legislative and Executive Authority of the Federation*

(i) it was agreed that the draft Constitution (Suspension and Modification) Decree, 1967, should take account of the Aburi decision of the Supreme Military Council to the effect that the legislative and executive authority of the Federation should vest in the Supreme Military Council.

(ii) On the exercise of the Supreme Military Council's legislative and executive authority, it was agreed that, in order to give full effect to the decision of the Supreme Military Council as recorded in paragraph 12 of the minutes of its Aburi meeting, it should be provided in the draft decree that in respect of the matters listed below, the Council should exercise its legislative and executive authority only with the concurrence of all the Military Governors:

(a) power to make decrees affecting the territorial integrity of a region or altering any of the entrenched provisions listed in the proviso to section 4 (1) of the Constitution of the Federation, 1963, to be revived with necessary modifications;

(b) power to make laws or to administer existing laws of an economic character affecting the whole country, for instance, laws with respect to trade, commerce, industry, transport and communications, labour, public service and public finance (other than the approval of the Federal estimates, but including the approval of new capital projects in such estimates);

(c) power to make new laws or to administer existing laws of international or security character affecting the whole country, for instance, laws with respect to external affairs, defence, naval, military and air forces, the Nigeria Police, arms and ammunitions, administration of the affairs of a Region, maintenance and securing of public order, public safety and essential supplies and services;

(d) power to make new laws or to administer existing laws of a higher educational or professional character, for instance, laws with respect to higher education generally, existing higher educational institutions and the professions;

(e) power to exercise executive authority affecting the country with respect to any of the matters mentioned in (a)–(d) above.

(iii) On the question of the delegation of the legislative and executive authority being vested in the Supreme Military Council, it was recommended that, for administrative convenience, the provisions of the draft decree enabling the Supreme Military Council to delegate some of its powers should be widened to include 'any other person or authority', provided that:

(a) it should not delegate any of its powers to make decrees;

(b) where it is considered necessary to delegate the exercise of its authority with respect to matters on which the concurrence of all Military Governors is required, such delegation should be effected only with the concurrence of all the Military Governors.

2. *Exercise of Executive Authority of Regional Governments and Emergency provisions*

In view of the divergence of opinion expressed on these matters, it was not possible to reach agreement as to whether or not to incorporate in the draft decree provisions identical to those contained in the suspended sections 70, 71 and 86 of the Constitution or to include the power to declare a state of emergency in any Region in the list of subjects in respect of which the concurrence of all Military Governors is required. It was, for this reason, agreed that the matter should be referred to the Supreme Military Council for determination and that the paper presenting it to the Supreme Military Council should set out the conflicting views which emerged at the meeting on the subject.

3. *Questions referred by the Law Officers to the Supreme Military Council for determination*

In respect of question (a) the meeting agreed that the Aburi decision with regard to the exercise of the Supreme Military Council's legislative and executive authority could not be construed as implying that a meeting of the Council could not be held or be properly constituted unless all the Military Governors were present. As for the other questions, it was considered that the issues raised were bound up with the manner in which the Supreme Military Council should exercise its legislative and executive authority and that the recommendations of the meeting on this issue would go a long way in resolving the doubts which existed in the minds of the law officers.

4. *Appointments to posts in the Federal Civil Service, Federal Statutory Corporations, Diplomatic and Consular Services and the Police*

(i) *The Federal Civil Service.* The expression 'super-scale posts' occurring in the relevant section of the minutes of the Aburi meeting was defined as 'all posts in the Federal civil service graded in Group 9 or above'. In keeping with the Aburi decision, therefore, it was recommended that appointments to these categories of posts in the Federal civil service should be made by the Supreme Military Council, the Federal Public Service Commission having for this purpose an advisory function. The expression 'appointments' was construed as including acting appointments, promotions, transfers and secondments. The powers of the Supreme Military Council in relation to posts falling within the categories specified above were thought to include the power to exercise disciplinary control on the officers concerned.

(ii) *Federal Statutory Corporations.* It was recommended that the authority of the Supreme Military Council with regard to appointments to senior posts in the Federal statutory corporations should be exercised within the same scope as for the Federal civil service. It was also recommended that consideration should be given to the establishment of a Federal Public Corporations Service Board to operate on the same lines as the Federal Public Service Commission. It was considered very desirable that each Region should be equitably represented on the proposed Federal Public Corporations Service Board.

(iii) *Diplomatic and Consular Services.* It was agreed that the Supreme Military Council should be responsible for making appointments to senior ranks in the diplomatic and consular services as recorded in the minutes of the Aburi meeting.

(iv) *The Nigeria Police.* It was agreed that appointments to senior ranks in the Nigeria Police should be made by the Supreme Military Council and that the Police Service Commission shall for this purpose have an advisory function.

5. *Federal Electoral Commission*

The meeting recommended that the Federal Electoral Commission should be abolished.

6. *The Supreme Military Council*

The necessity for an early meeting of the Supreme Military Council was unanimously appreciated and emphasized and the following agenda was recommended:

(i) Minutes of the Aburi meeting.
(ii) Draft Constitution (Suspension and Modification) Decree.

(iii) Disruption of essential services.

(iv) Maintenance of Public Corporations and other national institutions.

(v) Report of Finance Permanent Secretaries on the rehabilitation of displaced persons.

7. *The Problem of Displaced Persons*

It was agreed that a meeting of Finance Permanent Secretaries of the Federation should be held shortly after the present meeting to recommend to the Supreme Military Council ways and means of giving effect to the Council's decisions at Aburi on this subject.

[Source. *Meeting of the Nigerian Military Leaders held at Peduase Lodge, Aburi, Ghana.* Federal Ministry of Information, 1967]

APPENDIX F

The demand for the creation of more states has not been confined to the Northern and Eastern Regions. There are in the Western Region historical divisions and accumulated discontents which prompt demands for separate statehood. These came to be more openly expressed once the decision had been taken to create more states. Several petitions of this kind were addressed to Lt-Col Gowon in June and July 1967. There was for example a demand that the two provinces of Oyo and Ibadan be constituted into a separate central Yoruba state. Two of the petitions reproduced in this Appendix make this demand. The third, presented by the Yoruba East Movement and apparently written before June 1967, advocates that the Western Region be divided into three states. These three petitions, and others very similar, were published some time in 1968 by persons calling themselves 'Statists'.

Petition for the Creation of Yoruba Central State by Decree submitted by the Alafin of Oyo, Chiefs, and People of Oyo, to General Gowon, 20 June 1967

We, the Alafin and Chiefs on behalf of all the Chiefs and people of Oyo Division would like, first, to congratulate Your Excellency on your present promotion to the esteemed position of the Major-General of our Armed Forces. We also wish to thank you for the progressive and courageous step taken by you in carving Nigeria into twelve component States.

Sir, as people of the Yoruba Central State, we have been sorry and abject victims of an aggressive oligarchy from outside Ibadan; while our population is five and one quarter million of a total of nine million in the newly created Western State we are completely shut away from our natural rights and amenities and we are reduced to the position of mere second rate citizenship in a state of our birthright.

In Yorubaland it is the traditional right of the Alafin and the Yoruba Obas and Chiefs to appoint one of their sons to the exalted Office of the Are-Ona-Kakanfo. This ancient tradition was recently attacked by the appointment of a Leader of the Yorubas a direct affront to our tradition as Yorubas, and undue recognition being accorded a certain

personality by the Military Government of Western State. It is no
exaggeration to say that the minority in this State today controls our
Civil Service, the Police Force, the Local Government set up to the
detriment of the indigenous from the majority section which are the
proper Oyo and Yoruba Ibadan Provinces.

It is a pointer to the success and superiority of self-rule that only
when the Late Chief S. L. Akintola himself a native of Central Yoruba
area, became the Premier of Western Region that some of the towns
in the area have pipe-borne water and electricity.

Since the Army take-over, harsh hands of neglect have gripped our
area and we are choking under the throes of a ruthless Ijebu and Ekiti
Officialdom. The only solution to the problem is the creation of Central
Yoruba State by DECREE to comprise the Old Oyo and Ibadan
Provinces. The Central Yoruba area is now facing economic strangulation. In Government Contract awards, our people receive no patronage. Most industries which were in the Government blue-prints and
which were earmarked for Central Yoruba Areas were taken to Ekiti
and other areas. A case in point is the new Textile Factory at Ado-
Ekiti. A Shoe Company for which the Government of old Western
Region had suscribed £60,000 and which should have been producing
by now is decidedly put in the 'frigidaire' because it is located at
Ogbomosho. This, we are sure, is a way of stifling the economy and
prosperity of Yoruba Central Area.

The wave of violence, arson and atrocities unleashed on Central
Yoruba Area over the last four years is unprecedented and alien to us.
The perpetrators come from Ijebu, and Eastern Nigeria. They are
abetted by the arms of law. These atrocities never rear their heads in
Ijebu Areas. This is one way our people have been gagged and muzzled
so that the minorities can retain their predominance. We are confident
that in our own State these injustices and horrors will cease.

It baffles us how so few a group of people can have so much and
not be contented. The Ijebus are out for a rule of terror and
intimidation.

The so-called Western Leaders of thought is an Ijebu–Ekiti dominated
assembly which claims to represent us. Opposition elements were
bungled in prison—their papers were banned, their leaders blackmailed.
This is how the minorities obtain their mandate to impose their views
on the majority. The Federal Military Government is for a country
'where no man is oppressed' and therefore we are claiming our just
right; freedom from a minority rule, personal intimidation and economic strangulation. It is only the creation of a Central Yoruba State that
could solve the problem and save the country from future political
eruption.

We are not expressing mere sentiments. We have no chance of
survival in the new set-up of things in the Western State. Nothing short
of the creation of a Central Yoruba State will satisfy our aspirations.
We have the unflinching support of our people. We wish your good
self all succour and zest needed at this crucial moment. Our faith in
you and your Government will grow from strength to strength;
and we implore you to invoke your authority now and right-away
to create for us and our children the Central Yoruba State which will
include the Old Oyo and Ibadan Provinces—a population figure of
5.2 million.

In conclusion Sir, We like to emphasize that the creation of the
Central Yoruba State is being sought on the principles of:

1. Historical and Traditional ties;
2. Economic Viability;
3. Overall interest of the Federation as a whole—the principle being
that no one State should be too large to become a terror to its neighbours.

On behalf of ourselves and our people we remain, Sir.

*Petition for the Creation of Yoruba Central State by Decree submitted by the
Oshun Representatives' Committee to General Gowon, 28 June 1967*

We the representatives and elites of Oshun Division pray Your
Excellency our due homage and pray to God to assist Your Excellency
in the discharge of all your state duties.

2. The purpose of this petition is to pray Your Excellency to create
for us by Decree immediately the Central Yoruba State comprising of
the Ibadan Province and the Oyo Province with a total population of
5.2 millions.

3. This our demand cuts across party politics or party political
alignment. People with all shades of political opinion; non-politicians,
civil servants—and the masses of the Oshun Division support this
demand.

4. There are several reasons in support of our demand but we put
some of them before Your Excellency:

(i) The Western State as at present constituted is not as homogeneous as some people pretend and want the world to believe. The
bitterness is so deep that it is the Military Rule that ensure an uneasy
peace in a land where sectional interests and persecution had inflicted
serious wounds thereby driving sanity very far off.

(ii) Contrary to the propaganda of vested interests, we accept no
one leader in the West despite official and unofficial desperate efforts to
force one on us: A so-called leader who forgives no one, who is
arrogantly vindictive, who thinks he is wiser than everyone and who

equates himself with God can never be accepted by us, even if the Heaven falls.

(iii) The 2.6 million Textile Mill Factory was sited in Oshun Division during the Premiership of Chief S. L. Akintola; but no sooner the Ijebu and the Ekiti clique found themselves in power after the coup than they shifted the Mill to Ado–Ekiti.

(iv) The Federal Inter-Regional Secondary School for the West was sited by the Federal Government with the approval of the Western Government in Oshun Division which is one of the most backward in Educational facilities in the West—What do we find? The Ekiti-Ijebu axis had undone what the civilian government had done and transferred the school to Ijebu near Ikenne—Chief Awolowo Home Town. The Building Plans and the lands surveyed in our division for this purposes were abandoned.

(v) During the civilian regime, a Shoe Factory was started at Ogbomosho in a venture sponsored by the Western Government. It was half completed; now, it has been abandoned and jettisoned by the Ekiti-Ijebu alliance and all the money for it transferred to projects in Ijebu and Ekiti.

(vi) There had been a mass dismissal of corporation employees of Oshun origin. Reason? They come from Chief Akintola's Oshun Division. Therefore, regardless of merit, they must be persecuted. Some, as in the Housing Corporation who could not be dismissed outright were downgraded with contumely and effrontery in order to annoy them into resigning their job. The cars of these class of employee so disgraced were seized from them on the ground that their new downgraded grade does not entitle them to car advance, therefore the cars must be auctioned. The treatment given to them are reminiscent of those given to a slaves in the hey days of the slave trade.

Your Excellency could imagine the spectacle of adults weeping because of the humiliation brought upon them, for no other reason than that they come from Oshun.

(vii) Nine Judges were appointed to the High Court and the newly created Court of Appeal in the West not one is fit to come from our province even though we have eminent Lawyers of repute. What did we have? Lawyers who appeared in the Chief Awolowo's treasonable felony case and known Action Group minded lawyers were catapulted on to the Bench. This is neither just nor safe for our liberty and future.

(viii) The Ijebu-Ekiti minority in the West now controls: (a) The Judiciary; (b) The Political Power; (c) The Economic Power; (d) The Churches; (e) The Civil Service; (f) The Police Set-up. What then are we? Second class citizens! Without fair play for us!

(ix) The 80,000 General Hospital which the civilian regime earmarked for Ede in Oshun Division and the building of which had almost completed has been converted to a cottage hospital.

(x) Your Excellency should never listen to any Ekiti or Ijebu personality who may oppose our demand since they are the group who benefits from the present set up which is gross injustice to the Oyos.

5. What is the History of the Yorubaland? The history of we Oyo are synonymous with the history of the Yorubas. The Oyo empire is famous in African history being at par with Ghana, Mali, Ashanti, Bornu, and Sokoto Empires. The Oshuns, Oyos, Ibadans are all one constituting the hub of the Oyo Empire with Ekiti as our political colony where we installed Ajeles (Political Agents) for the purpose of collecting taxes and supplying us with the necessary slaves for sale to the Europeans. The Ijebus were mere traders selling to us ammunitions and when at Ode Remo, they wanted to impede our access to the coast, we fought them, defeated them and shot our way through.

These are the very clique who are lording it over us. People who dared not look our forefathers on the face. This must end Sir.

6. The Western State is a veritable combustible material in the Federation of Nigeria unless, Sir, more states are created therein.

7. A so-called Consultative Body set up in the Western State and consisting of 28 members have at least 22 known Action Groupers and Chief Awolowo too once boasted in the presence of the Governor that all the sixteen each representing an Administrative Division in the West are all known Action Groupers. Thus everything are being carefully tailored to suit a particular interest. We know some honest Action Groupers who resent this on the ground that the injustice is so palpable that if continued, the Region would soon be in flames.

8. We pray Your Excellency that for the sake of peace, fairplay, justice, good government and to avoid for all times man's inhumanity to man to please create by DECREE our Central Yoruba State without further delay.

Memorandum submitted by the Yoruba East Movement on the State Creation (Ondo Prov.) to General Gowon

We are convinced that the immediate cause of trouble in this country is the imbalance in political power in the country, the imbalance in the distribution of amenities among the various communities and the imbalance in the distribution of wealth among the citizens of the country.

But it is the view of the Union that these are mere by-products of the remote causes which are discrimination and isolation, hatred and jealousy, greed and selfishness.

In order to achieve unity, peace, even and orderly progress these remote causes must be removed. Discrimination should give way to identification or distinction; hatred to love; jealousy to healthy rivalry or competition, greed to contentment, selfishness to selflessness and service.

REMEDY

The country should be divided into administrative units consisting of states, so that groups of communities with identical yearnings, aspirations and problems can come together and develop their own lines in a free and peaceful atmosphere in order to catch up with others.

This division should be based on:—
1. the wish of the people
2. viability of the area
3. administrative convenience
4. geographical contiguity
5. historical association and lastly
6. common culture or language

PARAMOUNT FACTOR—ECONOMIC VIABILITY

The paramount factor is economic. Thus if it will be economically advantageous and advisable, and if an area will be economically viable, the case for creating the area into a state is justifiable.

Next is administrative convenience which of necessity takes account of (a) geographical contiguity (b) accessibility of one part to the other and (c) transport and communication facilities.

LANGUAGE—A SECONDARY FACTOR

The question of language is of secondary importance as food, clothing and shelter and the modern social necessities of life, can be provided without difficulty to people of divergent tongues, especially if they have a common language which they all speak, as is the case in Nigeria.

The same is true of culture and history. There is little room for culture where the basic needs of society are wanting. In fact culture and history go to the background when a people are struggling for mere survival. In any event when education, social and economic requirements of a people are adequately met they can create a new culture through modern avenues of music, plays, drama and dances games, pastimes and literature. These will supplement and enrich the old culture.

It is not unusual to have people of different languages and cultures in one political and administrative unit; equally it is not unusual that people speaking one language or having one culture should constitute more than one state (e.g. Australia) if the state will be viable and if their geography and administrative convenience, transport and communication are favourable.

The modern function of government, namely the provision of social economic and other needs of man do not fall along linguistic lines.

In the Northern Region especially in the Middle Belt several linguistic groups will have to be included in one and the same state and although Lagos and Ikeja speak Yoruba it is being suggested that a Lagos State be created distinct from the Western Region.

Both proposals go to confirm that people of different languages can, all other things being equal, be grouped together as one state while people of one language can be split into more than one state.

Finally it must be remembered that sentiments apart, English is, and will continue to be, the official language of Nigerians. Although the local language is a factor which may facilitate the communication of ideas, knowledge and information but if each citizen can have such items communicated to him in a language whether common to all or peculiar to his area then he will not complain. Also it is not imperative that all who speak one language must be in one state.

If this were so, Australia should not be a Federation but a unitary state. The Yorubas in Dahomey or the Hausas all over West Africa should form one country respectively.

IN THE WESTERN REGION THE YORUBA TERRITORIES OF NIGERIA SHOULD BE DIVIDED INTO THREE STATES NAMELY YORUBA SOUTH-WEST, YORUBA-NORTH AND EAST

When looked at from social, cultural, historical, geographical and economic considerations, the Yoruba country comprising the Western Region of Nigeria and the Yoruba territories at present in the Northern Region naturally falls into three areas or regions.

THE IJEBUS AND EGBAS—YORUBA SOUTH-WEST

The first is the South Western part known as 'Isale' (or Down Section) and comprising Ijebu and Abeokuta Provinces and the Old Colony Province.

This area produces gari, fruits and kola nuts. Generally the people are traders and merchants as they are near the coast and port of Lagos.

Their dialects are similar. They have advanced socially; the level of their educational and economic development is very high compared with other parts of Yoruba-land.

They are more sophisticated and Anglo-Saxon in outlook; rather far-sighted and dexterous. Practically all industrial, commercial and economic projects of the Region are sited in their area.

THE OYOS—YORUBA NORTH

The next is the Oyo area, comprising the Old Oyo Province (which includes the present Ibadan Province) and also the Yoruba speaking parts of Ilorin Province. Their dialect is identical or similar and is the so-called Yoruba Proper.

They produce cotton, cocoa, maize, yam and beans. They are conservative, easy going but diplomatic. They have large towns which attracted the early missionaries and colonial administrators leading to the building of Schools and other social institutions like St. Andrews College, Wesley College, Adeoyo Hospital, Moor Plantations and a host of Grammar Schools and other social institutions. They have long been enjoying electricity, pipe borne water and other social amenities.

THE IJESHAS, EKITIS, IYAGBAS, OWOS AND THE ONDOS AND OKITI-PUPA

The third group are the Ijeshas, the Ekitis, Iyagbas, Owos and the Ondos—the group of communities occupying the vast areas covered by Ondo Province, Ilesha Division and the Yoruba speaking area in Kabba Division (the Yagbas and the Northern Ekitis). These people are sturdy, simple and not sophisticated but plain, honest and frank. They produce cocoa, timber, cotton, palm oil and palm kernel for export overseas and yam, beans, maize, plantain, rice etc. for local consumption and export to other parts of the Region.

They occupy the Eastern part of Yorubaland. They have identical though slightly varying dialects. Their land is comparatively fertile, dotted with hills in the vast plains which are themselves divided or surrounded by thick evergreen forests. They did not have the advantage of early European contact and barring a few cases their towns are not as large as those in Oyo area.

They were neglected by the old colonial administration but have received worse discriminatory treatment from the regimes of the past 15 years when the Yorubas took over the reins. They have been treated as third class citizens in Western Nigeria, while the Oyos are regarded and treated as second class citizens and, of course, the Ijebus and Egbas are the first class citizens.

Not a single project or industry has been sited in these vast areas. The University for the Region which was and ought to have been sited in part of the vast areas, was sited in Ife to boost the prestige, economy and influence of that town. Many other social educational and economic projects which were earmarked for location in parts of these areas have had to be diverted to other parts of the Region. Although they account for over 50 per cent of the revenue of the Region they do not receive as much as 15 per cent of the benefits.

In order to ensure even and orderly progress, peace and harmony the West should be broken into three states: Yoruba South-West, Yoruba-North, and Yoruba-East so that each could plan its progress and advancement along the lines of its needs and aspirations and thus bridge the wide gap in the social and economic development among these territories.

This view is supported and subscribed to by practically all the illustrious sons and daughters of Yoruba Eastern State in their different social, cultural and other organizations throughout the length and breadth of the areas concerned.

Therefore the Yoruba East Movement categorically demands that a State should be created comprising Ondo Province, Ijesha Division to be named Yoruba East or such other suitable name as may be agreed. In support of its claims the Yoruba East State Movement submits the following seventeen reasons:

1. These areas comprise the Ekiti Parapo ethnic groups which fought the historic Ekiti Parapo wars and the people are homogeneous race.
2. They have identical cultural and social patterns.
3. They have a complementary economy.
4. They are contiguous.
5. They have identical yearnings, aspirations and objectives.
6. They have historical association as a federation of Kingdoms.
7. They have a large measure of community of interest namely:
   (a) Communication and Transport
   (b) Agricultural and industrial requirements
   (c) Local Trade and Commerce
   (d) Educational and Technological needs
   (e) Social and cultural attitudes
   (f) Religious beliefs.
8. If these areas are created into a state, the state will be economically viable for the following reasons:
   (a) The population is about 4,000,000
   (b) The area is over 10,000 sq. miles
   (c) The economic products are varied and substantial—
For export (i) Cocoa (ii) Timber (iii) Palm Produce (iv) Cotton (v) Tobacco. All these are produced and exported in large quantities producing in royalties, taxes and excise duties over 30 per cent of the revenue of the Region. The areas also produce (i) yam (ii) beans (iii) maize (iv) rice and plantain in such large quantities that are sufficient for local consumption and export to other parts of the country.
9. The transport and communication in the areas are good (although the roads are not well maintained) and every part is accessible to the other.

10. These areas have been neglected by successive Regional and Federal Governments such that the social, economic and educational development have been very slow and appalling in most cases although some desperate effort is now being made in certain parts in the realm of theoretical education.

11. The contribution of these areas to the wealth of the Region is considerably high being about 50 per cent whereas they receive less than 15 per cent of the benefits bestowed on the Region.

12. In plain words the wealth of these areas have been used to develop and feed other parts of the Region.

13. There is no single major or minor industry sited in any part of these areas.

14. These areas have illustrious sons and daughters who can plan and execute economic, social and educational developments and solve other problems posed by the areas so that the areas could catch up with other parts of the Region.

15. At present these areas are treated as colonies or at best as rural areas whose raw materials produce the bulk of the revenue and wealth of the Region, but who are given nothing more than the crumbs that fall from the master's table.

16. Decisions regarding the Region are often made without consulting the people of these areas or without ascertaining their views and such decisions are carried out irrespective of the views or feelings of the people of these areas and detrimental to their interest and

FINALLY

17. Unless these areas are constituted and created into a State of their own they will continue to be dominated, out paced and kept at the rear in all facets of life.